After Full Employment

Contemporary Politics

Series editors

David Beetham
Bob Jessop
John Keane
Anne Sassoon

Already published

The Context of British Politics
David Coates

The Power of the Powerless
Citizens against the state in central–eastern Europe
Vaclav Havel et al.
Edited by John Keane

After Full Employment
John Keane and John Owens

Contradictions of the Welfare State
Claus Offe
Edited by John Keane

The Myth of the Plan
Lessons of Soviet planning experience
Peter Rutland

Women and the Public Sphere
A critique of sociology and politics
Edited by Janet Siltanen and Michelle Stanworth

In preparation

The Rule of Law and the British Constitution
Norman Lewis and Ian Harden

Introduction to Soviet Politics
Peter Rutland

From a Women's Point of View
New perspectives on the welfare state
Edited by Anne Showstack Sassoon

After Full Employment

John Keane and
John Owens

Hutchinson

London Melbourne Sydney Auckland Johannesburg

Hutchinson & Co. (Publishers) Ltd

An imprint of the Hutchinson Publishing Group

62–65 Chandos Place, London WC2N 4NW
and 51 Washington Street, Dover, New Hampshire 03820, USA

Hutchinson Publishing Group (Australia) Pty Ltd
16–22 Church Street, Hawthorn, Melbourne, Victoria 3122

Hutchinson Group (NZ) Ltd
32–34 View Road, PO Box 40–086, Glenfield, Auckland 10

Hutchinson Group (SA) (Pty) Ltd
PO Box 337, Bergvlei 2012, South Africa

First published 1986

©John Keane and John Owens 1986

Set in Times by BookEns, Saffron Walden, Essex

Printed and bound in Great Britain by
Anchor Brendon Ltd, Tiptree, Essex

British Library Cataloguing in Publication Data

Keane, John, 1949–
   After full employment. — (Contemporary politics, V.6)
   1. Unemployment — Great Britain
   I. Title II. Series
   331.13'7941   HD5765.A6

ISBN 0 09 164091 1

Contents

Preface   7

Introduction: rethinking the employment society   9

1 The development of a full employment consensus   28
2 The social democratic vision   41
3 The era of full employment: from Attlee to Callaghan   53
4 The disciplinary state   74
5 The strong state and the free market   89
6 Populist Conservatism and jobless growth   103
7 Reagan's disguised Keynesianism   123
8 Labour's nostalgia for full employment   144
9 Beyond the employment society   160

Bibliography   181

Index   193

Preface

The return of mass unemployment to western European and North American societies since the early 1970s is stimulating a new and important controversy about the future of paid work. There is a growing recognition in these societies that the post-war policies guaranteeing full male employment through Keynesian welfare state arrangements are losing ground rapidly. Much less public recognition is presently being given, however, to the problem of whether the once widely endorsed policies of full employment can or should be restored. Indeed, in countries such as Britain and the United States, public discussion of this problem is virtually taboo. With few exceptions, debate within these countries focuses only on the *means* for achieving the goal of full employment. This goal, even when it is downgraded in favour of others (such as reducing inflation or increasing economic growth), is simply assumed to be desirable and possible. 'Getting the jobless back to work', in other words, resembles something of a settled issue – it is part of the framework of unquestioned assumptions which guide the policies of political parties, trade unions, businesses and governments.

The essays in this book are centrally concerned with exposing and challenging this assumption. At an introductory level, and with reference mainly to Britain and the United States, these essays describe and critically analyse four competing political interpretations of the causes of growing structural unemployment and the future of paid work: social democracy; free market liberalism; the theory of the disciplinary state; and utopian socialism. Considered together, we argue that these four interpretations are both illuminating and challenging, because they raise considerable doubts about both the viability and desirability of public policies designed to 'get the jobless back to work'.

These doubts feed into our central thesis, which is that the post-war policy of full male employment, as well as its political, economic and social preconditions, is not repeatable. Taking as our starting point Beveridge and Keynes's post-war vision of full employment, we explain why the full employment welfare states which developed in Britain and the United States have faltered under the weight of their own internal contradictions, to be replaced by the 'strong state, free market' programmes of Thatcher and Reagan. Our analysis of the Thatcher and Reagan strategies for reducing unemployment shows why their bold and innovative programmes have in turn been paralysed quickly by their own inconsistencies and consequences, as well as by long-term political, economic, social and demographic changes. We conclude that contemporary political commitments to 'full employment' (such as those of the British Labour Party) are far too optimistic and reveal a lamentable nostalgia for times past. Instead, we argue, it is essential and urgent that new political ideas and strategies for reducing and equitably redistributing paid work –for moving beyond a society of full male employment – become a central theme of contemporary politics in Britain, the United States and other employment societies.

This book has been developed from a course of lectures given to first year social science students at The Polytechnic of Central London in the autumn of 1984. Our primary debt, therefore, is to our students, and especially Véronique Duverger and Keith Lye, who read and commented carefully on most of the script. We also wish to thank Sarah Conibear and Claire L'Enfant at Hutchinson, as well as a number of colleagues and friends in Britain and elsewhere who helped in various ways with the preparation of this book: Nigel Amon, David Beetham, Johannes Berger, Nigel Bowles, Ian Gough, Phillip Hansen, Tim Hatton, David Held, Bob Jessop, Gareth Locksley, David McKay, Paul Mier, Howard Newby, Claus Offe, Margaret Owens, Ben Pimlott, Anne Sassoon, J. R. Shackleton, Michael Turner, Graham Wilson, and Nancy Wood.

John Keane
John Owens
London and Colchester, July 1985

Introduction: rethinking the employment society

Public concern with mass unemployment is today almost universal, and with good reason. In nearly all western countries, the level of registered unemployment has been rising steadily during the past two decades. During the past five years, unemployment rates have continued to increase in every country within the OECD (Organisation for Economic Co-operation and Development), except the United States and Finland, and further increases are widely anticipated. The average rate of unemployment in OECD countries is expected to rise from 5.1 per cent in 1979 to 8½ per cent by mid 1986; on these projections the overall number of officially unemployed persons will reach 35 million, over 20 million of these in western Europe, and 20,000 net jobs would have to be created every day until 1989 if unemployment is to be reduced to its 1979 level of 19 million persons.[1]*

The picture offered by these aggregate trends is disquieting, and yet it conceals the extent to which unemployment trends are uneven and dispersed in their extent and scope. OECD countries are presently experiencing not only rising, but also distinctively *uneven* patterns of unemployment. For instance, divergent patterns of unemployment are rapidly gathering momentum within the OECD, such that regions (e.g. Scandinavia) where joblessness has been relatively low are likely to experience a limited change in their rates of unemployment, whereas regions (such as south-western Europe) where there is already a high level of unemployment are expected to suffer further sharp increases in unemployment. Differences among particular countries are also striking. Whereas, for example, the rate of unemployment in Switzerland is less than 1 per cent (due partly to the expulsion of immigrant workers and restrictions upon women entering the labour market), double-digit unemployment prevails in eight other

---

* Superior figures refer to the Notes at the end of chapters.

western European countries, with a peak rate of nearly 20 per cent in Spain. Seriously uneven patterns of joblessness are also developing *within* most countries. In Britain, for instance, where nearly one in seven of the total paid work force (13.9 per cent) is jobless, unemployment levels of around 10 per cent are found in the most privileged regions of the South-East and East Anglia, whereas registered unemployment is above 19 per cent in the North-East and Northern Ireland.

These polarizing trends within and among countries are further deepened by diverging rates of unemployment among various social groups. By mid 1986, to cite the most prominent and disturbing example, youth unemployment in western Europe is expected to reach record levels. An estimated 44 per cent of unemployment in that region is presently accounted for by persons in the 15–24 age group, and unemployment rates among the young members of ethnic minorities are already of alarming proportions. Finally, when considering the extent and shape of the present unemployment crisis, the problem of concealed or 'hidden' unemployment should not be forgotten. Official unemployment data is notoriously misleading in this respect because it conceals the degree to which social groups (e.g. married women) without full-time jobs are not considered officially as jobless or as potential job seekers (despite their desire for employment); or have simply given up registering themselves as unemployed, and are presently working in the household or the so-called 'informal' or 'hidden' economy; or have been drafted into government job creation schemes; or have been redefined by government statisticians as no longer unemployed (as in Britain, where an estimated 200,000 persons over the age of 60 years are no longer required to register).

While these statistically defined unemployment trends are certainly helpful in clarifying the dimensions of the present unemployment crisis, they do not indicate the deeper reason why mass unemployment is presently generating such great public concern in most western countries. This has to do with the *trauma* of being unemployed – that is, with the widespread conviction that being employed is one of the main ways in which life can be made bearable and that, therefore, being flung into the ranks of the unemployed is a humiliating blow to one's very existence. The consequences of being unemployed are often deeply personal, and are by no means restricted to the difficulties generated by a serious reduction of income and consumer spending power. Certainly, as in the 1930s, the traumatic effects of being forced into joblessness are highly variable, clearly depending upon such factors as gender, the type of occupation in which one was previously employed, the degree of unemployment in one's geographic locality, and whether or not other members of one's household are presently working for a wage or salary.[2] Even when such factors are taken into account, however, it is clear that the unemployed often feel like passengers in an airborne plane with no landing gear. An acute sense of shock, panic, isolation, shame, lethargy, depression and fear of simply not being able to make ends meet is reportedly widespread among the unemployed; blood pressure, asthmatic difficulties, headaches, nervousness and other bodily ailments tend to increase; and young children of the unemployed are especially prone to disturbed feeding, sleeping difficulties and anxious behaviour.

The employment society

Why does the experience of being out of a paid job frequently have such traumatic consequences, and why do these consequences in turn generate a wider public concern about unemployment? This question is often considered to be so trivial that it is rarely asked. When it is, the most commonly offered answer goes something like this: 'Being unemployed is so stressful because it is only natural that people want a job. Without one, they rightly feel humiliated and depressed.'

A principal aim of this book is to show that this answer is seriously misleading, and that the desire for (and the fact of) employment that supposes it to be 'natural' has in fact appeared only under specific *historical* conditions. Public anxiety about unemployment, in other words, is not part of the natural order of things; it emerges as a publicly significant problem only when societies themselves become geared to the imperatives of employment. Any discussion of the contemporary problem of unemployment must recognize this striking fact: by contrast with all other past and present societies, the modern capitalist societies that emerged in full force in Europe and North America during the eighteenth and nineteenth centuries have been most concerned – some would say obsessed – with employment and its converse, unemployment. These societies can be called *employment societies*, for it is only within them that the fact of paid work – being employed as a worker for a wage or salary within a labour market geared to agricultural, manufacturing or service production – emerges on a large scale and as an activity separate from other institutions such as the household and the state.

The emergence of employment societies, in which most people, for at least some of their lives, work for a wage or salary within a labour market, was a wholly new development. If one compares modern employment societies – post eighteenth-century Britain or the United States, for instance – with hunting and gathering societies and contemporary Soviet-type regimes, to mention two randomly chosen examples, the contrast is striking. Anthropologists have pointed out that the members of hunting and gathering societies spent little time each day on subsistence activities – about four to five hours of intermittent and undemanding work in the case of the surviving Australian aborigines – and that, compared with our own employment societies, 'work' in these tribal societies did not at all have the same meaning for those engaged in it.[3] Work – the production of the felt necessities of life – was intermittent and discontinuous, ceasing at the moment when it was not required. It was not an activity performed for pay in a separate sphere of life – an 'economy' – because being 'a worker' was not a socially ascribed status in itself. The tribal members worked, or produced, only in their capacity as mothers, fathers, brothers, sisters or as members of other kinship groupings. Whatever work the tribal members performed was an expression of pre-existing community relations, and not the reverse. Hence to work in hunting and gathering societies did not mean to engage in 'a job', and it certainly carried no positive status. Terms such as 'worker' and 'employee', or phrases such as 'the right to work', 'the dignity of work' and 'the tragedy of umemployment' were simply meaningless to the members of tribal societies.

If we jump forward in time to contemporary Soviet-type regimes such as Czechoslovakia or the German Democratic Republic, the contrast with employment societies such as Britain and the United States is also very marked.[4] It is true that (unlike hunting and gathering societies) both types of social systems are geared to constantly expanding production of goods and services. Soviet-type regimes nevertheless differ from employment societies in at least one respect: they are characterized by the state's (attempted) control of every sphere of life and, hence, by the virtual liquidation of market mechanisms, private property and waged and salaried work. In Soviet-type regimes, it makes no sense to speak of workers being employed for a wage or salary within an 'economy' separate from the state, for there is no officially tolerated labour market and, hence, no officially recognized unemployment (although various forms of 'hidden unemployment' are rampant). Producers neither contract with an employer for 'a job' nor, conversely, can they be fired or made redundant by management. Producers (and managers) are subject constantly to the commands of the state authorities, who routinely restrict the free geographic movement of producers, allocate them to particular projects and industries, conscript them into the army and, in extreme cases (the so-called Gulag Archipelago is an example) confine them in institutions where they perform slave labour. In contemporary Soviet-type regimes, then, the absence of an institutionalized labour market and overt unemployment has its high price: producers are not allowed officially to bargain collectively or individually over their pay or conditions. Their pay and working conditions are determined for them by the Party-supervised state. In contrast to employment societies, producers also cannot withhold their capacity to produce. Striking is considered by the political authorities as treasonable. At most, producers can withhold their capacity to produce from this or that enterprise for a time, or engage in such forms of guerrilla action as absenteeism, go-slows, 'homing' (producing objects for household use by utilizing the factory's machines and materials) and, especially, giving the appearance of working. (As the Russian novelist Zinoviev has observed, it is virtually impossible in these countries to tell the difference between a person who is working and a person who is pretending to work.)

By contrast with hunting and gathering societies and contemporary Soviet-type regimes, modern employment societies compel or induce large numbers of men and women to spend a considerable portion of their daily lives within an institutionally distinct labour market. The development of employment societies in this sense dates only from the eighteenth and nineteenth centuries. From this time on, 'work' comes to have a special meaning. It ceases to mean (as it had done, say, in the vocabulary of old English) being engaged in any activity and effort, especially that aimed at satisfying the necessaries of life (cf. Shakespeare's *Henry IV*: 'Fie upon this quiet life, I want worke'). Work instead assumes a special and much more restricted meaning: paid employment. Work comes to mean 'having a job', and those who are engaged in paid employment are from hereon described as workfolk, workpeople, workers or working class. To be a worker, in other words, is to be employed, whereas the activity of a woman who runs a household, services men and brings up children, for instance, is consigned officially and arbitrarily to the category of non-work. There are some exceptions to this modern restriction of the sense of work to paid employment; even today, for instance, we still speak of 'housework', 'working around the home' or 'working in the garden'. But these are exceptions, which unfortunately (in view of their decisive importance in all people's lives), are not given official recognition or status. Within employment societies, household and other non-market forms of work such as cooking, cleaning and child-care are consigned by private employers and state policy-makers to the shadowy realm of non-work, as if they did not exist. Work is seen officially as synonymous with employment in a labour market, and it thereby becomes a pressing fact in people's lives, regardless of whether they are inside or outside the labour market. As workers, individuals are compelled or encouraged to sell their capacities to private or public employers in return for a wage or salary; if they refuse, or if they cannot find work, and therefore remain unemployed, they risk going without income and, hence, without the basic necessities of life for themselves and their household dependants.

The development of employment societies shaped by labour markets separate from households was without historical precedent. Never before had work in the sense of paid employment existed on such a scale and intensity in any society; never before or since has work and its traumatic converse, unemployment, come to be such a crucial factor in individuals' lives. Nor has 'work' ever been so celebrated, by the most powerful social groups at least, as the goal of life itself, and not merely its means. As employment societies began to emerge in full force during the eighteenth and nineteenth centuries, work came to be seen as a blessing. Many who celebrated the activity of work – Adam Smith and other writers within the new eighteenth-century discipline of political economy are only among the best known – defined human beings as *homo faber*, as makers and users of tools. As the following passage from Benjamin Franklin's *Auto-biography* makes clear, some writers went much further, regarding paid employment as not only natural, but as an enobling and deeply satisfying form of activity: 'When men are employed they are best contented; for on the days they worked they were good-natured and cheerful, and, with the consciousness of having done a good day's work, they spent the evening jollily; but on our idle days they were mutinous and quarrelsome.'

The official celebration of paid work as the goal, and not merely the means of life, distinguishes modern employment societies from all others. This fetish of employment within a labour market found its earliest expression in the so-called Protestant work ethic. As Max Weber showed in *The Protestant Ethic and the Spirit of Capitalism*

(1904–5) the belief that (male) individuals had a 'calling' to serve God through their work was invented and popularized by the Protestant middle classes. From the seventeenth century onwards, the faithful Christian was seen by these classes as one who worked not in order to live, but who lived in order to work. No longer was work viewed as an undignified necessity (to be performed only by slaves, women and other non-citizens, as in classical Greece). Nor was it any longer interpreted (as it had been in the early Judaeo-Christian tradition) as the curse of Adam, as the consequence of human beings' fall from grace ('in the sweat of thy brow shalt thou eat bread'). Instead, work came to be regarded as the means of future salvation, as the most certain sign of genuine faith.

Guided by this deep conviction, the Protestant middle classes condemned the waste of time through idle talk, and they despised both the frilly luxury and sexual indulgence of the aristocracy, as well as the drunken laughter of idling commoners in the public house. The hardworking Protestants insisted that every hour squandered could have been an hour of work to the glory of God. This celebration of work, Weber pointed out, contributed crucially to the early development of employment societies. Protestantism functioned to legitimize the new wealth and power of the male, property-owning classes; their attempts, as private entrepreneurs, to accumulate wealth and make profit within the market appeared to be the work of divine providence. Protestantism also provided a justification of the poverty and powerlessness of the lower classes, whose obedience to God was said to be conditional upon hard work, low wages, sobriety and – when necessary – confinement within workhouses which taught them the virtues of paid work. Through time, Weber concluded, it was not only the Protestants who regularly confirmed their image of themselves in the mirror of employment. The Protestant ethic also slowly became a conviction of the lower social ranks, thereby providing employment societies with conscientious, well-disciplined and punctual workers willing to work hard for an employer's wage or salary: 'The treatment of work . . . as a calling became as characteristic of the modern worker as the corresponding attitude toward acquisition of the business man.'

The full employment welfare state

Weber's conclusion presents a rather exaggerated picture of the extent to which the less powerful social ranks willingly or resignedly embraced the Protestant ethic. More recent research indicates that well into the nineteenth century the so-called working classes of modern employment societies found ways of evading the pressures and moral imperatives of regular and full-time employment. In fact, contrary to what is commonly supposed, only a minority shared the crushing fate of the early nineteenth-century factory workers who were often employed up to eighty hours a week.[5] The less powerful social groups *normally* had access to several types of employment during the year; well into the nineteenth century, for instance, copper workers in South Wales often abandoned their employers during the summer months in favour of healthier open-air employment such as stacking hay and fishing. These groups also *typically* worked in the labour market only on a seasonal or sporadic basis, and only until the point at which their traditionally-defined needs were met.* Many paid homage to 'Saint Monday' and most continued to work and to have access to food resources and 'an extra bob or two' *outside* the labour market. Work performed by men and women in households was especially crucial; activities such as domestic service, laundry work, homeworking for the textile trade and gardening operated as a kind of unemployment insurance system, ensuring that those who became unemployed were not necessarily without work and, hence, without the necessities of life.

This ability of individuals to subsist by moving, often on a seasonal basis, between the labour market and non-market institutions (such as the household) began to decline rapidly in the second half of the nineteenth century. Consequently, employment and its converse, unemployment, loomed larger in the social lives of most workers. Henceforth, workers experienced increasing difficulties in making ends meet outside the labour market. These difficulties were due largely to the pressures of accelerating urbanization, the rapid growth of industrial manufacturing, new and stricter forms of factory discipline, and because the compulsory schooling of children and the

---

* No doubt, this is why the eighteenth- and nineteenth-century advocates of industrial employment argued for keeping wages low. They feared, with considerable justification, that raising the wages of workers employed in the labour market would encourage them to work *less* in the labour market and *more* in non-market institutions such as households. The traditional (and misleading) view that full-time factory employment was the norm for nineteenth-century workers is discussed and criticized by J. D. Chambers, *The Workshop of the World* (London, 1961), pp. 21–2, and R. Samuel, 'Workshop of the World: steam power and hand technology in mid-Victorian Britain', *History Workshop*, no.3 (spring 1977), pp. 6–72.

exclusion of women from the labour market severely squeezed the earning capacity of households. These factors are discussed in detail in Chapter 1, where they are also seen as the decisive background against which demands for 'full employment' guaranteed by the state began to develop during the 1880s within the trade union movement and among various political and social reformers. This late nineteenth-century conviction that governments could do something to remedy unemployment – that they could reform employment societies so that there would no longer be societies of unemployment – had earlier roots. The questioning of unemployment (in England, at least) was already prominent in the 1820s and 1830s among trade union associations and radical and Owenite circles, which attacked the view, associated with Malthus and others, that unemployment was either a natural problem or due largely to a 'surplus' of population among the lower classes.[6] These early nineteenth-century circles insisted, correctly, that unemployment is caused by the operation of modern employment societies themselves, and in so doing exposed a basic contradiction which has threatened employment societies until today – that these societies have typically failed to generate enough of the paid work that they at the same time depend upon and celebrate officially.

What was new about the talk of 'full employment' after 1880 was the suggestion that this contradiction, and therefore the inconvenience or trauma of being unemployed, could be overcome by *state* policies aimed at guaranteeing every adult male individual a full-time job that provided a wage or salary sufficient for himself and his household dependants. Chapters 1–3 examine the factors in Britain which stimulated acceptance of this ideal of full male employment through state intervention. They demonstrate how political support for the ideal of the full employment welfare state gathered momentum, sometimes against considerable political resistance, between the years 1880 and 1940. They also indicate the ways in which this broad full employment consensus was linked closely to the increasing social power of the trade union movement, fears of social unrest, two world wars, the experience of economic crisis, changing party policies and, by no means of least importance, to pathbreaking proposals by J. M. Keynes, William Beveridge and others for maintaining high levels of employment through welfare state regulation of the labour market. Finally, these chapters emphasize the *novelty* of the full employment welfare state. They show how, in the years after 1945, modern employment societies such as Britain and the United States entered an unprecedented historical phase, in which governments more and more attempted to provide full-time jobs for all adult men by policies designed to, first, stimulate private capitalist investment, second, provide a voice for trade unions in matters of collective bargaining and public policy making and, third, secure the health, transportation and education needs of citizens.

Problems of the full employment welfare state

In a number of employment societies the commitment to high levels of male employment through welfare state intervention was attained only with great difficulty, and lasted for only a relatively brief period of two decades or less. While countries such as Britain, Australia and Sweden secured relatively low rates of unemployment after the Second World War, unemployment rates in other countries such as Canada and Italy remained quite high (6 per cent–10 per cent) throughout the 1950s. Indeed, in the United States, it is arguable whether, aside from the Kennedy–Johnson administrations in the 1960s, full male employment was ever achieved. Even during their heyday in the period 1955–65, moreover, the 'model' full employment welfare states such as Britain and Sweden were sometimes criticized by employers, politicians and others advocating a return to less state regulation of the labour market.

Since the early 1970s, public criticism of the full employment welfare state has increased greatly, both in volume and scope. While the vaguely defined goal of 'full employment' remains for the most part a settled issue, the old consensus about achieving this goal through welfare state regulation has everywhere and from all sides begun to crumble rapidly. Almost everything that appeared uncontroversial about this welfare state has become contested, subject to public debate and political struggle. Rising levels of unemployment have played a major role in stimulating this controversy although, throughout this book, we argue that the factors responsible for this controversy about *how* to restore full employment run much deeper. Some of these unsettling factors are no doubt unique to particular countries or regions; examples include the long-standing and now acute 'deindustrialization' of the British and American economies (discussed in Chapters 3, 6, 7 and 8) and the particularly strong West German environmental movement against nuclear energy and unbridled economic growth (themes considered in Chapter 4). Notwithstanding such local variations, a cluster of difficulties *generally* confronts the employment societies of the OECD at the present time.

Three broad types of difficulties – economic, political and social – are discussed in this book, and each is viewed as a source of disruption of the full employment welfare state arrangements, as well as a reason why these arrangements *cannot be repeated* in their old post-war form. As a guide to understanding the chapters which follow, these economic, political and social difficulties are summarized briefly below.

1 The massive post-war wave of economic growth within the employment societies began to be replaced during the 1970s by deep stagflationary trends – sluggish economic output combined with high levels of unemployment and price inflation. These stagflationary trends have had an unsettling effect on the whole global economy, and they have also severely undermined the capacity of the welfare state to effectively fulfil its various functions, including its commitment to high levels of employment. Several of the most important *economic* sources of stagflation are summarized below:

(*a*) Markets for certain types of durable consumer goods (such as automobiles and refrigerators) have in recent years become relatively saturated, and the demand that presently exists for their replacement is more and more satisfied by imports from Third World countries, where they can be produced more cheaply. In order to stimulate a new wave of investment *and* employment in the leading employment societies, mass markets for new (labour-intensively produced) consumer products would have to be developed. However, adequate substitutes for the old employment-generating durable consumer goods appear nowhere on the horizon.

(*b*) During the past two decades, the propensity of privately-owned business firms to invest has tended to decline, due in part to the strengthened position of trade unions in the process of bargaining over wages and conditions. The relative advances of trade unions during the era of the full employment welfare state have been an especially unsettling factor in the economy, because private firms' attempts to recoup the gains made by trade unions, for example, their attempts to maintain their profit levels by raising prices or making workers redundant, have in turn directly resulted in increases of price inflation and rising levels of registered unemployment.

(*c*) Many private firms have also attempted to reverse the relative gains of trade unions by removing all or part of their investments to the Third World. This is presently resulting in a new international division of labour.[7] This trend is evident in the transfer and decline of corporate investment and employment in the old industrial heartlands of western Europe and North America and the simultaneous growth of industrial investment and employment in Third World countries. Profound changes in the world economy are resulting from this trend towards trans-national production: national and multinational companies are moving all or part of their production processes out of high-wage economies (such as Britain, West Germany and the United States), into countries (such as Mexico, Brazil and Malaysia) where there is an unlimited industrial reserve army of workers to keep wages down (to usually less than £0.40 per hour) and working hours long (sixty hours per week are common). In other words, companies' production processes are being split more and more into sub-processes which are carried out anywhere in the world, according to where the most profitable combination of capital and workers can be found. For instance, shirts are cut out in the Federal Republic of Germany, air-freighted to Tunisia, where they are sewn together and packed and then flown back to Germany for retailing. Or, an American electronics company manufactures wafers and masks for integrated circuits in America (a highly automated process), flies them to the Philippines, where they are soldered into capsules (through labour-intensive processes), after which they are returned to the United States for testing and marketing.

(*d*) The trend towards trans-national production intensifies pressure on companies everywhere to 'modernize' by reducing their labour costs by substituting capital for workers. This has contributed greatly to breakthroughs in the micro-electronics industry and robotics. The pace and extent of introduction of new types of labour-saving devices in industrial manufacturing and service industries is sometimes exaggerated by both their defenders and critics. The job-reducing effects of a particular technology often vary from one sector of the state or economy to another, depending on such factors as how and where it is applied within the factory or office, the power of trade unions (where they exist), as well as the strength of demand for the goods or services being produced with the new technology. Nevertheless, there can be no doubt that the new types of labour-saving devices (such as robots) do not lead in the short run to a net gain in the overall number of jobs. Rather, these devices are currently producing dramatic increases in both unemployment and productivity – propelling a form of 'jobless growth' which shakes the full employment welfare state to its foundations.

(*e*)   The hope that welfare state intervention would ensure continuous prosperity and full male employment has also been dashed by major changes in the international monetary and trading systems. During the post-war period, the relaxation of tariffs and exchange controls resulted in large increases in capital movements and international trade (exports of OECD countries as a whole increased from 11 per cent of gross domestic product (GDP) in 1954 to almost 17 per cent of GDP in 1973). This had the long-t erm effect, ironically, of exposing the national economies of employment societies to the ravages of uncontrolled competition, in much the same way that they were exposed before the 1930s. This competition was manageable so long as the United States remained the predominant western economic and political power, acting effectively as the western world's banker. But with the deterioration of the balance of payments of the United States, and the emergence of Japan and western European countries as its strong trading competitors, unhindered trade and capital movements have become a major destabilizing force within the OECD. The suspension, in 1971, of the convertibility of the US dollar into gold signalled the end of an era that began with the Bretton Woods agreement signed in 1944. The OECD now resembles a highly fragile monetary and trading system without a centre, and matters have been made only worse by the abandonment of fixed exchange rates, increasing reliance on private banks for government financing, currency speculation, renewed fears about international debt, and growing protectionism. For the time being, little relief from these dangerous centrifugal trends can be expected. This is despite the fact that closer consultation, new stabilization programmes and greater central co-ordination of the monetary and trading systems would seem to be in the interests of many employers, private banks and OECD governments.

2   These economic difficulties confronting the full employment welfare state have been compounded by a cluster of *political* difficulties arising from the growing power and scope of the state itself. The following chapters discuss four interrelated types of problems generated by the interventionist welfare state:

(*a*)   In attempting to perform its various functions, including the maintenance of high levels of male employment, the welfare state has greatly extended the grip of unaccountable government and para-government institutions over its clients and citizens. The welfare state has consequently undermined some of its earlier popularity; there has developed a certain loss of popular trust in the apparatus of government, which comes to be viewed by many citizens as synonymous with red tape, surveillance and bureaucratic control. The growth of unaccountable and unpopular state power was neither fully anticipated nor seen to be problematic by the early advocates of the full employment welfare state. It has nevertheless provided a platform for its critics, on both the left and right, to publicly accuse the full employment welfare state of paternalism, of being a recipe for less democracy and more bureaucratic regulation and closed government.

(*b*)   The decline in popularity of the welfare state has been exacerbated by a definite discrepancy between its promises and actual performance. Early defenders of the welfare state pointed to its ability to achieve full male employment and greater equality of opportunity for all. This had the effect of heightening many social groups' expectations of what could be achieved through welfare state regulation. Yet in view of the evident failures of the welfare state to either maintain full employment for men or to reduce gender, class, regional and ethnic inequalities, these heightened expectations have remained in practice unsatisfied. Frustration and disappointment have resulted, and in certain cases (the rebirth of the women's movement is a good case in point) this has been followed by active political attempts to remedy social grievances and discriminations.

(*c*)   By reducing the anticipated duration of unemployment, and by providing a cushion of social policies for many employed and unemployed workers, the welfare state helped for a time to strengthen the hand of trade unions against private firms. By regularly involving trade unions in state policy-making processes, and by removing the whip of unemployment, the welfare state increased the chances of a retaliatory investment 'strike' by private firms against trade unions – thereby paralysing its own attempts to maintain private investment, permanent economic growth and full male employment.

(*d*)   This inability of the welfare state to maintain an accord with trade unions and business has been exacerbated by a basic contradiction within many of its interventions in the capitalist economy. Described simply, this contradiction is one in which the full employment welfare state has attempted during the past four decades to do the impossible: it has tried to regulate *publicly* and even restrict the market economy so as to ensure that it functions spontaneously as a *privately-controlled* economy. In other words, the welfare state tried to reach the objective of full male employment by both underwriting the power of private enterprise *and* weakening and counteracting its negative effects, such as unemployment and environmental pollution. This contradiction was not anticipated fully by Beveridge and other early advocates of the full employment welfare state (see Chapter 2). They assumed, incorrectly, that the welfare state could perform its various tasks (stimulating capitalist investment, recognizing trade unions, maintaining full employment, providing for various collective needs) by simultaneously limiting *and* respecting the power of private capitalist firms to invest, to create jobs and, thus, to support or undermine government policies.

3   These economic and political problems confronting the full employment welfare state have been reinforced by a number of *demographic and social* developments, two of which are given special emphasis in the following chapters:

(*a*)   Demographic trends have added to the pressures on nearly all full employment welfare states. Within the OECD countries, there has been a steady increase in the overall size of the labour force during the past two decades: between 1970–80, for instance, the estimated total labour force rose from 308 million to 349 million persons.[8] The most important factor in this increase was the growing number of young people reaching the age of employment, reflecting the baby boom of the 1950s and early 1960s. The increased part-time or full-time employment of women, particularly married women, has also been crucial. The supply of (potential) employees within employment societies is likely to continue to rise during the remainder of this decade, even if more slowly than in the past. The main reasons for this slowing down include disproportionate increases in redundancies among older employees, a tightening of (discriminatory and often racist) immigration policies, and a lower outflow of labour from the agricultural sector. But these three factors are likely to be at least counter-balanced by continuing increases in the numbers of young employable people (a trend expected to continue until the early 1990s), a further rapid rise in the rates of participation of women in the labour market, and reduced accessibility of young people to higher education.

(*b*)　Since the 1960s there has been a vigorous growth of social movements, such as feminism, the peace movement and environmentalism.[9] These movements draw their support from across class boundaries, they place a high value upon grass-roots, local, informal and often publicly 'invisible' or 'submerged' forms of organization, and they consequently tend to be suspicious of business, trade union hierarchies, political parties and state bureaucracies. While (with the clear exceptions of feminism and environmentalism) these movements are not principally concerned with matters of unemployment and paid and unpaid work – this is one of their present blindspots – they nevertheless contribute decisively to the erosion of the welfare state consensus. They publicly question the confident post-war view that the good life is equivalent to permanent economic growth, full male employment, constantly rising consumption and passive citizenship. Few institutions of the welfare state today escape their criticism. Contrary to the claims of its early post-war defenders, the full employment welfare state does not guarantee social and political tranquillity and public satisfaction with the status quo. It is instead confronted by movements of citizens who force a reconsideration of the overall meaning of 'welfare', press for more democracy and greater social and political equality, and, in the case of the feminist and environmental movements, challenge the assumption that work is simply equivalent to employment.

The uncertain future of full employment societies

These three broad sets of problems presently confronting employment societies – stagflationary and jobless growth trends within the economy, controversies surrounding the welfare state, and demographic and social developments – are at the centre of the following discussion of a range of proposed political remedies for mass unemployment. Our argument is that these difficulties confronting the full employment welfare state are presently forcing the old, peculiarly modern problem of unemployment to resurface, and that this problem is likely to remain a major public issue throughout this decade, at least. For the reasons summarized above, the ideal of full male employment guaranteed by the welfare state appears no longer realistic. Nor does it serve as an effective peace-formula among citizens, political parties, trade unions and business, as it did for almost three decades after the Second World War. The swaggering confidence of the full employment era is rapidly disintegrating; in its place, there is emerging an uneasiness about the future, as well as new political controversies about how – or whether – full employment should be restored.

The outlines of this emerging debate are critically examined in the following chapters. The differing political views on the present unemployment crisis are introduced by considering (in Chapters 1–3) the origins, development and breakdown of the post-war social democratic model of the full employment welfare state. We show that, since the early 1970s, the failures of the social democratic model have been exposed and attacked publicly by *three* post-social democratic political tendencies. Advocates of the *disciplinary state* were among the first to criticize the full employment welfare state for its inability to govern and its contribution to stagflation and, as we show in Chapter 4, they recommended a tougher and more interventionist state capable of restoring 'full employment' and establishing a new, compulsory accord among state decision-makers, trade unions and businessmen. Chapters 5–7 examine the theory and practice of the *strong state, free market* strategy for reducing unemployment. Its vigorous defence of free market capitalism guarded by the strong state is considered, and its serious weaknesses are illustrated and explained in case studies of the Thatcher and Reagan administrations.

Chapters 8 and 9 consider the deep uncertainty and often confused responses of the left, in Britain for instance, to the present unemployment crisis. These chapters also propose some ways in which this uncertainty and confusion might be positively overcome. The prevailing nostalgia of the Labour Party in Britain for restoring full employment is contrasted, in the final chapter, with some *utopian socialist* proposals for reducing and equitably redistributing waged and salaried work. The main weakness of these proposals, we argue, is that they beg many questions about political strategy, that is, questions about the means for moving towards a society without mass unemployment. Notwithstanding this weakness, these utopian socialist arguments are seen to be invaluable contributions to the task of stimulating public discussion about alternatives to full male employment. In direct contrast to social democratic, disciplinary state and free market proposals, utopian socialism boldly rejects the ideal of full male employment. It consequently points – in our view correctly – to the need to move towards a type of post-employment society, in which individuals would be able to choose freely whether or not (or how much) they wished to engage in paid work.

Notes

1   Organization for Economic Co-operation and Development, *OECD Economic Outlook*, **36** (Paris, 1984), pp. 49–58; *The OECD Observer*, **130** (September 1984), pp. 5–10.

2   See the famous study of 1930s unemployment in Britain conducted by the Pilgrim Trust, *Men Without Work* (Cambridge, 1938), especially pp. 143–79, and, more recently, Margaret Mitchell, 'The effects of unemployment on the social condition of women and children in the 1930s', *History Workshop*, **19** (spring 1985), pp. 105–27.

3   See, for example, Marshall Sahlins, 'The original affluent society', in his *Stone-Age Economics* (London, 1974), pp. 1–40.

4   The best recent discussion of the functioning and limits of these regimes is Ferenc Fehér, Agnes Heller and György Márkus, *Dictatorship over Needs* (Oxford, 1983). Independent (i.e. non-state) studies of working conditions within these regimes are rare; one of the few and most stimulating examples is Miklós Haraszti, *A Worker in a Worker's State* (Harmondsworth, 1981).

5   The brutal, time-governed exploitation of factory workers by private employers in the early nineteenth century was described passionately by Marx in the first volume of *Capital, A Critical Analysis of Capitalist Production* (Moscow, 1970), pp. 252–3:

> In its blind unrestrainable passion, its were-wolf hunger for surplus-labour, capital oversteps not only the moral, but even the merely physical maximum bounds of the working-day. It usurps the time for growth, development, and healthy maintenance of the body. It steals the time required for the consumption of fresh air and sunlight. It higgles over a meal-time, incorporating it where possible with the process of production itself, so that food is given to the labourer as to a mere means of production, as coal is supplied to the boiler, grease and oil to the machinery. It reduces the sound sleep needed for the restoration, reparation, refreshment of the bodily powers to just so many hours of torpor as the revival of an organism, absolutely exhausted, renders essential. It is not the normal maintenance of the labour-power which is to determine the limits of the working-day; it is the greatest possible daily expenditure of labour-power, no matter

how diseased, compulsory, and painful it may be, which is to determine the limits of the labourers' period of repose. Capital cares nothing for the length of life of labour-power. All that concerns it is
simply and solely the maximum of labour-power, that can be
rendered fluent in a working-day. It attains this end by shortening the
extent of the labourer's life, as a greedy farmer snatches increased
produce from the soil by robbing it of its fertility.

6   See E. P. Thompson, *The Making of the English Working Class*
    (Harmondsworth, 1972), pp. 853–4n. Thompson here criticizes the view
    of G. M. Young (*Victorian England*, Oxford, 1936, p. 27) that 'unem-
    ployment was beyond the scope of any idea which Early Victorian refor-
    mers had at their command, largely because they had no word for it'.

7   Folker Fröbel *et al.*, *The New International Division of Labour*
    (Cambridge, 1980), esp. chs 1–2.

8   *The OECD Observer*, **115** (March 1982), pp. 8–9.

9   The best single account is provided by Alain Touraine, *The Voice and the
    Eye. An Analysis of Social Movements* (Cambridge, 1981).

Further reading

Nixon Apple, 'The rise and fall of full employment capitalism', *Studies in
    Political Economy*, **4** (autumn 1980), pp. 5–39.
Laura Balbo, 'The servicing work of women and the capitalist state', *Political
    Power and Social Theory*, **3** (1982), pp. 251–70.
Tom Forester (ed.), *The Information Technology Revolution* (Oxford,
    1985).
Maurice Godelier, 'Work and its representations: a research proposal',
    History Workshop, **10** (1980), pp. 164–74.
Krishan Kumar, 'The social culture of work : work, employment and unem-
    ployment as ways of life', *New Universities Quarterly* (winter 1979),
    pp. 5–28.
Claus Offe, *Contradictions of the Welfare State*, edited John Keane
    (London, 1984).
R. E. Pahl, *Divisions of Labour* (Oxford, 1984).
Joan Robinson, 'What has become of employment policy?', in Joan Robinson,
    Contributions of Modern Economics (Oxford, 1978), ch. 23.
E. P. Thompson, 'Time, work discipline and industrial capitalism', *Past and
    Present*, no. 38 (1967), pp. 56–97.

1 The development of a full employment consensus

It is the orthodox Treasury dogma, steadfastly held, that whatever might be the political or social advantages, very little additional employment and no real permanent additional employment can, in fact, as a general rule, be created by State borrowing and State expenditure. [Chancellor of the Exchequer Winston Churchill, British House of Commons, April 1929]

For many years, at least since the 1880s in Britain, full employment had been a political objective not only of those most likely to find themselves unemployed, but of social reformers of many political persuasions. It was, however, the events of the First World War and the subsequent depression which pushed the problem of mass unemployment to the top of the political agenda in the 1920s and 1930s. Once there, it stimulated a sense among electorates and government policy-makers of the need for more systematic and viable schemes designed to maintain full male employment. Focusing on Britain, this chapter examines the slow and convoluted process through which political support for government guarantees of full male employment widened during the inter-war years; how the emergence of this broad political support was linked inextricably to the development of new proposals by J. M. Keynes and others for managing and stabilizing the economy, and achieving full employment of labour and capital; and how the realization of these proposals was initially impeded by changes in the party system.

The roots of the full employment ideal

It is still often thought that the ideal of full employment guaranteed by the state originated during the 1920s and 1930s. This assumption seems based mostly on the fact that the harsh experience of unemployment during these decades still evokes bitter memories today –

and for good reasons. Between 1921 and 1932 registered unemployment in Britain averaged 14 per cent of the workforce (reaching 22 per cent in 1932). Once the depression began, there were never less than 1 million men unemployed, and in September 1932 unemployment rose to its worst level of 3.75 million.[1]

This harsh inter-war experience of unemployment was not responsible, however, for the development of the full employment ideal. This ideal in fact was invented and popularized during the nineteenth century. Through the course of that century, the rapid growth of an employment society, set in train by the twin processes of capitalist industrialization and urbanization, made unemployment in Britain a more intractable problem as well as an important source of political unrest. Under pressure from urbanization and the rapid growth of industrial manufacturing, ways of making ends meet *outside* the labour market disappeared for many workers. Their 'free' access to seasonal jobs and resources in the countryside was more and more restricted during the nineteenth century. At the same time, they were confronted increasingly with employers' demands for greater job specialization and stricter work discipline. This 'de-casualization' of paid work severely reduced the capacity of workers to make a living by moving to and fro between the labour market and their households; employment and its converse, unemployment, thereby loomed larger as apparently *inescapable* facts of workers' everyday lives. The earning capacity of households, for so long the material refuge of the unemployed, was also squeezed during the last decades of the nineteenth century by the compulsory schooling of children and the exclusion of many women from the labour market. It is estimated that at the beginning of the nineteenth century at least half of all married women in Britain were employed in the labour market; by mid century, this proportion had declined to one-quarter and, by 1911, to just 10 per cent.[2] This development had negative consequences for many women, who increasingly lost their freedom to move between the household and the labour market.

It was not long before these economic and social changes stimulated political demands for full employment among not only those who found themselves unemployed, but also among social reformers and pamphleteers. As early as 1848, the popular scientific writer Hugo Reid demanded that the state should 'fulfill its task of finding employment at a sufficient rate of wages' for those unable to do so themselves. How the demand for full employment was subsequently transformed from a preoccupation of the unemployed and a few radical sympathizers in the mid nineteenth century to being a major concern of politicians, government policy-makers and businessmen by the turn of the century was a complex process involving many factors.

One important factor was the behaviour of government itself. Although the 'Treasury view' remained adamantly opposed to state spending to reduce unemployment – maintaining that if people were unemployed it was because they demanded too high wages, and that governmental efforts to create employment would only make matters worse for business – nineteenth-century governments occasionally conceded that unemployment was due not to the personal inadequacies of the unemployed but, rather, to changes in economic conditions. Thus, the economic consequences of the Irish famine and political unrest in the 1840s, the Crimean War in the 1850s and the American Civil War in the 1860s persuaded governments to succumb to public pressure and approve public works legislation.

A second important factor was the increasing body of humanitarian literature focusing on the harsh social consequences of unemployment. This literature argued the need for social reform and prompted voluntary activity to find paid work for the 'deserving unemployed'. More generally, it raised public awareness about the plight of the unemployed, suggesting that 'work for all' should be a central objective of government policy.

The powerful voice of the emergent trade union movement, combined with recurrent bouts of high unemployment after the 1870s, provided additional weight to existing demands for full employment to be placed high on the political agenda. The opening address of the Trades Union Congress in 1879, for instance, demanded to know whether it was really necessary that 'every few years large multitudes of the people should, through no fault of their own, be reduced to such a destitute position'. Pressured by trade unionism, and in the context of growing awareness of relative industrial decline, businessmen, politicians and government policy-makers increasingly viewed unemployment as not only wasteful of economic resources, but feared its political and social consequences.

All these factors combined to ensure that by the end of the nineteenth century unemployment was a major public issue, and that demands for full employment were impassioned and pressing. A growing body of social and political opinion rejected the view that unemployment was due to personal inadequacies among the unemployed – either their lack of effort and initiative or their tendency to produce large families – or that it was the inevitable result of a natural tendency towards increased economic growth and prosperity. Even so, the various remedies for unemployment promoted in the late nineteenth and the early twentieth centuries (protectionism, public guarantees of the right to work, direct job creation by the state, naval and military conscription, and progressive taxation combined with counter-depressive public works) were largely rejected by Conservative and Liberal governments imbued with the earlier nineteenth-century public philosophy which defined unemployment as primarily a short-term and recurrent economic problem which entailed unavoidable, if harsh, social consequences. While these governments purportedly conceded the state's responsibility for unemployment and welfare, their policies appeared more concerned with maintaining free markets for labour and disciplining workers through intrusive although fairly extensive welfare policies. Thus, although the Liberal governments between 1905 and 1916 introduced new small-scale public works schemes, established labour exchanges to help the unemployed find jobs, and initiated an unemployment insurance scheme for workers in major industries, their basic approach to budgetary policy was wholly orthodox.

Full employment on the political agenda

Even the mass mobilization of men and women during the First World War,[3] guaranteeing jobs for all who wanted them, did not improve the immediate prospects for government guarantees of full employment. When the war ended, each of the main political parties accepted the 'Treasury view' that the solution to post-war unemployment lay in dismantling wartime controls over production, prices and labour, reducing public expenditure (to achieve a balanced budget) and real wages, restoring free market principles and business confidence at home, and re-establishing the pre-war international financial and trading system abroad.

These policies were underpinned by the assumption, derived from the economic orthodoxy of the day, that full employment was 'natural' in employment societies because, following Say's Law, supply created its own demand. As unemployment rose, increasing the supply of 'idle' labour, it was argued, wages would fall, thus allowing more workers to be employed. In this way, government policy-makers and most economists assumed that the sharp rise in unemployment following the post-war boom would be temporary, and that, as before 1914, public works would need to be introduced only to relieve social distress and reduce the risk of political unrest. When unemployment continued to rise in the 1920s, however, the Treasury would not agree to further increases in state spending or relaxation of its monetary policy. 'Money taken for government purposes', the Conservative Chancellor of the Exchequer, Stanley Baldwin declared, 'is money taken away from trade, and borrowing will thus tend to depress trade and increase unemployment.' Even the Labour governments of this period accepted this view.[4] As far as the Treasury was concerned, a balanced budget, low interest rates, and returning Britain to the Gold Standard (at the pre-war value of sterling) were the primary economic tools used to deal with depression and unemployment throughout the 1920s.

Nevertheless, the sharp rise in the level of unemployment after the First World War prompted major re-examinations of the prevailing orthodoxy about the role of the state, especially in the areas of economic management and social welfare provision. Two distinctive critiques of Treasury economic and social policy emerged in the 1920s and 1930s. First, 'imperial visionaries' [Constantine] such as Leo Amery, Neville Chamberlain, Lord Beaverbrook of the *Daily Express*, the Labour politician J. H. Thomas and, in 1930, the Trades Union Congress openly challenged the orthodox perception of unemployment as a short-term problem to be remedied by free trade. They argued that the state should play a more active role in encouraging trade within the British Empire. By converting the Empire into a much more economically self-sufficient unit, disentangled from the international economy, Britain would be able to compete much more aggressively, thus realizing a higher level of employment.

The second group of critics of the prevailing economic and social orthodoxy also rejected the idea that governments should basically sit back and wait for an inevitable recovery in the trade cycle. Largely influenced by J. M. Keynes, these critics began to explore the heretical concept of state management of the economy.

In his writings from the mid 1920s, and most famously in *The General Theory of Employment, Interest and Money* (1936), Keynes introduced the concepts of aggregate economic demand and demand deficiency. Challenging the prevailing orthodoxy that full employment was part of the natural state of affairs, Keynes argued that there is no effective and automatic mechanism for ensuring optimum use of aggregate resources in a market capitalist system.

Instead, he argued, the employment level is a function of the level of economic output, which in turn is a function of the amount of goods and services that individuals and businesses buy for the purposes of consumption or investment. When consumption or investment are increased or reduced, there is a corresponding ripple or 'multiplier' effect throughout the economy which raises or decreases output and employment. Thus, when there is insufficient consumption and investment (demand deficiency) – as Keynes argued was the case in the 1920s and 1930s – the 'multiplier' process operates in reverse, producing falls in output and employment. Business investment is notoriously erratic, Keynes argued, because firms must always buy goods and services at one point in time in order to produce goods and services for sale in the future. Employment levels thus depend on a basically unstable factor in the economy. In order to maintain aggregate demand and full employment, or so Keynes argued, governments must do what private business will not do. They must henceforth make themselves responsible for *regulating the level of aggregate demand in the economy*, by varying disposable income, not only through changes in interest rates, public works projects or direct credits to consumers, or by cutting taxes, but also *by expanding and contracting government revenue* so as to counteract the cyclical booms and slumps (and uncertainties) of a market economy. Contrary to Say's Law, Keynes argued, if the level of demand in the economy was high and continuous, optimum levels of supply would follow.

Keynes's ideas appealed particularly to the radical wing of the Liberal Party under Lloyd George, to figures such as Sir Oswald Mosley and John Strachey (then members of the Independent Labour Party), and to Ernest Bevin, General Secretary of the Transport and General Workers' Union. At first, only the Liberals were willing to endorse such ideas as official party policy. Once Lloyd George became party leader in 1928, he recruited Keynes to his Liberal Industrial Inquiry. The product of this inquiry was the famous Liberal 'Yellow Book' of 1928 which drew heavily on Keynes's ideas by calling for a vast programme of public works, *financed by deficit spending*, to provide work for the unemployed. Just over a year later, in the 1929 general election campaign, this programme formed the basis of the Liberal Party's manifesto, *We Can Conquer Unemployment*. In their campaign statements, Liberal leaders also assumed the power of the Keynesian multiplier. They calculated that for every £1 million spent by government 5000 men would be set to work, half of them directly and half indirectly in producing the materials required for the additional jobs. Lloyd George told Liberal candidates in 1929:

If instead of an allowance of one pound or twenty-five shillings a week, a man brings home three pounds a week from his job, you double and treble his purchasing power. The mills, the factories, the workshops will derive benefit from it. The result will be you will start a round of prosperity.

Throughout the 1920s and the early 1930s, however, Keynes's ideas were not accepted by Treasury policy-makers. Labour and Conservative governments of this period implemented new public works programmes but refused to endorse deficit financing. As a result, the programmes were too small in scale to produce much effect on unemployment. Although the 1929 Labour government doubled its expenditures on public works in response to ever-rising unemployment (almost 2 million men by 1930), the main thrust of its economic policy was protectionism (high import tariffs) and a balanced budget. Government ministers and Treasury officials simply did not believe that public spending could in the long-run influence the level of demand and employment. Indeed, on the contrary, they held firmly to the pre-Keynesian belief that government income must match government expenditure. In keeping with this belief, Labour's Chancellor Philip Snowden appointed the former chairman of the Prudential Assurance Company to seek savings in government spending.* In contrast, Keynes advocated a protectionist revenue tariff (essentially import duties) coupled with an expansionary fiscal policy. His pro-

---

* Recent re-examinations of economic policies in the 1930s have suggested that Lloyd George could not have fulfilled his claims to reduce unemployment to pre-1914 levels, partly because the multiplier effect of loan-financed public works which he advocated would have been much less than has been previously assumed, partly because the scale of Keynes's solution would have created serious balance of payments problems [Glynn and Howells] and partly because Britain was suffering not from one type of (cyclical) unemployment problem but many, including 'structural' unemployment in its export sectors [Booth and Glynn]. Lloyd George's proposals were, moreover, formulated before the steep rises in unemployment in the late 1920s when unemployment was about 1.5 million. At that time, a reduction in unemployment of some 400,000–500,000 would have been substantial; the effect would have been much less substantial in the early 1930s, when unemployment was over 3 million. See T. Thomas 'Aggregate demand in the United Kingdom 1918–45', in Roderick Floud and Donald McClosky (eds.), *The Economic History of Britain since 1700*, vol. 2 (Cambridge 1981), pp. 332–46.

posal attracted little enthusiasm from Snowden who, like his Treasury colleagues and the Bank of England, feared the effects of deficit financing (on top of an already high national debt) on the financial stability of the country. Equally, the radical proposals of Mosley, a former Conservative MP who had joined the Independent Labour Party in 1924, found little support from either Labour's parliamentary leaders or the party outside parliament. Drawing on the ideas of Keynes and the 'underconsumptionist' theories of the radical economist J. A. Hobson, Mosley called in his 'Birmingham Proposals' for nationalization of the banks and 'vigorous expansion of the national credit to create demand' among the less well-off. Mosley resigned from the Labour government in 1930 and within a few months formed his fascist New Party.

Despite these promptings and increasing unemployment, the policies of the Labour government in 1931 were barely different from those of the Conservatives in 1925. Almost monotonously, Treasury orthodoxy dictated policies based on sound government finances and a fatalistic reliance on a revival in world trade. Thus, in the depths of the depression income tax and excise duties were *raised* in 1930. Indeed, the Conservatives' 1929 campaign slogan, 'Safety First', made a positive virtue of this approach. Like Labour, they accepted the argument that deficit spending would merely transfer equivalent resources from the private sector to the state, thus realizing no net increase in employment.[5]

Keynes, rearmament and the achievement of full employment

The National Government (essentially Conservative but led by the Labour leader MacDonald) formed after the financial crisis of 1931 showed some signs of accepting Keynes's analysis that the national fund of capital was not being fully employed. However, the economic policies that were pursued between 1931 and 1935 were largely conventional. The National Government moved to reduce interest rates by taking Britain off the Gold Standard. Although this served to stimulate domestic investment, the government's cheap money policy was essentially a by-product of its foreign exchange policy and it steadfastly refused to endorse Keynes's complementary argument for reflationary fiscal policy based on deficit spending. Following the May Committee's report, public spending, particularly on salaries and transfer payments, was severely reduced. Only when war seemed inevitable after 1936 did the government (after 1935 a Conservative one led by Baldwin) allow deficit spending (but not of the Keynesian type) in order to finance rearmament.

The National Conservative governments of the 1930s also responded to growing public concern over unemployment by directing spending to the most depressed areas. This was the aim of the Special Areas Act of 1934, which marked the beginning of a regional aid policy. In 1937, when the economy was growing sharply (albeit at a lower level of employment than in 1929), the Treasury went some way towards accepting Keynes's idea of using public works expenditure to offset fluctuations in the trade cycle, but the proposals were very modest. The intellectual conversion to Keynesian economic thinking among government policy-makers remained far from complete. Indeed, until 1937 and with continually high levels of unemployment, the government actually ran budget surpluses. It did not accept overall responsibility for achieving and maintaining full employment. Various schemes were designed specifically to provide work for the jobless, but they were introduced piecemeal and small in scale. Government policy retained its basic adherence to the prevailing economic orthodoxy, relying primarily on tariff barriers to protect the home market and the promotion of trade and employment through rationalization of export industries and encouragement of labour mobility.

However, there were elements within all three major parties that dissented increasingly from the Treasury orthodoxy during the 1930s. Since the late 1920s, dissident elements within the Conservative Party had been attracted increasingly to Keynes's ideas. Politicians such as Macmillan, Boothby and Butler eschewed 'free' market orthodoxy and called for governments to use monetary and fiscal techniques, together with minimum wage legislation and generous welfare allowances, to raise and sustain the level of demand and employment. Their proposals were published in books such as *Industry and the State – A Conservative View* (1927), written mainly by Boothby, and in Macmillan's *The Middle Way* (1938).

Resistance to Keynesian proposals remained steadfast within the Conservative Party hierarchy throughout the 1930s. Not so among Labour, which since the 1920s had become the main opposition party. MacDonald's desertion in 1931 stimulated some reappraisal of the party's policies. Although Labour's major policy documents of the decade – *For Socialism and Peace* (1934) and *Labour's Immediate Programme* (1937) – continued to stress the importance of public ownership for the achievement of socialism, a number of party influentials, including Dalton, Morrison and Bevin, were drawn increasingly to Keynes's economic thinking and the possibility of state-managed capitalism. These party influentials wanted greater social equality, and advocated public investment and central direction of the economy to achieve it. They perceived that Keynes had provided them with the economic rationale for their essentially humanitarian policies. Yet, Labour leaders had to decide first whether they still wanted to abolish capitalism or, as Keynes wanted, to reform it. Their answer became increasingly clear during the 1930s and 1940s. Much to the annoyance of Labour's left, they opted, albeit somewhat uncertainly, for Keynes.

It was the experience of the Second World War that ultimately legitimized the goal of the full employment welfare state. The complete mobilization of the country in conditions of total war reduced the level of registered unemployment to just 60,000 in 1943; most of this figure was accounted for by people moving between jobs. Women re-entered the labour market on a massive scale. (By 1943, nine out of ten single women between the ages of 18 and 40, and eight out of ten married women were in the armed forces or working in factories and offices.) From 1943 onwards, moreover, the government was consuming about 60 per cent of GNP, while taxation accounted for over one-third of national income. Complementing this massive financial intervention, government exercised direct control over the flow of most goods and services. One-third of consumer expenditure was subject to rationing; and imports and most building required government licences. What was produced, moreover, was determined by government controls over raw materials, factory space, labour, prices, and retail outlets. Under these conditions, the economy quickly reached full employment and workers found themselves much better off financially than ever before. Indeed, Ernest Bevin, as Minister of Labour, pursued a deliberate policy of improving the pay of low-paid workers and extending collective bargaining to those who had prevously been poorly organized.

It was also during the Second World War that budgetary policy assumed a central role in government finances. The lines of policy were explicitly Keynesian. Keynes had outlined his ideas on how to pay for the war in articles to *The Times* in 1939 (published in 1940 as *How To Pay For The War*). The massive increase in state spending, he argued, would create more demand than the economy could meet and lead to inflation, unless private spending were to be adequately restricted by taxation. Churchill, Prime Minister in the wartime

Coalition government, was not greatly interested in government finance, and in any case he was generally receptive to unorthodox views. Keynes and other Keynesians were brought into the Treasury in 1940 with the result that government officials came under mounting pressure to apply a general theory of the behaviour of economic aggregates (national income, gross domestic product and so forth) and devise policies for the *total* economy. During 1941 the Treasury produced its first Keynesian budget – the so-called 'stabilization' budget of 1941 – accompanied by a White Paper providing estimates of national income and expenditure. Such estimates were essential prerequisites for Keynesian policies directed towards monitoring and sustaining aggregate demand, and marked the elevation of the budget to a new role in British economic policy. These innovations marked the beginning of a process wherein government accounting and economic practices would be adapted gradually and incrementally to the requirements of aggregate demand management. From this time onwards, governments were no longer concerned only with their own finances and balancing their budgets, but with the total economy and with ensuring adequate demand in order to secure the full employment of capital and labour. Due to Keynes's influence, wartime financial policy also embraced new approaches to monetary policy and the determination of interest rates, as well as the notion that the economy and its principal aggregates would be monitored closely and integrated into monetary and budgetary policy-making.

The experience of total war, the success of so-called 'physical' or administered controls over economic resources, Keynesian budgeting and other initiatives persuaded Labour, Liberal and Conservative politicians, as well as the wider public, that the problem of mass unemployment was neither natural nor insuperable. These wartime developments also bred confidence that government could guarantee full employment and that the broad parameters of policy and political arrangements of the war should be continued in peacetime as a means of avoiding a return to the dark days of depression.

These perceptions were confirmed subsequently in Churchill's Four Year Programme published in 1943, the Coalition government's *Employment Policy* White Paper and, most influentially, in Beveridge's *Full Employment in a Free Society*, to whose highly elaborate vision of the full employment welfare state Chapter 2 turns.

Notes

1 These aggregate data conceal considerable disparities between the depressed areas which had flourished in the mid and late nineteenth century and other regions and towns where there was considerable prosperity. Thus, while one in three men (38 per cent) were unemployed in Wales in 1932, the ratios for south and east England were one in eight (13.1 per cent).

2 E. H. Hunt, *British Labour History 1815–1914* (London, 1981), p. 18.

3 Between 1914 and 1918, the number of married women working outside their homes increased from 5.7 million to 7 million (3 million of whom were working in industry).

4 On his first appearance in the House of Commons in February 1924 as Prime Minister, MacDonald declared that the first Labour government would 'concentrate not first of all on unemployment [which was then about 11 per cent], but on the restoration of trade'. In 1923, however, the Labour Party conference had approved an executive committee motion calling for extensive public works in order to enlarge employment 'up to the point of absorbing every willing worker'. The motion also called for provision of training for unemployed women and juveniles.

5 It has recently been argued, however, that the Treasury view was not as simplistic as many (Keynesian) writers have suggested. See Roger Middleton, 'The Treasury in the 1930s: political and administrative constraints to acceptance of the "new" economics', *Oxford Economic Papers*, new series, **XXXIV** (1982), pp. 48–57.

Further reading

Derek H. Aldcroft, *The Inter-War Economy: Britain 1919–1939* (London, 1970), ch. 9.

Stephen Constantine, *Unemployment in Britain Between the Wars* (London, 1980).

Robert Skidelsky, *Politicians and the Slump: The Labour Government of 1929–1931* (London, 1967).

John Stevenson, 'The making of unemployment policy, 1931–1935', in Michael Bentley and John Stevenson (eds.), *High and Low Politics in Modern Britain* (Oxford, 1983).

Michael Stewart, *Keynes and After* (Harmondsworth, 1967), chs. 3–5.

Jim Tomlinson, *Problems of Economic Policy 1870–1945* (London, 1981), chs. 1 and 5.

Jim Tomlinson, 'Where do economic policy objectives come from? The case of full employment', *Economy and Society*, **12** no. 1 (February 1983), pp. 48–65.

2 The social democratic vision

The only sovereign remedy yet discovered by democracies for unemployment is total war.   [William H. Beveridge, 1944]

It has sometimes been claimed that the emergence of full employment as a central objective of state policy did not depend upon a clear case having been made for its desirability in political and economic terms.[1] The great political influence of William Beveridge's *Full Employment in a Free Society* (1944) suggests otherwise. *Full Employment in a Free Society* laid out in a most detailed and publicly accessible form a comprehensive criticism of inter-war government policies in Britain as well as specific proposals for achieving the objective of full employment. Most of the arguments of this book were not original, however. A whole body of writing on the problem of remedying unemployment had already been developing for more than half a century. Especially after 1880, there was a very rapid growth in the literature on the plight of the unemployed. Some of this literature took the form of systematic theoretical defences of the ideal of full employment written by economists, social researchers, and publicists from various political parties. The political influence of this theoretical literature should not be underestimated. Between 1880 and the end of the Second World War, this writing not only helped to define and stimulate public anxiety about unemployment; it also facilitated the transformation of the vision of full employment into the prevailing common sense of practical politics. As a result, unemployment could no longer be viewed so easily as an inevitable or desirable phenomena; instead, it came to be regarded as the negative and *avoidable* consequence of the failure of politicians to make 'work for all' a central objective of state policy.

It is important to reconsider this early theoretical literature in defence of the full employment welfare state, since it helps to highlight several of the reasons why the whole political doctrine of full employment has subsequently come unstuck. From the beginning, we would claim, the twentieth-century ideal of the full employment welfare state contained the seeds of its own destruction, and that, consequently, it was able to survive as a workable ideal only for a relatively short time and only under special political, economic and social conditions – which no longer prevail. Nowhere is this point more clearly evident than in William Beveridge's classic report, *Full Employment in a Free Society*. Written under conditions of total war, and anticipating the transition from war to peace, the arguments of this book explain and in a sense summarize the essence of the social democratic case for full employment through welfare state intervention. Like his earlier work, *Unemployment: A Problem of Industry* (1909), this book does not develop many new political or theoretical insights on unemployment. Its real achievement is rather to be found in the fact that it skillfully synthesized, in a language accessible to the reading public, the theory of unemployment developed by J. M. Keynes during the 1930s, Beveridge's own earlier, rather different analysis of the causes of unemployment, and an explicit, highly detailed contribution to the social democratic case for the full employment welfare state which had been developing since the late nineteenth century. *Five* interrelated themes in Beveridge's argument seem in retrospect to be especially crucial. They illustrate well what the term full employment has meant to most social democrats during the past four decades.

1   Inequality based upon economic privilege is viewed by Beveridge as the major blot on contemporary capitalist societies. Economic privilege, the unequal distribution of material wealth is the root of 'the giant social evils of Want, Disease, Ignorance and Squalor'. It is also the source of the angry clamour associated with lock-outs and strikes and the bitter reactions to the hunger marches, dole-queues and soup kitchens generated by mass unemployment. Economic misery generates social animosity and political breakdown, says Beveridge, and he sees this equation to be especially evident in the experience of being unemployed: 'The greatest evil of unemployment is not physical but moral, not the want which it may bring but the hatred and fear which it breeds.' It follows from this that greater material equality based on full employment ('freedom from Idleness') is a necessary condition of a welfare society, in which fear, jealousy and the corrupting effects of mass unemployment will have been finally eradicated. According to Beveridge's vision, every male individual who works while he can and contributes from his earnings

to state revenue should be entitled to an income 'sufficient for the healthy subsistence of himself and his family, an income to keep him above Want, when for any reason he cannot work and earn'.

Notice how Beveridge portrays full employment (for *men*, at least) as subversive of class relations in capitalist society. The equal possibility of all adult male individuals finding a job in the labour market will likely lead to greater social equality, he argues, for differences in monetary reward for variations in work effort and skill do not of themselves create class distinctions. However, he does emphasize that once freedom of entry into the labour market is guaranteed, competition among busy and productive (male) individuals cannot be allowed to operate in unrestricted form. This competition within the labour market must be moderated and under-pinned by various government policies – Beveridge especially had in mind a system of children's allowances and a comprehensive health and rehabilitation service – to whose benefits all employed workers and their household dependants should be *entitled*. Only in this way could full employment have genuinely equalizing consequences.

2   The achievement of greater social equality through full male employment and a system of social security is seen by Beveridge to depend upon stimulating capitalist economic growth. The full employment of waged and salaried labour can and should be achieved through the full employment of *private* capital. It should be mentioned in respect of this second theme that the *degree* of reliance upon private capitalist enterprise was always, and remains to this day, a contro-versial issue among social democratic advocates of full employment. Beveridge by no means evades this controversy. Indeed, at one point in *Full Employment in a Free Society* he says that 'if . . . it should be shown by experience or by argument that abolition of private property in the means of production was necessary for full employment, this abolition would have to be undertaken'. However, this possibility is not central to Beveridge's argument. His general view is that rising levels of capitalist production are a necessary condition of abolishing joblessness.

Beveridge's main argument is this: in order to bring about a smooth transition from total war to peace, the full employment welfare state will have to rely upon the co-operation of private capitalist firms. This is because the financing of the programmes of the welfare state (its building of hospitals and its provision of unemployment insurance, for instance) depends crucially upon the volume of contributions and social security taxes that are extracted from the wages and salaries of the employees of private capitalist firms. To move suddenly against those firms would risk provoking an immediate unemployment crisis, since they would probably take retaliatory action by laying off their employees in large numbers. In turn, this would threaten the state's main source of taxation revenue, and so a fiscal crisis of the state – its inability to either borrow from private banks or to pay for its social security programmes – would soon follow. This scenario can be avoided, Beveridge argues, if the state actively solicits the *co-operation* of private corporations by involving them in its policy-making and administration procedures. In his view, the war effort in Britain confirms that full employment and equality of opportunity in the labour market do not require the full socialization by the state of the production process. A third way – which by-passes the old political choice between market capitalism and state-directed socialism – is possible and desirable.

3   Although full employment of labour crucially depends upon fostering and maintaining capitalist investment, this can and should only be achieved, or so Beveridge insists, through government regulation of the economy – through conscious and continuous 'intelligent flexible planning' co-ordinated by the welfare state. To count on competing individual firms to always invest their profits productively and to maintain a permanently high demand for workers is unrealistic. Only the full employment welfare state can ensure this outcome. Here Beveridge draws explicitly upon Keynes's belief that unemployment was caused primarily by inadequate investment by private capitalists and deficiencies of effective demand for labour and its products (see Chapter 1). Processes of market competition among capitalists, Beveridge says, cannot keep the demand for and supply of workers in equilibrium, let alone ensure equality of opportunity of all (male) workers in the labour market. Indeed, deficiency of total effective demand, both for labour and its products, has always been a chronic problem in unplanned capitalist systems. What is now required, therefore, is a 'mixed economy' wherein government strives to stimulate and regulate private economic growth in order to 'socialize' demand rather than production. Only in this way can the full employment of capital and paid labour be ensured. Beveridge quotes with approval the principle laid down by Alvin Hansen, a contemporary American economist: 'Private industry can and will do the job of production. It is the responsibility of the Government to do its part to ensure a constant demand.'

Beveridge proposes the following package of interventionist state policies designed to regulate and stimulate private capitalist investment:

a the internal reorganization of the state apparatus (the establishment of departments for controlling and co-ordinating public expenditure and encouraging industrial investment, for instance) so as to ensure its effective and efficient operation;

b the expansion of flexible, selective and planned state policies – concerning such matters as military defence, transport, agriculture and foreign trade – which aim to encourage private investment and the spending of public or private money on the products of capitalist industry;

c controlling the location of capitalist industry through urban and regional planning, and facilitating the organized mobility of labour by means of job retraining schemes and (perhaps compulsory) registration at employment exchanges;

d redistributing wealth and enhancing consumer spending power through increased taxation of property owners and the very rich;

e the selective transfer of strategic industries, such as transport and power production, from private to public ownership;

f the stabilization and expansion of international trade through bilateral or multilateral agreements with other states;

g the guarantee of greater equality of opportunity in the labour market by providing unemployment insurance, health care, housing and rehabilitation services;

h facilitating full freedom of entry (of men, at least) into the labour market by means of a state-organized system of education.

Considered as an overall programme, these policies illustrate one of Beveridge's most basic political points: just as the state is presently expected to defend its citizens from attack from abroad and at home, so in future the state must defend them against booms and slumps, mass unemployment and inequality of opportunity. While Beveridge did not believe that either seasonal unemployment or 'frictional unemployment' – short-term unemployment due to changes of job preference and uneven growth among different sectors of the economy – could be entirely eliminated, he did consider that serious progress towards the eradication of unemployment was possible. (Beveridge envisaged a reduction in the level of unemployment in Britain to not more than 3 per cent; this compared with the levels of

10–22 per cent in the inter-war period.) State invervention could ensure that there was always more vacant jobs than unemployed men – Beveridge's definition of full employment – such that the labour market would always be a seller's market rather than a buyer's market. At worst, unemployment would be reduced to short intervals of idleness; the misery, humiliation and bitterness formerly associated with being jobless would disappear, as individuals found themselves both eligible for unemployment insurance and able to very soon find jobs for which they are qualified. In sum, thanks to the full employment welfare state management of capitalist markets, inequality and unemployment would wither away. The division of employment societies into two hostile classes, one having a large appetite and hardly any dinners and the other large dinners and virtually no appetite, would become a thing of the past. Class divisions and conflict would be superseded by a 'busy productive and contented' society.

4　Full employment and greater equality of opportunity for men, Beveridge insists, are goals to be attained through instalments and 'realistic' reforms enacted and legally secured by social democratic governments and their working-class, trade union and middle-class supporters. Reaching and maintaining full employment does not require revolutionary upheavals and drastic alterations of the status quo. Progress towards the full employment welfare state is necessarily a gradual, piecemeal and level-headed process. It is a matter of time, patience and popular willingness to elect and return social democratic governments committed to reform. 'Full productive employment in a free society is possible, but it is not possible without taking pains. To win full employment and keep it, we must will the end and must understand and will the means.' The full employment welfare state is not a wildly utopian vision; by actively seeking public support for it, and by developing detailed policy programmes, it *can* be achieved.

5　Finally, the maintenance of parliamentary democracy is viewed by Beveridge as a necessary condition and outcome of the full employment welfare state. The negative example of Nazi totalitarianism – a type of society 'completely planned and regimented by an irremovable dictator' – is invoked to drive home the point that a sudden move to destroy the existing parliamentary democratic system, thereby antagonizing the settled opinion of the majority of people, would almost inevitably result in new forms of political dictatorship. Full employment must be achieved and maintained by the state, under the supervision and guidance of the existing political framework of freedom of public assembly, periodic elections, competitive party democracy, and parliamentary and cabinet government. This is what Beveridge means by the phrase 'full employment in a free society': the freedom of (male) individuals to enter and circulate in the labour market, and the right of all adult citizens, male and female, to choose periodically those who are to govern and administer them.

Considered together, these five themes in *Full Employment in a Free Society* illustrate well the *political* vision underpinning Beveridge's social democratic views on full employment. The ideal of full employment is not seen narrowly by him as an *economic* reform, but as part of a much broader social and political programme leading to a society which guarantees justice and freedom for all individuals. Considered in retrospect, these five themes in Beveridge's classic book also indicate several fundamental weaknesses of the vision of the full employment welfare state. In our view, the social democratic formula wherein government (with the co-operation of private enterprise and trade unions) is to be the benevolent father of full employment, greater social equality and democratic liberty is in several respects quite unconvincing, even self-contradictory. In fact, the formula contains at least three blindspots.

First, it is clear that Beveridge inadequately recognized the undemocratic consequences of the full employment welfare state. He failed to see that, in order to carry out its various functions, the welfare state would be likely to undermine some of its own popularity by extending the grip of unaccountable government and para-state institutions over the daily lives of their clients and citizens. The growth of a powerful bureaucratic state was neither fully anticipated nor seen to be problematic. According to Beveridge's social democratic formula, the populations of welfare state countries could interest themselves in politics, attend public meetings and periodically exercise their rights to vote. Beyond minimal levels of political activity, however, they were supposed to be *policy-takers* and not *policy-makers*; that is, they were not required to be active and informed decision-making citizens, but the passive objects of welfare state monitoring and regulation. 'Acceptance by the State of responsibility for full employment is the final necessary demonstration that the

State exists for the citizens – for all the citizens – and not for itself or for a privileged class.' This sentiment is repeated several times in Beveridge's argument for the full employment welfare state. What is striking about it is the degree to which it truncates the rich meaning of the term democracy. Democracy – the most important political weapon yet invented for limiting the arbitrary exercise or abuse of power – is seen by Beveridge to be inapplicable to the spheres of the household and the economy. Having been restricted by him to the sphere of state institutions, democracy also comes to mean not much more than passive citizenship, a deference to public policy-makers and administrators who seek to secure capitalist investment, reduce unemployment and expand welfare opportunities.

As Chapter 5 explains, this basic political weakness of Beveridge's social democracy – that it speaks the language of democratic freedom while at the same time implicitly recommending its restriction in prac- tice, by calling for the considerable expansion of bureaucratic and unaccountable state power – has been successfully, if opportunistically, exploited by market liberals such as Milton Friedman, who claim that the full employment welfare state is leading us along the road to bureaucratic slavery. This deficiency, as our discussion of the work of André Gorz makes clear in Chapter 9, is also emphasized by new socialists, as well as by environmentalists and many activists within the new social movements. These 'left-wing' critics of the full employ- ment welfare state emphasize that not only the practice, but also the theory of social democracy must be criticized as paternalistic, as blindly in love with bureaucratic state power.

The second blindspot in Beveridge's argument concerns the way in which the full employment welfare state stimulated expectations which it subsequently failed to satisfy. The emphasis placed by Beveridge and other social democrats upon the achievement of full employment and greater equality of opportunity has had the (unin- tended) effect of heightening the expectations of certain social groups; in view of the evident failures of the welfare state to maintain either full employment for men or to eradicate class, regional, ethnic and gender inequalities, these heightened expectations have remained in practice unsatisfied. Women's experience of the labour market and the welfare state is a good case in point of this 'frustration of heightened expectations' effect. Beveridge and other social demo- crats justified the full employment welfare state in terms of such *universal* goals as employment for *all* and freedom and equality for *every* person. At the same time, they also envisaged a post-war world in which *men* would be fully *employed* while most women would be *occupied* (with the unpaid household work tasks of shopping, washing, cleaning, preparing food and caring for children), and therefore unable to participate fully and equally in the labour market. During the years after 1945, however, large numbers of women chose (or were forced for financial reasons) to remain in (or enter) the labour market as either full-time or part-time workers. Women's migration into the labour market normally did not reduce the quantity of the work they performed at home. What is more, their migration into the labour market was highly structured along gender lines. For instance, women presently make up 51 per cent of all non-manual workers in Britain, and only 28 per cent of all manual workers. More than half of manual-working women are employed in catering, cleaning, hairdressing or other services described as 'personal'. In non-manual work, over 50 per cent of women are employed in clerical and related occupations. Three classifications of employment – clerical work and catering, cleaning and hairdressing, and welfare – account for over two-thirds of all women's jobs.[2] The net result has been that many women are not only faced with limited pay, promotion and job improvement prospects in the labour market, but also with the necessity of performing *two* types of work – paid as well as unpaid – at the same time. This 'overworking' of women has arguably been one important factor in the rebirth of the women's movement during the past two decades. Since the 1960s, in particular, many women have come to recognize that their actual living conditions openly contradict one of the highest ideals of the full employment welfare state: freedom of choice and equality of opportunity of all individuals in the labour market.

This contradiction between social democratic principles and the actual performance of the full employment welfare state has also been experienced by other social groups, such as working-class youth and ethnic minorities, and it has in no small measure helped to produce a serious decline of trust in the welfare state among these groups. Their disenchantment has often been translated into political action to redress their social grievances. These groups suspect, not inaccurately, that the major beneficiaries of the full employment welfare state did not include women, unskilled workers, and ethnic minorities but, rather, the male, white, urban, professional middle classes.

The final blindspot in Beveridge's vision concerns his assumption that the full employment welfare state would be able to maintain an accord between trade unions and private capitalist corporations, as well as ensure the friendly, if self-interested co-operation of private capitalist corporations with the state. In particular, Beveridge asked few questions about the enormous power of capitalist firms to directly determine levels of investment and employment and so indirectly affect the level of taxation revenues accruing to the state. This power of capitalist firms was assumed to be compatible with the vision of a full employment welfare state. True, Beveridge harboured a few doubts about the difficulty of maintaining full employment in a parliamentary democratic society. He asked, for instance, whether industrial discipline and paid workers' incentive to work would be undermined by the welfare state's removal of the whip of hunger and unemployment, and how, under peacetime conditions, when full employment and free collective bargaining between trade unions and employers become the norm, 'irresponsible' trade union action and inflationary wage spirals could be prevented. He also pondered the adequacy of state controls over prices of essential goods and services in containing wage-generated inflation; whether the right of trade unions to negotiate and strike would need to be limited (by compulsory arbitration, for instance) in order to ensure full employment; and whether capitalists would attempt to sabotage the full employment welfare state.

Beveridge raised these crucial questions, but he failed to pursue them in any detail. In particular, he neglected to discuss whether his proposed strategies for managing the capitalist economy might lead, in the longer term, to a breakdown of the accord between business, trade unions and the state.[3] As we have pointed out already in the introduction, this is precisely what has happened in western Europe and North America during the past decade. By reducing the expected duration of unemployment, and by providing a cushion of social policies for many employed and unemployed workers, the welfare state helped structure capital–labour relations in a manner potentially disadvantageous to the profit and investment interests of private firms. It did this by facilitating confident trade union demands for higher wages and improved conditions, thereby increasing the likelihood of a retaliatory investment 'strike' by private capitalists against trade unions and the full employment welfare state. In this sense, therefore, the welfare state may be said to have encouraged indirectly – and inadvertently – faltering economic growth and the instability of the accord between trade unions and business which Beveridge considered to be one of the mainstays of a full employment welfare society.

Beveridge did not anticipate this self-paralysing dynamic of the full employment welfare state. With the benefit of hindsight, and taking into account the contemporary economic crisis, the social democratic faith in capitalist investors' loyalty to the welfare state is unconvincing. In consequence, a new series of political questions, which point beyond social democracy, has emerged since the mid 1970s. In view of the current economic pressures on the welfare state, especially the flight of certain types of business investment from the industrial heartlands of western Europe and North America, is Beveridge's vision of the full employment of labour and capital still realistic? Given the fact that large numbers of women have entered, on a full-time or part-time basis, the labour market, and are likely to resist being forced back into the household, must not the ideal of full male employment be abandoned as an undesirable masculine dream? And granted that the quickening pace of automation since the 1960s is likely to continue, blocking any further substantial growth of employment in both the industrial and service sectors, can full employment in Beveridge's sense – a 35–40 hour per week job for all adult men guaranteed by the welfare state – be restored in the near future?

These questions seem to be especially troublesome for latter-day supporters of Beveridge, such as the Cambridge group in England.[4] While admitting the need for government to deal with international movements of currency and capital, to co-ordinate and regulate international trade and production, and to 'reach agreement with all social classes', the Cambridge group supposes that political support for the full employment welfare state can be restored, despite the three serious political problems mentioned above. The Cambridge group also makes the questionable assumption that increased state investment in the economy will lead quickly to faster economic growth (without serious environmental damage) and *therefore* to higher rates of employment, greater job security, higher wages and enhanced social policy provision (see Chapter 5).

We are highly sceptical of these latter-day social democratic claims. In view of the three 'blindspots' of the social democratic programme outlined in this chapter, it is extremely doubtful whether the Beveridge vision of full male employment is either a viable or desirable political option for the coming years. In order to further explain and justify this doubt, Chapter 3 illustrates, in the form of a case study of the post-war British welfare state, how Beveridge-type ideals and strategies worked in practice, as well as why they had begun to break down by the mid 1970s.

Notes

1 See, for example, Jim Tomlinson, 'Where do economic policy objectives come from? The case of full employment', *Economy and Society*, **12** no.1 (February 1983), pp. 48–65.

2 Sheila Allen, 'Gender inequality and class formation', in *Social Class and the Division of Labour*, edited by A. Giddens and G. Mackenzie (Cambridge, 1982), pp. 137–47; George Joseph, *Women at Work. The British Experience* (London, 1983).

3 This possibility was first discussed in the theory of a 'political business cycle' developed by the Polish economist, Michal Kalecki. See his classic essay, 'Political aspects of full employment' (1943), reprinted in his *The Last Phase in the Development of Capitalism* (New York, 1972), pp. 75–85.

4 See, for example, Francis Cripps and Terry Ward, 'Government policies, European recession and problems of recovery', *Cambridge Journal of Economics*, **7** (1983), pp. 85–99.

Further reading

William H. Beveridge, *Full Employment in a Free Society* (London, 1944), esp. pt 1.
Herbert Gintis and Samuel Bowles, 'The welfare state and long-term economic growth: Marxian, Neoclassical, and Keynesian approaches', *American Economics Association Papers and Proceedings,* **72** no.2 (May 1982), pp. 341–5.
José Harris, *William Beveridge: A Biography* (Oxford, 1977).
John Keane, *Public Life and Late Capitalism* (Cambridge, 1984), ch. 1.
Krishan Kumar, 'Unemployment as a problem in the development of industrial societies: the English experience', *The Sociological Review*, **32** no.2 (May 1984), pp. 185–233.

3 The era of full employment: from Attlee to Callaghan

The maintenance of full employment will be an integral part of the Government's economic, financial and industrial policy.   [Ernest Bevin, Memo to Cabinet Committee, 1943]

The cosy world we were told would go on forever, where full employment would be guaranteed by a stroke of the Chancellor's pen, ... is gone.   [Prime Minister James Callaghan to the Labour Party Conference, 1976]

Beveridge's case for full employment through economic demand management and welfare state intervention, summarized in *Full Employment in a Free Society*, fired the imagination of policy-makers and the public in Britain during the 1940s, helping make the goal of the full employment welfare state part of a new emerging public philosophy which rejected unemployment as an inevitable consequence of a market capitalist economy. From 1944 onwards, all three major parties as well as trade union and business leaders supported the view that post-war governments should guarantee a job to all those adult males who wanted one. By reviewing post-war employment policies in Britain, this chapter demonstrates how Beveridge's vision of the full employment welfare state was translated into practice by governments from Attlee's to Callaghan's, why Britain enjoyed three decades of full male employment after Beveridge, and why the three blindspots identified in the previous chapter became increasingly apparent, especially after the 1960s.

Full employment policy

The collapse of Chamberlain's Conservative government in 1940 provided the opportunity for Churchill to become Prime Minister as head of a coalition government. At a time when military defeat in the war against Nazism seemed possible, Churchill accepted that representatives of the working class in the Labour Party and the trade unions needed to be brought into government decision-making in order to achieve maximum support for the war effort. Under the influence of these leaders, and at the prompting of many Conservative backbenchers, the government was persuaded to make fairly elaborate plans for the post-war social and economic reconstruction of the country. Labour's effective dominance of the Cabinet's Reconstruction Committee (through the activities of Bevin, Attlee and Morrison), the reality of wartime full employment fostered in large part by Bevin's effective manpower policies, the bitter memories of mass unemployment during the 1920s and 1930s, a determination to avoid another post-war depression, Keynesian influences within the Cabinet's Economic Section, and the general wartime emphasis on 'fair shares' at a time of grave physical danger were all crucial factors pressing government leaders into a commitment to post-war full employment. Indeed, once the government became aware of the nature of Beveridge's private inquiry, Churchill became so eager to endorse the commitment to full employment that he insisted his government's White Paper on *Employment Policy* be published before Beveridge's *Full Employment in a Free Society*.

Despite its broad support for the ideal of full employment, it is important to note that the Churchill government's commitments to full employment, embodied in its 1944 White Paper *Employment Policy*, were much more equivocal and significantly weaker than those demanded by Beveridge and Keynes, and by many politicians in the Labour and Conservative parties. Since it was the result of compromises between different government departments and personalities, the White Paper only committed the government and, therefore, whichever party won the next general election, to 'accept[ing] as *one* of their primary aims and responsibilities the maintenance of a high and stable level of employment after the war' [our emphasis]. There was no commitment to the maintenance of full employment as the *overriding* goal of government economic policy; and, moreover, no consistent commitment to the political ideas of Keynes or Beveridge. Indeed, although conceding the political significance of the government's commitment, Beveridge derided it as 'a public works policy, not a policy of full employment'. Much to Beveridge's (and Keynes's) annoyance the statement conspicuously failed to endorse the principle of government responsibility for stimulating and stabilizing economic demand in the event of another post-war depression.

While Keynes's or Beveridge's ideas failed to register the dominant influence on the 1944 White Paper, Keynesian economic thinking slowly became the dominant influence on wartime financial policies. The success of these financial policies in facilitating the war effort against Germany (as well as so-called 'physical' or administered controls over economic resources) made it virtually inevitable that future government policy-makers would feel that such policies could be used to eliminate unemployment after the war. In the 1945 general election, the main issues were social security, housing and full employment – in fact, Beveridge's agenda. Although both major parties committed themselves to the maintenance of full employment and state welfare, it was Attlee's Labour Party which surprisingly won the election. Apparently, Labour was thought more likely to honour its pledge to full employment than the Conservatives, who were identified as the party which had tolerated mass unemployment in the 1930s. It had been Labour rather than Conservative ministers, moreover, who had been most closely identified with government commitments to the establishment of the welfare state. Labour identified itself and was identified with Beveridge, and accordingly reaped its electoral rewards.

Despite the increasing wartime influence and use of Keynesian financial techniques, however, the new Labour government's programme was not immediately Keynesian. Instead, Labour emphasized planning and the continuation of 'physical' controls. According to Labour's programme, adopted just seven months before the 1945 election at its 1944 Party Conference,

full employment and a high standard of living for those who work by hand and brain c[ould] only be secured *within a planned economy, through the maintenance and adaptation of appropriate economic controls* after the war, and above all by the transfer to the State of power to direct the policy of our main industries, services and financial institutions [our emphasis].

Indeed, in its first few years of office, the Labour government managed the potentially difficult problems of demobilization and reconstruction primarily through 'physical' controls. They did this not by employing Keynesian demand management policies (which relied on the market and were therefore viewed by many socialists, including Chancellor of the Exchequer Dalton, with suspicion). Moreover, Dalton's budgets were based on pre-Keynesian or even anti-Keynesian premises, relying as they did on cheap money rather than overall economic management. Nevertheless, the 1945 Labour government remained committed to full employment throughout its period of office, even when it faced an acute economic crisis (in February 1947, due to severe weather and fuel shortages, unemployment rose temporarily to just under 2 million, or 12½ per cent of the workforce), persistent demands for rearmament and, eventually, fierce resistance from the City. Fearing immediate post-war deflation, Dalton's 'manpower' budgets of 1945, 1946 and 1947 emphasized the social rather than the economic consequences of financial and monetary policy and were specifically designed to maintain high levels of employment.

The economic crisis of 1947 nevertheless persuaded the Labour government to adopt Keynesian financial policies to increase the budget surplus (by raising taxes) to restrain domestic consumption in order to stem rising inflationary pressures resulting from a rising overseas trade deficit. Faced with rising wages and prices, a mounting balance of payments crisis, increasing unemployment and the failure of both 'physical' and strict budgetary controls to restrain and rearrange the pattern of aggregate demand (so as to hold inflation down), the Attlee government also introduced the first of a succession of post-war wages policies. Any future wage increases, the government warned, would depend on increases in productivity. In the Labour government's so-called 'austerity' policies of 1947–50, therefore, can be seen most of the elements of post-war (Keynesian) economic policy: government regulation of aggregate demand through fiscal policy (primarily alterations in taxation), the emphasis on controlling inflation through a wages policy, government promotion of exports, and the appointment of 'working parties' to study the problems of particular industries. Labour also pursued a vigorous regional policy directing job opportunities to depressed areas in Scotland, Wales and northern England.

Aided by massive economic infusions through the Marshall plan and American stockpiling, Labour could rightly claim credit for the achievement of full (male) employment after six years of government, and despite the demobilization of millions of men and women. After 1947, export-led economic growth encouraged by the adoption of Keynesian demand management techniques and Dalton's Distribution of Industry Act of 1945 effectively reduced registered unemployment to 1.5 per cent in the years 1948 to 1950 and to just 1.2 per cent in 1951. In north-eastern England, where unemployment had been 38 per cent in 1932, only 3 per cent were without jobs in 1949. The success of the Attlee government's employment policies were nevertheless less than favourable to certain social groups, especially women. The post-war baby boom and the resurgence of patriarchal and discriminatory social attitudes ensured that married women were systematically excluded from the labour market during these years.[1]

The construction of the full employment welfare state along the lines of the Beveridge Report, and successful management of the economy to achieve economic growth were the main policy objectives not only of the Attlee government but also, until the mid 1960s, of successive Conservative and Labour governments. Throughout this period, governments accepted these objectives not only because it now seemed practicable, but because apparently it was expected of them. As a consequence, British governments became more and more involved in a mass of detailed management of economic and social life: directly nationalizing industry in some cases; limiting consumption by rationing and allocation; providing subsidies of various kinds; controlling building and supplies of raw materials; overseeing the movement of capital and labour; influencing investment decisions; determining the location of new industrial development; improving the organization and efficiency of firms by stimulating mergers, giving financial aid and imposing job-training schemes; developing research and science-based industries; restricting imports and the flow of foreign exchange; and so on. While there were shifts in emphasis from time to time, the general code of government policy appeared to be immutable and highly workable.

Encouraged by their earlier successes, the two main political parties remained committed to full male employment throughout the 1960s and early 1970s. During this time, they could rightly claim to have been successful in keeping their commitments. There was sustained full male employment (the number unemployed averaging 1.7 per cent between 1948 and 1964, four-fifths of whom were out of work for less than a year), rising money wages and low inflation (kept down by falling import prices) in an economy which was growing steadily. When it seemed necessary, governments regulated their own expenditure to ensure a high level of effective demand and employment. Thus, when in 1963 unemployment rose to more than 3 per cent for the first time since the war, the Conservative government increased social benefits and reduced taxes in order to increase demand and employment. The conclusion was drawn by most commentators and policy-makers that, since governments using such Keynesian techniques were able to keep unemployment low and maintain prosperity, these policies must, therefore, ensure these conditions.

With the benefit of hindsight, however, it is clear that post-war governments' spiralling self-confidence in their ability to manage the unemployment problem was misplaced. As the following discussion demonstrates, the so-called 'golden age' of full employment rested on a conjuncture of many other (more important) economic, social and political factors besides Keynesian demand management policies. Once these supportive factors weakened in the late 1960s and early 1970s, the political commitment to the full employment welfare state became increasingly problematic.

The post-war conditions of full employment

Undoubtedly, the prime *economic* characteristic of the 'golden age' of the 1950s and 1960s was the extraordinarily high levels of growth[2] and business profitability, particularly in manufacturing. Through a combination of American financial assistance, backlogs in potential growth, a generally high level of investment reflecting businessmen's heightened expectations, and the application of relatively new technology derived from the war, British companies were able to take advantage of the unprecedently high and stable levels of demand to expand employment opportunities. As a result, the overall level of employment rose from 22.4 million in 1950 to a high point of 25.0 million in 1966.

Levels of economic growth also remained high and stable because of the favourable growth expectations created by the revival of liberalism in international finance and trade. Until its collapse between 1971 and 1973, the post-war international payments system (established by the Bretton Woods Agreement of 1944 and based on the international hegemony of the American dollar) proved an effective vehicle for promoting free trade. (Although in creating the Overseas Sterling Area as a monetary union with sterling as its reserve currency, Britain also sought to insulate colonial and former colonial markets from foreign – especially American – competition.) Because the United States was willing to guarantee dollar convertibility for gold held by foreign central banks, currency exchange rates were stable and business confidence to invest and market was high. In consequence, as the Introduction pointed out, the proportion of countries' output which they traded increased (although in Britain's case, this benefit was offset by an overvalued currency in the 1950s and 1960s). This post-war impetus to international trade was also facilitated by tariff reductions by the EEC and GATT, and technological diffusion and investment from the United States, particularly in leading sectors such as vehicles, electrical products, chemicals and consumer durables. In turn, these international developments further encouraged the transfer of resources, primarily labour, within and between countries, especially from low productivity sectors, such as agriculture, to high productivity areas such as manufacturing.

British governments' commitments to full employment and growth through Keynesian demand management policies provide a second, *political* reason for the high level of demand and full employment during the 1950s and 1960s. Through their public spending, taxation and other macro-economic policies, domestic demand and business profits were maintained at high levels. For Britain, however, it is important not to overestimate the effect of such 'pump-priming'.* At best, it seems Keynesian policies made only marginal, short-term adjustments in the aggregate level of economic activity, even though, in sharp contrast to inter-war policies, post-war policies were not deflationary.

Despite the concern of Beveridge and others that, under conditions of full employment, inflation would become a serious problem during this 'golden age', it was not. For a variety of economic, political and social reasons, prices remained within acceptable limits. This was to do with the fixed exchange rate system which acted as a sort of proxy for strict monetary restraint, the tremendous increases in productivity, the stable prices of basic commodities, such as food and oil, the easy expandability of the labour supply through increased female participation and large-scale immigration from the West Indies and Asia, the favourable climate for wage bargaining, and low inflation expectations.

---

* Matthews has shown that between 1945 and 1964 British governments usually ran budget *surpluses*. He argues that faster growth was due not to government injections of net demand into the economy but because of a spontaneous investment boom initially stimulated by government wartime spending and subsequently sustained by a backlog of wasted investment opportunities and by a supposed acceleration of technological innovation; see R. C. O. Matthews, 'Why has Britain had full employment since the war?', *Economic Journal*, **LXXVIII** no.3 (September 1968), pp. 555–69.

Emerging problems of the full employment welfare state

All these economic, political and social factors combined to ensure a high level of full-time male employment during the post-war period. During the post-war period, however, the political commitment to the full employment welfare state, as well as these factors underpinning such policies, became increasingly problematic. The previous chapter anticipated three crucial reasons for this development: the likelihood that the policies and mechanisms for achieving full employment would enhance the power of bureaucratic state institutions over various social groups and ultimately undermine at least some of the policy's popularity; the likelihood that full employment would raise popular expectations which could not be realized; and the underestimation of the difficulties which would be encountered in producing a political accord between government and business, and government and organized labour. To this list can be added a fourth: in trying to resolve these problems and yet maintain their full employment commitments, governments in Britain were faced by the 1970s with an industrial economy showing increasing signs of major new structural weaknesses.

The remainder of this chapter focuses on these four problems. It shows how each quickly became a major preoccupation of governments after the mid 1960s, prompting them to adopt new and sometimes contradictory policies. In these circumstances, government itself increasingly came to be identified as the problem. Because government had accepted so many new responsibilities in the post-war period – including responsibility for maintaining full employment – the political system, it was argued, had become effectively 'overloaded', while society itself was made 'ungovernable'. As subsequent chapters will show, it was this political climate which provided a golden opportunity for critics of social democracy to press for alternatives to the full employment welfare state.

Rising popular expectations

One important consequence of government commitments to full employment was to raise popular expectations which could not subsequently be realized. Initially, this raising of expectations manifested itself primarily through trade unions' demands for better wages and conditions and in increasing industrial unrest. Later, as racial minorities and women became more politically active, governments' commitment to full employment came under additional strain from new directions.

From the moment leaders of the labour movement entered government circles during the Second World War, the problem of rising expectations was already apparent. As Beveridge had predicted, the power of organized labour in conditions of full employment increased greatly. Even during the war, rank and file trade unionists demanded their traditional bargaining rights, defying the government's notorious Regulation 1AA prohibiting strikes, and receiving support from Aneurin Bevan and others on the left of the Labour Party.

As post-war governments committed themselves to maintaining full employment, the bargaining strength of the unions was considerably enhanced, not only through power exercised by union leaders in negotiations with government ministers (discussed in the next section), but also through the negative economic power exercised by rank and file trade unionists at the workplace. It was not long before this increased power at the shop floor level became a problem for governments and union leaders. Notwithstanding the close formal links between the Labour Party and the unions, the Labour government of 1945–51 found itself prevented from renewing its voluntary wages policy in 1950 by a vigorous shop floor revolt. Indeed, another fifteen years passed before a government could reach a similar agreement.

During the 1950s, the Conservative governments basked in the glow of prosperity resulting from the massive growth in world trade. Memories of two world wars and the depression appeared to fade as nearly everyone's living standards and expectations increased year after year. When, however, world trade slackened in the late 1950s, the hefty pay increases which had been paid during the early 1950s could not be continued without fuelling inflation. Yet, workers' expectations of ever-higher wages had been raised and, in response, unions demanded further increases which subsequently could not be met. When the Conservative government attempted to halt this process through voluntary wage restraint, they were rebuffed by shop floor opposition, which in the public sector was particularly severe. In 1955, the train drivers called the first national strike in twenty years and in 1957 the number of working days lost through strikes rose to almost 8½ million – the highest level since 1926.

Throughout the 1960s and 1970s, high wage expectations continued unabated and, in many ways, were further encouraged by union militancy stemming from the growth of the shop stewards' movement in the 1950s and the resulting leftward shift within trade union leaderships from the 1960s onwards. To these pressures were added the heightened expectations of women and racial minorities, who from the 1960s onwards constituted an increasing proportion of the paid workforce. Encouraged by increased opportunities for part-time employment, especially in the services sector, less time-consuming home work (due to the spread of labour-saving domestic appliances and the limited growth of child-care facilities outside the home etc.), their increased desire to fulfil themselves in work outside the home, and the need to supplement family income,[3] married women entered the labour market on a massive scale. Between 1961 and 1971, thus, married women increased their participation in the labour market from 29.7 per cent to 42.9 per cent. Between 1971 and 1977, this percentage rose further to 50 per cent. Little reliable data exist on the number of black people in the labour market, although most estimates place the total between 2 and 3 million (approximately 7 per cent of the labour force), most of whom arrived in the country during the so-called 'golden age' of the 1950s and 1960s.[4] They increasingly demanded the same rights and employment opportunities as indigenous white workers, especially during the 1970s.

The swelling of the full employment welfare state

In order to fulfil their commitments to full employment and to accommodate the rising tide of expectations, post-war British governments increased their expenditures continually[5] and extended their power over various social groups. Increasingly, the acquisition of one set of powers stimulated a need to acquire new and additional powers. Some of these new powers were relatively minor irritants to those they affected. For example, the adoption of national income accounting methods required businesses to provide government with the economic data (employment, investment, production levels) necessary to compute these aggregates. Other policy initiatives resulted in the wholesale expansion of the state's regulatory coercive powers.

Perhaps the most striking example of the swelling of the full employment welfare state concerned wage levels and the role of the trade unions. Faced with the difficulty of combining full employment with moderate wage increases, post-war governments resorted increasingly to wages policies in their attempts to constrain inflation. In the late 1940s, during a period of austerity, the Labour government found trade union leaders willing to co-operate in voluntary wage restraint. During the 1950s, Conservative governments sought to pursue wages policies in combination with more conventional Keynesian techniques of economic management in order to resolve recurring balance of trade problems attributed to large wage increases. Although they were able to impose limits in the public sector, in these more prosperous times these governments failed to gain unions' agreement to voluntary restraint in the private sector. Anticipating later developments (see Chapter 6), they attempted to shift the main onus for maintaining full employment on to the unions by pursuing restrictive monetary policies. Faced with rising union militancy following a period of unrivalled prosperity – a possibility hinted at by Beveridge – the Conservatives under Macmillan also began to entertain ideas of 'reforming' the trade unions by statute.

As inflation continued to rise and the balance of trade worsened, the 1964–70 Wilson Labour governments resorted to voluntary then statutory wages and prices controls supported by a new Prices and Incomes Board. At the same time, the Wilson government appointed the Donovan Commission to investigate the trade unions, with a view to curtailing their powers. Following a period of considerable industrial action (especially unofficial strikes) and the need to placate foreign holders of sterling, the Labour government proposed restrictive legislation in its White Paper *In Place of Strife*. Subsequently, the Heath Conservative government faced with the same problems pursued policies even more restrictive than those proposed by Labour. The Industrial Relations Act of 1971 was an attempt to make the unions subject to a tightly woven net of legal controls supervised by the courts.[6] Strikes continued, however, and, in three instances in 1971 and 1972, the government declared a State of Emergency. After 1972, the Heath government also resorted to the most comprehensive attempt to date to control wages, prices, profits and dividends.

Although the Wilson–Callaghan governments of 1974–9 repealed the Conservatives' industrial relations legislation, they also introduced wage and price controls, on this occasion with the support of the trade unions as part of their 'Social Contract' policies. Threats of state sanctions, however, were never far in the background. Indeed, when wages continued to rise above the stipulated percentages, the Callaghan government threatened to nullify the extra increases by additional taxation and contemplated penalties against employers conceding wage demands in excess of the specified limits. After 1978, all private companies signing contracts or sub-contracts to supply goods or services to government were required to limit their workers' pay increases in accordance with government limits. For public sector pay, the Labour government imposed cash limits on public expenditure and in 1979 established the Clegg Commission to examine comparability with the private sector.

Post-war British governments' increasing resort to state-imposed restrictions to pay and prices well illustrate one of the basic contradictions of Beveridge's full employment welfare state. In order to maintain their commitments to full employment *and* low inflation, post-war governments were increasingly required to try to extend their reach over the daily lives of their citizens through means which seriously threatened the legitimacy of the full employment welfare state itself. This contradiction was identified in Chapter 2: Beveridge's social democratic formula was silent on the possibility – indeed likelihood – that the policy-taking citizens of the full employment welfare state – trade unionists, for example – would refuse to accept state policy-making. The discussion in this section has demonstrated the reactions of post-war British governments to this contradiction: the state increasingly tried to use unaccountable means and coercive forms of governing. However, as this discussion has also demonstrated, the ability of post-war British governments to implement these new forms of control policies was until 1979 always constrained by the considerable industrial and political power exercised by the trade unions.

Organized labour was not the only object of the swelling paternalism of the full employment welfare state. Labour's nationalization of vital industries in the late 1940s – coal, gas, electricity, iron and steel, and rail – certainly enhanced direct state control over workers, particularly when governments wanted to restrict pay. Governments of both parties have also pursued regional and industrial policies (costing some £2 billion a year by the end of the 1970s) through a whole plethora of new and existing departments and agencies designed to change (sometimes through coercion) the behaviour of firms in matters of investment, employment levels, and the location of plants (e.g. the Distribution of Industry Act in 1945, the Local Employment Act of 1960, the Industrial Development Act of 1966, and the Industry Acts of 1972 and 1975). To these policies and agencies were added, as unemployment rose in the 1970s, new job creation schemes such as the Special Temporary Employment Programme (STEP), the Youth Opportunities Programme (YOPs) and other schemes operated by the Manpower Services Commission.

It is clear, therefore, that since 1945 there has been a steady increase in both the size of government and the functions it performs. This growth of state power is a direct result of governments attempting to maintain full employment. As the discussion of trade union resistance illustrates, this swelling of the full employment welfare state not only produced employment-related policies and agencies whose effectiveness was highly suspect, it also tended to undermine the popularity of governments. Government intervention increased particularly in industrial relations and industrial policies but also in other areas (for example, employment protection, racial and sex discrimination legislation). Although this increase in government intervention typically fell far short of outright state control (nationalization), the degree of state control over social groups was enhanced to an extent not anticipated fully by Beveridge or Keynes. High political and economic costs were incurred, in terms of higher taxation, increasing resistance from these social groups – particularly trade unionists, but also businesses – and a fiscal crisis of the state.

The increasing fragility of corporate bias

As Beveridge had anticipated, governments' commitment to full employment implied the need to recognize the economic power of the trade unions and to accept them alongside private capital in the corridors of power. The Second World War not only facilitated the establishment of a political consensus or settlement between government, business and labour, but also a commitment to maintain these tripartite arrangements for the development of post-war full employment policies. As a result of these commitments, the trade unions were able to increase their membership and exercise unprecedented power both on the shop floors and as partners with government and business in the formation of economic policy. Trade union leaders demanded and received extended representation on the increasing number of para-state agencies concerned with economic and social policy. They gained access to information about how the political and economic systems functioned and, in the process, acquired new status and power in British society.

These political arrangements, based on what Middlemas has described as 'corporate bias', reached their apogee during exactly the period when full employment was achieved. During this 1945–65 period, a prevailing 'cult of equilibrium' [Middlemas], underpinned by the unprecedented prosperity of the period, tended to reduce class conflict and ensure a broad policy consensus based on commitments to full employment and the welfare state. It also led to a narrowing of party differences, best epitomized in the 'Butskellism' of the 1950s.[7] Both the main parties (for different reasons) endorsed these arrangements and policies.

Yet, as the discussion in the previous section has shown, the system of corporate bias showed increasing signs of stress. Occasionally, governments sought to re-establish the arrangements on new and firmer ground. Each of the Labour and Conservative governments of the 1960s and 1970s managed somewhat ingenious re-formulations based on government restrictions of wages linked to new investment and price controls. Their successes, however, were temporary because although they could often persuade union and business leaders to co-operate in deflationary policies, these leaders typically found they could neither sustain the active support of their respective memberships nor prevent them from utilizing the means available to them to evade agreements. By the 1960s, moreover, as the next section outlines, domestic and international economic conditions were deteriorating visibly, thus making impossible the maintenance of a Butskellite consensus.

Declining industrial performance

After 1965, the supposed inverse relationship between inflation and unemployment (a relationship described by the so-called Phillips curve)[8] became increasingly expensive. The level of registered unemployment in Britain rose steadily: to a mean of 2.6 per cent between 1965 and 1973 and 4.7 per cent from 1974 to 1979. Similarly, prices increased by a mean of 6.1 per cent between 1966 and 1973, and by 15.7 per cent between 1974 and 1979.

These stagflationary trends evidently had their origins in governments' use of Keynesian/Beveridge-type techniques for maintaining full employment. To begin with, by stimulating demand and economic growth through fiscal and monetary policy – as in 1953–4, 1958–9, 1962–3, 1972–4 and 1978–80 – governments almost invariably increased the country's imports, which then threw the balance of payments into deficit and precipitated runs on the foreign exchange reserves. Post-war governments were thus frequently faced with the difficult choice of either allowing the exchange rate to decline or deflating the economy – as in 1955–6, 1960–1, 1964–71 and 1975–7 – so as to reduce expenditure on imports relative to exports. This was the dilemma which confronted the Conservative Chancellor of the Exchequer Thorneycroft in 1957. He argued for deflation (thereby abandoning his government's commitment to full employment) in order to reduce inflation. Prime Minister Macmillan was not willing, however, to see unemployment rise. The proposed cuts in public expenditure and the money supply were not made and Thorneycroft and the entire Treasury ministerial team resigned. Relatively high inflation (3 per cent in 1958) would continue to be tolerated.

Stagflationary trends also derived from the labour market policies of the 1950s and 1960s. Governments' commitments to full employment by inducing high levels of demand for goods and services encouraged employers to concede substantial wage increases (especially in engineering) unrelated to productivity. These commitments also encouraged employers to hoard their scarce skilled labour in the expectation that continued economic growth would enable them to cover their increased costs through higher sales and profits. Even in the public sector, the Conservative governments succumbed to union pressures and bailed out the nationalized industries. In a technical sense, therefore, the so-called 'golden age' of the British economy during the 1950s and early 1960s was most likely based on *over full* employment, which permitted inefficient businesses to survive. When domestic and international demand fell after the mid 1960s, Labour and Conservative governments found themselves constrained to place a higher priority on reducing inflation and balancing the value of imports and exports than on maintaining full employment. In consequence, firms were compelled to shed their surplus labour, whereas the sustained demand of the earlier period had encouraged them to retain it. This is why the 1966–70 Labour government's wages and prices policies led to substantial increases in unemployment, as did the Heath and Wilson–Callaghan governments' deflationary policies in the 1970s.

The cumulative consequences of demand management policies are, however, only part of the broader reason for economic decline. Since the mid 1960s, 'core' or 'structural' unemployment (as distinct from 'cyclical' unemployment) has increased steadily and independently of the general level of demand in the economy. According to one estimate, this core or 'structural' unemployment rose from a rate of 3 per cent (575,000) in 1967 to 4.3 per cent (over 1 million) in 1973, and then to 5 per cent in 1977.[9] There has also been an increase over this period in long-duration unemployment. Between 1966 and 1973, the percentage of unemployed men aged 25 to 50 on the register for more than six months rose from 23 per cent to 39 per cent; by 1979, the figure had increased to 45 per cent. This net increase in unemployment has been part of a longer term, accelerating process of *de-industrialization* which has resulted in the industrial share of GDP and employment falling in virtually all OECD countries, including Britain, since the mid 1960s. Between 1966 and 1977, British manufacturing industry suffered a *net* loss of almost 2 million jobs (21 per cent), most of them held previously by men. Until 1974, the expansion of service industries (which offered job opportunities particularly to women), together with people leaving the labour market, absorbed much of the net job losses in manufacturing industry. After 1974, this ceased to be the case. One effect was the net increase in 'structural' unemployment. Another effect was that at about this time Britain began to import many more manufactured goods than it exported, with the result that British manufacturing exports were making progressively smaller contributions to pay for imported raw materials and food. Declining performance in the manufacturing sector, therefore, not only had the immediate effect of reducing job opportunities, it also jeopardized future opportunities in manufacturing by damaging foreign trade, upsetting the balance of payments, constraining domestic demand, and enhancing the overall stagflationary trends.

Undoubtedly, the major reasons for the increase in 'structural' and long-duration unemployment were the exhaustion of the growth potential of existing (oil and electricity-based) technologies, the relatively lower job-creating capacities of the new technologies (based on micro-electronics, telecommunications and nuclear energy) and the further centralization and rationalization of production which resulted from these technical changes. The sharp rises in world commodity and oil prices exacerbated these trends, so that business profitability declined sharply. Firms – particularly those producing steel, ships and chemicals which had over-expanded in the 1960s and early 1970s – moved in the mid and late 1970s to reduce their costs by shedding their labour and by trying to hold down real wages. However, these same firms found they could not easily reduce their real wages costs because of the industrial strength of the trade unions and government policies. As a result, business profitability and capital investment fell even more sharply than in most other OECD countries. In the manufacturing and distribution sectors, for instance, companies' pre-tax real rates of return on capital fell from about 10 per cent in the mid 1960s to about 5 per cent by 1979. This reduction in the share of profits prompted a further decline in invest- ment (especially labour-using investment) after the mid 1960s and this led indirectly to yet higher levels of structural unemployment. Far from ameliorating this 'structural' unemployment problem, govern- ments' financial and technical support for older or newer industries probably made matters worse by enhancing the pace of industrial centralization and rationalization, politicizing the relations of produc- tion and dramatically increasing the size and cost of the state.

The abandonment of full employment

All these problems – rising popular expectations, increasingly unpopular state intervention, inherently fragile 'corporate bias', and stagflationary trends within the economy – were momentarily obscured in the mid 1970s, when trade union and Labour Party leaders reached another *rapprochement*, which subsequently became the centre-piece of the new Wilson government's policies in 1974. Under the terms of the so-called 'Social Contract' formulated in the early 1970s, Labour leaders promised to pursue expansionary social and economic policies, to introduce a package of items demanded by the unions (including the repeal of the Conservatives' 1971 Industrial Relations Act and the statutory wages policy, and new legislation strengthening unions' and workers' rights), in return for which the unions would agree to some measure of pay restraint. What followed, however, was more or less a repeat performance of union– government confrontations of the late 1960s and early 1970s.

Within several months of the February 1974 general election, the TUC fulfilled their part of the 'Social Contract' by publishing volun- tary guidelines for pay. These guidelines, however, were notoriously ineffective in keeping wages down. As a result of the substantial wage rises which followed (and the huge increases in oil prices in 1973), inflation rose in 1975 to an unprecedented 25 per cent. Registered unemployment also rose to almost 1 million (4.2 per cent). Business firms, faced by government restrictions on prices on the one hand and high wage claims on the other, faced serious profitability problems. In these circumstances, the government contemplated penalties against employers giving wage increases beyond the TUC's limits, but then rejected this course under pressure from the TUC. Instead, the government embarked on a deflationary policy, cutting public expen- diture and raising taxation.

In order to prevent a further deterioration in their relations, Labour government and union leaders negotiated a new 'Social Contract', which to all intents and purposes accepted the government's arguments relating inflation to wages and unemployment to wages. Under the terms of the new contract, wages would be restricted to stipulated percentages, prices would be controlled, restrictions would be imposed on the nationalized industries and local authorities, food and rent would be subsidized, and employers would be compensated for not making their workers unemployed.

During 1976 and 1977, even though trade union leaders' influence in government circles was equal to that enjoyed by their predecessors between 1945 and 1950, wages were cut severely. The government was forced by a run on the pound to seek a huge foreign loan (from the IMF) – the alternative outlined by the Callaghan Labour government was 'savage deflationary cuts and three million unemployed'. It was not long before opposition among rank and file trade unionists began to mount. The chief architects of the 'Contract', Jones and Scanlon (the leaders of the Transport and General Workers and Amalgamated Engineering Workers, respectively), retired, and Prime Minister Callaghan announced what to many was an absurdly low pay limit making it certain that the unions would not renew their agreement and demand instead a return to free collective bargaining. With the government determined to set its new pay limit regardless of union opposition, there followed a whole series of strikes culminating in the so-called 'Winter of Discontent', threats of a government-imposed State of Emergency, and the defeat of the government in the House of Commons. These circumstances, together with rising unemployment, high taxation and mounting public concern over excessive union power, became important vote-winning issues for the Conservatives at the 1979 general election.

This brief history of the 'Social Contract' illustrates dramatically the impossibility of governments pursuing full employment welfare state policies with a powerful decentralized trade union movement in circumstances of economic decline. Labour's unhappy experience with the 'Social Contract' also served, rather ironically (bearing in mind Labour's claim to be able to 'handle' the unions), to undermine the logic and legitimacy of the full employment welfare state. It demonstrated that, to a great extent, the post-war political consensus was only viable and legitimate while full (male) employment could be maintained and living standards improved. As this chapter has demonstrated, however, after the mid 1960s the chances of realizing those objectives visibly decreased as Britain's industrial decline continued. Once unemployment rose to 3, 4 and then 6 per cent in the 1970s, the terms of the consensus were bound to be challenged and its fragility exposed. The birth and death of the 'Social Contract' demonstrated fairly conclusively that the full employment welfare state's political arrangements were neither fully viable nor legitimate. It also demonstrated that the incorporation of organized labour into government was neither a guarantee to male and female workers that full employment would remain a priority for governments nor, to those more sceptical of these 'corporatist'-type arrangements, that trade unions' influence would be a positive step towards economic growth, industrial harmony and social progress.

The consequence of all this was that many of those who had previously identified themselves with Beveridge's vision perceived the need for something stronger, in the form of a disciplinary state. At the same time, those always opposed to the full employment welfare state were provided with a golden opportunity to press their case for an alternative pre-Keynesian 'free market' political economy and new controls over the unions. It is these alternative visions of an employment society to which we turn in the following chapters.

Notes

1   Between 1943 and 1951, the proportion of women aged between 20 and 45 working outside the household fell from over 80 per cent to 43 per cent. Thus, whereas eight out of ten married women were working outside the household in 1943, barely two out of ten were doing so in 1951. Among single women, however, the ratio hardly changed during this period. These changes are discussed in Denise Riley, 'The free mothers : protonatalism and working mothers in industry at the end of the last war in Britain', *History Workshop* 11 (spring 1981), pp. 59–118.

2   Although Britain's annual growth rate was lower than those of every other major industrial country between 1950 and 1970, the rates achieved during this period were unprecedented in Britain. GDP grew by 2.8 per cent per annum during this period, compared with 1.3 per cent between 1913 and 1950 and 1.9 per cent between 1870 and 1913.

3   Because of the structure of the British tax system, the net income to a family from a wife working part time is much greater than if the husband worked overtime for the same additional gross pay, albeit probably for a small number of hours.

4   Stephen Castles, *Here For Good. Western Europe's New Ethnic Minorities* (London, 1984), esp. ch. 5.

5   Current government expenditures on goods, services and transfer payments rose from 30.1 per cent of GDP in 1950 to 40.8 per cent in 1977.

6   Unions were required to register with a new Registrar of Trade Unions, under threat of losing existing legal immunities. Once registered, however, unions were required to adopt new rules, particularly on calling strikes, and to take disciplinary action against any of their members who went on strike in breach of the new rules. Meanwhile, unions which remained unregistered lost a number of rights, including their immunities from legal action in trade disputes. Union 'closed shops' were made illegal, although registered unions were allowed to retain some of their restrictive practices. Leaders of registered and unregistered unions were also required to restrain their members from taking industrial action against a legally binding agreement between employers and workers.

7   The term derives from the names of R. A. Butler, the Conservative Chancellor of the Exchequer after 1951, and Hugh Gaitskell, the shadow Chancellor and later leader of the Labour Party. It denotes their respective endorsements of the 'mixed' economy and the full employment welfare state advocated by Beveridge.

8   This relationship derives from the empirical work of the economist A. W. Phillips, who discovered a long-term statistical correlation between rates of change in wages and unemployment rates. Phillips's work became famous because a *causal* relationship was assumed by many Keynesians to exist between these two factors, so that inflation (measured by wage levels) could be reduced by raising unemployment; and vice versa.

9   S. J. Nickell, 'The determinants of equilibrium unemployment in Britain', *Economic Journal*, **92** no.3 (September 1982), pp. 555–75.

Further reading

Samuel H. Beer, *Britain Against Itself. The Political Contradictions of Collectivism* (London, 1982), intro., chs I and II.

Colin Crouch, *The Politics of Industrial Relations* (London, 1979).

Keith Middlemas, *Politics in Industrial Society* (London, 1979), chs 13 and 14.

Claus Offe, 'Theses on the theory of the state', in *Contradictions of the Welfare State*, edited by John Keane (London, 1984).

Kerry Schott, 'The rise of Keynesian economics: Britain 1940–64', *Economy and Society*, **11** no.3 (August 1982), pp. 292–316.

Robert Skidelsky, 'The decline of Keynesian politics', in *State and Economy in Contemporary Capitalism*, edited by Colin Crouch (London, 1979).

Michael Stewart, *Keynes and After* (Harmondsworth, 1967), ch. 7.

Donald Winch, *Economics and Policy. A Historical Study* (London, 1969), chs 12–14.

4   The disciplinary state

Under pressure from the type of problems sketched in the previous chapter, it is hardly surprising that the terms of the full employment welfare state consensus were challenged increasingly during the 1970s. One of the first, and most influential, types of reaction against the social democratic model of the full employment welfare state was outlined in a 1977 report of the OECD, *Towards Full Employment and Price Stability*.[1] This widely read and highly controversial report certainly shares certain views of Beveridge and post-war social democrats – notably, their stated commitment to full male employment, economic growth and political stability. Consistent with this commitment, the report analyses the problems facing major OECD countries, and suggests new government policies for achieving a 'more orderly economy' based on non-inflationary economic growth and rising high levels of employment. This continuity with the goals of social democracy is limited, however. *Towards Full Employment* is in several important respects highly critical of the full employment welfare state, clearly abandoning, for instance, the egalitarian and parliamentary democratic assumptions of Beveridge's social democratic vision, sketched in Chapter 2. This chapter argues that the report defends a vision of the *disciplinary state*, and for this reason requires separate consideration as a second contemporary model of how to secure full employment. Five connected themes in *Towards Full Employment* illustrate well the basic message of this disciplinary state model – that full employment can be restored only by *more* and *tougher* state control over the economy, and by *abandoning* the commitment to the social democratic principles of social equality and active parliamentary democracy.

1   *Towards Full Employment* begins its diagnosis of the present crisis with some qualified praise for the achievements of the post-war full employment welfare state. During this period, the industrialized

world enjoyed economic growth and employment levels to an extent unprecedented in modern times. The authors' claim that this post-war boom was primarily due not to factors such as post-war reconstruction, rapid technological changes, stable and cheap supplies of energy and raw materials, and the rise in volume of international trade, but to the full employment welfare state itself. The most developed capitalist states everywhere adopted more interventionist economic policies, which were crucial for creating a favourable economic climate – first, by their active commitment to the full employment of labour and capital and, second, by their commitment to free trade and co-operation with one another. According to McCracken and his co-authors, the steady growth of state intervention during the era of full employment (see Figure 1, which is taken from the report) has virtually dissolved the distinction between the public sphere of state institutions and the private realm of civil society. The welfare state has become the key organizer of the economy, the agent of voluntary class co-operation and the guarantor of social harmony in general. Consequently, the state has come to be regarded more and more by numerous economic and social power groups as an unlimited liability insurance company, an arrangement that is supposed to underwrite various social institutions and provide coverage against risks such as unemployment, bankruptcy, poverty and environmental damage. This trend is strengthened by competition for electoral support among political parties, whose attempt to outbid each other's promises serves to stimulate voters' expectations.

2　As a consequence of the post-war integration of state and civil society and the expanding range of matters for which the full employment welfare state is seen to be responsible, the report observes, electorates and economic and social power groups become addicted to government, which is consequently under constant pressure to provide bigger and better 'fixes' to satisfy their clients' ever increasing expectations. The full employment welfare state generates a 'build-up of demand pressures and stubborn inflationary expectations'. This build-up of political demands and expectations is seen by the report to be the major cause of the present crisis of the full employment welfare state. The growing pressures on the state ('expectational inflation') results in a decline in political authority or effectiveness; the business of government becomes more and more difficult, and its ability to manage the capitalist economy declines. The 'sharing-out' function of government – its involvement in allocating resources through its taxation and spending policies, and its direct interventions in social and economic life – becomes excessively burdened. Like the proverbial sorcerer who became the victim of his own powers, government is besieged by policy failures (in matters such as industrial strategy and incomes policies) as well as 'overloaded' by demands and opposition from social power groups who obstruct or refuse to co-operate with the state. Due to the growing size and complexity of the web of involvements and responsibilities within which government is ensnared – and, therefore, made more vulnerable – 'big government' is prevented from operating 'authoritatively' and effectively. The full employment welfare state, contrary to the rosy expectations of its social democratic defenders, strengthens the trend towards clumsy and ineffective policy-making, contradictory policy measures that are also highly vulnerable to external 'shocks' (the report mentions examples such as harvest failures and the explosive rise in oil prices in the early 1970s), and growing disrespect for political and social authority. Public confidence in the ability of government to govern thereby wanes.

3   The build-up of political expectations and demands upon the state also leads to a serious deterioration of *economic* performance, which further 'overloads' the spending, taxation and administrative capacities of the state. According to the authors of *Towards Full Employment*, welfare state governments have made major 'errors' of economic policy. (The report points to the US government's failure to finance adequately both the Vietnam War and new social policy programmes through higher taxation, as well as the futile attempt by western governments to maintain an exchange rate system pegged to the US dollar, despite declining confidence in it.) The destabilizing consequences of these economic policy errors were compounded by accelerating inflation and declining business confidence. Rising inflation during the 1970s was caused partly by a rise in popular expectations generated by the growth of governmental functions and expenditures. As electorates' expectations adjusted in the post-1945 period to full (male) employment, expanding economic growth and welfare state spending, their demands increased steadily – both for privately-provided consumer goods and services as well as for greater state provision of goods and services. Governments and political parties only exacerbated this problem by whetting democratic appetites and failing to exercise discipline over their domestic money supplies; rates of monetary expansion grew rapidly and excessively. The expectation that governments would constantly increase their

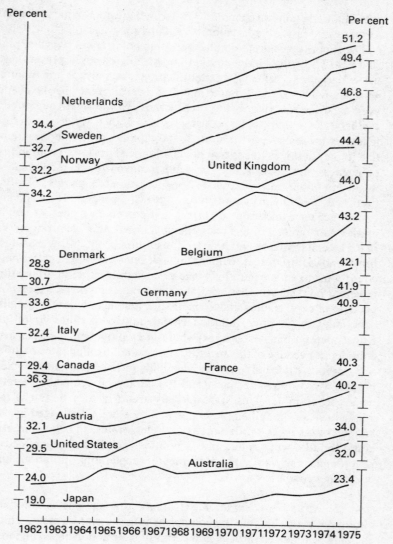

Figure 1 *Evolution of general government expenditure 1962–75 in per cent of trend GDP at current prices. (Public expenditure here includes transfers. Each line is plotted on a different vertical scale. Countries are ranged by the ratio of expenditure to trend GDP in 1975.)*

spending and maintain economic growth and full employment also led to more aggressive trade union bargaining for wages.

The report gives great emphasis to this point about 'wage explosions' and growing labour market unrest: 'increasingly present-day wage bargaining reflects a determination not only to maintain a certain money wage level but to maintain a certain real wage level and even a certain rate of growth of real wages'. Both private and public sector trade unions press constantly for higher wages, and this tendency for real wages 'to increase too rapidly', or 'to increase relative to output prices' leads to a decline in the short-term profitability of business firms. As a result, firms either make workers redundant or avoid employing new workers. 'The expectation of high rates of inflation and pessimism about future growth generated by recent experience have undermined normal, self-correcting forces present in market economies.' In this uncertain and unbalanced environment of rising unemployment, inflation and declining profitability, business firms tend to raise prices to maintain their rates of profit. Yet this only contributes to an accelerating wage-price spiral; inflation originating in labour markets stimulates inflation in product markets. Moreover, because of close trading and financial ties among industrial capitalist economies, wage-price inflation is transmitted to other countries. Consequently, businesses everywhere in employment societies lose confidence because of the uncertainties created by high rates of inflation, militant trade unionism and declining rates of profitability; their propensity to invest declines, and the edifice of free trade thereby begins to crumble. This stagflationary trend in turn threatens the whole basis of the full employment welfare state. Challenged by the actions of business, trade unions and electorates, the social democratic 'middle way' enters into a political cul-de-sac of ineffective government, growing unemployment, accelerating inflation and declining economic growth.

4 *Towards Full Employment* argues that these stagflationary trends seriously threaten the commitment to full employment, which can only be renewed through new forms of state action based on more stable and restrained demand management policies. The expansionary demand management policies of the full employment welfare state must be modified. What is urgently required, the report insists, is *restrictive* (i.e. more cautious and proscriptive) demand management policies. In this respect, the report openly rejects the proposals of Friedman and other market liberals (see the following three chapters),

who argue for a renewal of 'free' capitalist markets and, thus, a deepening of the division between civil society and the state. According to the report, the state's growing interdependency with civil society is irreversible. Contrary to the claims of market liberals, the present crisis of the full employment welfare state cannot be entrusted to the self-equilibrating mechanisms of the capitalist economic system. The present unemployment crisis can be solved only if governments improve the (cost) effectiveness and efficiency of their own programmes and, at the same time, play a more active and interventionist role in civil society by stabilizing expectations, defending the principle of 'economic and political realism', rebuilding business confidence and, thereby, setting economies on the road to increased investment, full employment and price stability.

The report defends a vision of a powerful disciplinary state, one which is capable of pursuing steady long-range plans, and imposing in the short run the sacrifices vital for the long-run achievement of full employment, economic growth and political stability. It insists that what is needed is not less but *more* state intervention, an expanded and more effective use of state instruments for managing economic and social life. Specifically, the following package of new policies is recommended:

Publicly announced targets for the growth of the monetary aggregates; a fiscal policy geared to a budget target designed to avoid giving an inflationary stimulus over the medium term; a prices and incomes policy designed to clarify the kind of price and wage behaviour consistent with achieving and maintaining full employment; and measures to reward or penalise those who conform to guidelines for prices and incomes or fail to do so.

The report urges that excessive burdens should not be placed on the redistributive functions of the state, lest conflicts among social and economic groups and between social and economic groups and the state become insupportable. Governments must attempt to reduce the 'expectational inflation' which parliamentary democratic processes have directly promoted. For the time being, electorates must in general learn to accept greater economic restraint and fewer benefits; they must come to understand that parliamentary democracy is only one particular way of constituting authority and that, in many areas of government policy, the claims of expertise, seniority and experience should override the claims of parliamentary democracy. Politicians must also be prepared to make 'unpopular' decisions, to resist the temptation of promising bigger and better policies in order to assure their own popularity and election. Equally, governments should aim at a gradual winding-down of inflationary economic expectations and an improvement of business confidence and industrial competitiveness by actively seeking ways of ensuring that the most powerful economic groups co-operate with each other as well as with state policy-makers.

5   Central to the disciplinary state strategy is the recommendation that governments strive to establish a new accord among state decision-makers, trade unions and businesses concerning the need for a return to full employment by means of a (perhaps compulsory) prices and incomes policy, higher profit levels, and a restructuring of the economy through improved investment in capital goods and new technology. (Essentially, the report calls for a new form of *corporatism*, that is, a particular type of decision-making process based upon organized bargaining among the representatives of the state and the most powerful social groups, a mixed or hybrid system of public-private decision-making. This would lead to the fusion of social power and state power by encouraging the direct representation of major social interests within the state, as well as the direct intervention of the state within civil society.)

Within the terms of this corporatist framework (or 'concerted action approach', as the report calls it), public and private sector trade union leaders would be encouraged to learn to avoid inflexible and 'unrealistic' demands. They would be prompted to understand that their actions and expectations reduce competitiveness, scare off business investment and render state power ineffective. Meanwhile, within this state-guaranteed corporatist framework, the report envisages businesses being reassured of firm government support and determination to restrain rises in real wages, to reverse the recent serious decline of profit rates and, in general, to defend private enterprise. The report recommends a package of pro-business policies, including new and more vigorous (nuclear?) energy policies to overcome likely future shortages; policies aimed at encouraging business competition by removing tariffs and non-tariff barriers to imports; and improving the flexibility of capital markets by eliminating tax disincentives and reducing restrictions on share ownership.

An accord that favoured government, business and trade unions – a form of *selective* corporatism – would clearly have direct negative implications for such unorganized interests as the unemployed, part-time employed, women, and minority social groups. *Towards Full Employment* acknowledges the need for 'employing under-privileged groups' by means of subsidies to firms who employ new workers, and for public sector emergency job creation measures (worked out through tripartite negotiations among businesses, trade unions and government). Through such state-initiated means, it is hoped that the present number of unemployed can be reduced. However, the report sees such direct measures for alleviating mass unemployment as being limited in scope. Effectively, the disciplinary state strategy supposes that the unemployed as well as marginal or unorganized groups would have to learn, for the time being at least, to make do and to expect less from government. They, too, must appreciate that no government or economy can survive the present crisis without a tightly administered anti-inflation programme which emphasizes monetary restraint and privileges businesses and trade unions in the making and administering of government policy.

The upshot of McCracken's and his co-authors' call for restraint is that full employment cannot be guaranteed regardless of developments in the areas of investment, prices and wages and that, therefore, the unemployed must not expect to become employed *immediately*. In the words of the report, 'As compared with a strong front-loaded recovery followed by an early recession, what is involved is accepting, reluctantly, a less rapid reduction of unemployment now, in order to achieve lower levels of unemployment later on. The correctly-judged recovery track is one which will *minimise average unemployment over the recovery period as a whole*' (original emphasis).

Towards the disciplinary state?

The authors of *Towards Full Employment* argue that this overall strategy of containing the range and quantity of social and economic demands through the disciplinary state would help to restore the authority and effectiveness of state power, as well as to ensure reasonable rates of economic growth and a steady return to full employment. In this way the report claims to have found a way out of the dilemma of stagflation in which employment societies such as Britain and the United States became trapped during the 1970s. By adopting a narrower and more disciplined path to growth, this dilemma – that increasing the pace of private economic activity will be likely to stimulate inflationary expectations and a loss of business confidence, whereas failing to do precisely this will be likely to keep business confidence low, thus perpetuating stagnation – could be overcome successfully. A strategy which avoided highly expansionary and inflationary fiscal and monetary policies would solve the central problem of how to regenerate economic growth and set unemployment on a downward trend without setting off an explosion of inflationary social demands.

This disciplinary state strategy clearly differs from the social democratic view of how to achieve the goals of political stability, economic growth and full (male) employment. While both approaches view these goals as achievable and desirable, the disciplinary state strategy insists that they can be achieved only by devaluing the principles of redistribution (greater social equality) and active parliamentary democracy that were central to the vision of Beveridge and other post-war social democrats. In this exact sense, the disciplinary state model is a challenging attempt to deal with two serious practical and theoretical weaknesses of the full employment welfare state. First, the vision of the disciplinary state freely concedes the undemocratic consequences of the full employment welfare state, and consequently argues for *less* citizen control of state policy-making and administration in order to prevent the 'frustration of heightened expectations' effect (Chapter 2). Second, the disciplinary state strategy rejects the unrealistic assumption, made by Beveridge and other social democrats, that the loosely organized full employment welfare state is capable of maintaining an accord between trade unions, private capitalist corporations and the state; a more active and powerful state is seen to be the only way in which class co-operation – and, hence, a return to full employment – is possible.

In these two respects, the vision of the disciplinary state sharply exposes several of the key contradictions of the full employment welfare state. The disciplinary state strategy for restoring full employment is none the less not without equally serious difficulties, the most important of which are summarized below.

1   Although *Towards Full Employment* admits the need for *ad hoc* state policies designed to make 'polluters pay', it fails to consider the probable negative environmental effects of attempting to return to full employment through a new and more vigorous round of economic growth. The report confidently defends the traditional aim of employment societies growing their way out of trouble:

Continued economic growth in the industrialised countries, providing for a reasonable rate of expansion in the available supply of goods and services, remains an essential objective. It is needed to satisfy people's aspirations for a

rising standard of living and to provide adequate employment opportunities.

We can leave aside here two of the report's very questionable
assumptions: that continued economic growth will create more jobs
(see the discussion of 'jobless growth' in the Introduction and Chapters 5, 6 and 9); and that rising levels of goods and services will serve
to increase the overall level of consumer satisfaction.[2] It sufficies only
to point out that one does not have to make doomsday predictions to
see that the report's call for higher levels of production and consumption could be achieved only through the more rapid depletion (or
costly replacement) of exhaustible natural resources and, above all,
the further deterioration of our natural environment. The disciplinary
state model of full employment blindly ignores the tentative conclusions of recent ecological science: that there are some tolerance limits
in the ecosystem, even if these are not fully known; that the economies
of employment (and Soviet-type) societies are presently testing and
violating at least some of these limits; and that it is, therefore, unwise
to follow the present path of quantitative economic growth until those
limits are violated fully, since by that time it may be impossible to
undo the environmental damage, or to do so only at the cost of cata-
strophic social and political disruption.

If extreme negative environmental and socio-political consequences
of this type are to be avoided, the simple-minded call (defended by
Towards Full Employment) for a 'return to full employment' through
higher levels of economic growth will have to be reconsidered. In our
view, the post-war era of full employment simply cannot be repeated
without immense environmental risks. To say this leads to the conclusion, conversely, that a move towards a more ecologically sensitive
society would recognize the need to reconsider the quality of work
performed by individuals. It would acknowledge that the goal of full
employment at any environmental price would have to be abandoned,
and that, instead, priority would need to be given to types of paid
('formal') and presently unpaid ('informal') work that utilized renew-
able resources, conserved the use of non-renewable resources and, in
general, helped to reverse the present-day poisoning and over-
simplification of the ecosystem.

2   Despite the occasional references to the principles of 'quality
of life' and enhancing 'social welfare' through state unemployment
and assistance programmes, *Towards Full Employment* fails to spell
out clearly the *deepening* inequalities that would be likely to result

from attempts to implement the disciplinary state model. It is not only that the report is silent about the glaring inequalities of property, power and status which the full employment welfare state failed to eradicate. The report also assumes that a further 'dualization' between the core policy-makers and the peripheral policy-takers is a necessary condition of resolving the present crisis of the full employment welfare state. Effectively, the disciplinary state strategy is a recipe for further selective impoverishment and a widening of the gap between the most powerful economic and social groups, who have access to the state, and the rest. Those unorganized social groups (such as the part-time employed, ethnic minorities, women, and consumers of social services) who are presently disadvantaged, and who would certainly have limited or no access to the state-organized framework of bargaining among the major economic and social power groups, would be expected to 'get by' and fend for themselves – no doubt under the watchful eye of the government administrator, social worker, judge and police officer of the disciplinary state.

This scenario also offers little in the way of greater equality of opportunity for the presently unemployed. As we have seen, *Towards Full Employment* speaks of the need for gradually alleviating mass unemployment through state-sponsored measures. Even assuming that such measures could be implemented successfully, it is very likely that they would be counteracted by a further loss of jobs (or a slowdown in the rate of creation of new jobs) due to the continuing flight of capital overseas and 'technology bite', that is, unemployment resulting from investment directed to reducing labour requirements in the state and private sectors. The new international division of labour and increased technological unemployment are not considered at all by the report,[3] which is why its gradualist approach to job creation seems to offer little too slowly to the unemployed.

There are also nagging doubts about the likely negative redistributional effects of disciplinary state measures aimed at 'getting back to full employment'. Defenders of these measures usually extol their cost-effectiveness, their capacity to develop a better-trained work force and, above all, their compatibility with the post-war ideal of full employment. The last of these claims is especially misleading, a depressing triumph of hope over experience. Even if the emergency job creation measures recommended by *Towards Full Employment* were expanded in scope and developed more quickly (so as to counteract job loss trends), they would most likely serve to institutionalize, and deepen, the existing highly unequal patterns of access to the paid labour market. In other words, they would probably serve to strengthen the present trend towards a dual society: the gap between workers employed in the most privileged core sector of the labour market (where jobs are full time, covered by union contracts and relatively secure and well-paid) and those confined to its marginal sector (of precarious, poorly-paid, part-time, non-unionized and state-subsidized jobs) would become even wider. Indeed, emergency job creation measures (as the rapidly expanding Community Programme and Youth Training Scheme in Britain suggest) are less a means of 'getting back to full employment' (a phrase which has all the Beveridge-type connotations of greater liberty and equality of opportunity for the disadvantaged) and more a short-term recipe for state disciplining and managing of the unemployed. In these *corvée* programmes, the unemployed would be required to perform, at low wages and with every prospect of returning to the ranks of the unemployed, the 'task work' that the able-bodied unemployed used to be required to perform under the Poor Laws.

3   The degree of economic and political stability that would result from a disciplinary state strategy is considerably exaggerated by the authors of *Towards Full Employment and Price Stability*. Indeed, there is considerable evidence that the corporatist arrangements upon which they pin their hopes would be likely to generate new contradictions and heighten distributional conflicts. These outcomes would be likely despite the fact that corporatist bargaining mechanisms are relatively flexible and often equipped with powerful sanctions (e.g. the withdrawal of public recognition and subsidies against those economic groups, especially trade unions, who attempt to disrupt or withdraw from them). As the failure of the 'Social Contract' in Britain suggests, corporatist-type arrangements are nevertheless particularly vulnerable to breakdown, and their successful and continuous implementation seems to be possible only under exceptional historical conditions.[4]

In addition to the practical or strategic question of whether corporatist mechanisms *can* be implemented (despite opposition from within by trade unions, business representatives and civil servants, and pressure from without by other traditional interest groups, newer single-issue social movements, established political parties and elected parliaments), the disciplinary state strategy for achieving political stability, economic growth and full employment is likely to be plagued by a serious *legitimacy problem*. This problem is not unrelated to the second problem of inequality that was described above. It derives from the elitism, secrecy, 'pragmatism' and pro-business (and sometimes pro-trade union) bias which are typically associated with the corporatist arrangements that the authors of *Towards Full Employment* consider to be central for restoring full employment. Briefly, this legitimacy problem of corporatist arrangements can be explained through the following questions. According to which normative principles or criteria are the proposed decision-making privileges (of state administrators, trade unions and business) to be justified? Why are the 'needs' of certain groups to be selectively screened out or given less priority? Why, for instance, should the case put forward by anti-nuclear power groups for an ecologically sensitive economy be subordinated to the demands of high-growth, pro-nuclear governments, trade unions and businesses? Why should the special concerns of women be considered of little or no importance in 'tripartite' forums to discuss pay and employment? In short, why, aside from their obvious power resources, should certain social groups be active policy-makers while others are relegated to the role of passive policy-takers?

These questions remain unanswered in *Towards Full Employment*. It assumes that the goal of full employment and growth without inflation guaranteed by the disciplinary state is already agreed upon by all social groups, and it thereby fails to give normative reasons for its particular version of a form of *selective* corporatism. This is a fundamental flaw in the vision of achieving full employment through the disciplinary state – that it does not provide compelling reasons for investing a *few* privileged groups with the authority which should rightly be opened up to discussion and criticism by a *plurality* of social groups, that is, to an openly *democratic* decision-making process. Indeed, a more comprehensive and democratic bargaining process of this type would directly contradict the terms of a disciplinary state strategy: it would give the rights of veto and initiative to exactly those groups whose self-restraint, relative powerlessness and marginalization is assumed to be a necessary condition of the successful return to full employment.

Considered together, these three weaknesses of the disciplinary state strategy for achieving full employment are monumental, raising doubts about whether 'getting back to full employment' in this particular way is either a workable or desirable goal. It was perhaps because of these serious weaknesses that the overall recommendations of *Towards Full Employment* were shelved for the time being by state policy-makers in Britain and the United States. In these two countries another, more formidable, type of challenge to the post-war vision of the full employment welfare state – the strong state, free market approach – quickly developed into a new political and economic orthodoxy. Its strengths and weaknesses are the subject of the following three chapters.

Notes

1 Paul McCracken *et al.*, *Towards Full Employment and Price Stability* (Paris, Organization for Economic Co-operation and Development, 1977) hereafter referred to as *Towards Full Employment*. This report is based on a range of views of eight economists, including university teachers, senior government advisors, the former Vice-President of the Commission of the European Economic Community, and the former Governor of the Bank of Italy.

2 This assumption has been criticized brilliantly and rejected by Fred Hirsch, *Social Limits to Growth* (London, 1978), p. 67:

> Increased material resources enlarge the demand for positional [i.e. prestige] goods, a demand that can be satisfied for some only by frustrating demand by others. The intensified positional competition involves an increase in needs for the individual, in the sense that additional resources are required to achieve a given level of welfare . . . . Individuals chase each others' tails. The race gets longer for the same prize.

3 *Towards Full Employment* ignores the contribution made by the new international division of labour to the unemployment problem in employment societies. It assumes, naively, that the 'developed world' will aid economic growth in the 'developing countries' by increasing their exports and exporting capital to them. The report is also starry-eyed about the employment potential of bigger and better research and development 'programmes' and the development of new technology. It underestimates seriously the present trend towards 'jobless growth', whereby investment is mainly directed to saving labour costs rather than to expanding capacity by creating additional jobs.

4 The best recent discussions of the self-paralysing tendencies of corporatist mechanisms are: *Patterns of Corporatist Policy Making*, edited by Philippe C. Schmitter and Gerhard Lehmbruch (London, 1982); and Claus Offe, *Disorganized Capitalism*, edited by John Keane (Cambridge, 1985), ch. 8.

Further reading

William Leiss, *The Limits to Satisfaction: An Essay on the Problem of Needs and Commodities* (Toronto, 1976).

Paul McCracken *et al.*, *Towards Full Employment and Price Stability* (Paris, 1977).

Claus Offe, *Disorganized Capitalism*, edited by John Keane (Cambridge, 1985), esp. ch. 8.

Philippe C. Schmitter and Gerhard Lehmbruch (eds), *Patterns of Corporatist Policy Making* (London, 1982).

Social Democratic Party, *Economic Policy* (London, 1984).

5 The strong state and the free market

Government is today the major source of economic instability.
  [Milton Friedman]

During the past two decades, a serious political challenge to the full
employment welfare state has emerged from right-wing movements
and governments. In several countries and regions of western Europe
and North America, this so-called New Right has managed to dis-
place social democracy as the dominant public philosophy. The
novelty of this development should not be exaggerated. The central
belief of the New Right – that the non-state sphere of civil society is
more and more being swallowed up by the bureaucratic state and that,
consequently, 'free markets' and individual initiative and self-help
need to be renewed – is a rather old and recurring political theme. It
dates back to the last quarter of the nineteenth century – to precisely
the period (as Chapter 1 has shown) when the vision of the full
employment welfare state was first elaborated systematically. The
emergence in this period of a right wing, pro-market reaction against
the vision of state-guaranteed full employment was by no means
fortuitous. From the beginning, this pro-market reaction was, and has
remained until this day, a rebellious child of social democracy, a pro-
test against the growing state regulation of civil society associated
with full employment welfare state policies.
  Herbert Spencer's vitriolic attack on state coercion in *The Man
Versus the State* (1884) is one of the earliest examples of this type of
pro-market reaction against the emerging full employment welfare
state. Written by one of the most prominent and influential
nineteenth-century English thinkers, this essay contains a central and
surprisingly contemporary argument: that the reliance upon bureaucratic state means to guarantee the 'welfare' of individuals has
become an end in itself, thereby contradicting the original liberal goal
of maximizing individual liberty and equality of opportunity. According

to Spencer, rapidly multiplying dictatorial state measures are tending continually to reduce the liberties of individuals. The steady expansion of the bureaucratic state – its establishment of Factories Acts, compulsory vaccination and schooling, its attempts to define and regulate matters as diverse as the consumption of alcohol, prostitution, chimney sweeping and the lives of the unemployed – is seen by him to be producing an alarming increase of compulsory (or 'socialistic') governmental power, and a corresponding diminution of social space within which each individual citizen can enter voluntarily into contractual relations with others. Spencer warns against a new form of 'state socialist' slavery masked by the principle of 'the welfare of the many' and administered by a new class of officials: 'Socialistic arrangements necessitate . . . enslavement . . . ; and towards such an enslavement many recent measures . . . are carrying us.' He urges that freedom and justice in modern society cannot be guaranteed or developed through state or 'collective' action. The liberty and equality of individuals are at bottom dependent upon their private activities and spontaneous co-operation. These, in turn, can be developed only through a carefully defined strong state, which respects the independence of a system of 'peaceful industry' and protects the life, property and freedom of each hardworking and resourceful individual. The friends of liberty, says Spencer, must therefore strive to minimize the present state compulsions and restraints upon individuals. They must reject the 'socialist myth' that state power should in principle be unlimited, and their motto must be 'Individualism *versus* Socialism'.

A century has passed since Spencer's polemic against the embryonic full employment welfare state, and yet it still has a strikingly contemporary ring about it. The arguments of the contemporary American 'Chicago School' political economist, Milton Friedman, have helped to ensure this. As government adviser and media personality, Friedman has proven himself to be one of the most convincing and influential advocates of the free market and the strong state. This chapter examines and criticizes his views on the failures of the full employment welfare state, the causes of unemployment and the future of paid work. In preparation for the case studies of the policies of the Thatcher and Reagan administrations (Chapters 6 and 7), this chapter pays special attention to the strengths and weaknesses of his criticisms of the full employment welfare state. Friedman summarizes his criticisms in the following proposition: 'Two aspects of the growth in government's role – the expansion of transfer payments and the growing rigidity of the price system – are . . . the fundamental reason why the level of unemployment has been trending up.' His claim amounts to a vigorous defence of 'free market capitalism' guarded by the strong state. In order to assess its validity, the prior assumptions and arguments upon which it rests will be examined briefly.

1   Friedman's criticism of the full employment welfare state may fruitfully be introduced and explained by means of a thought experiment. Imagine a simple society comprising a collection of interacting Robinson Crusoe-like individuals. Imagine also that these rational, calculating individuals are willing and able to work, and have their own adequate resources (of land, tools, materials etc.), such that they are able to produce sufficient goods and services *either* directly for themselves *or* for exchange with others. According to Friedman, an important consequence would follow from this allegedly happy situation. Since these rational, calculating individuals need not enter into any exchanges with others unless they see themselves as benefiting from such transactions, no exchanges will in fact take place unless they are mutually beneficial and chosen freely. Under such circumstances there may be some higgling and a few open quarrels, and yet individuals will generally pursue their own interests by exchanging their products and services voluntarily and co-operatively. That is to say, transactions among producing and consuming individuals will be achieved without coercion or exploitation; their freedom and equality of opportunity will be maximized.

2   The same principles of equal and voluntary exchange apply in modern capitalist economies, or so Friedman claims. Note the rather giant leap in his argument. Modern capitalist economies, their much greater complexity and productivity notwithstanding, resemble a simple society of Robinson Crusoe-like individuals, since both are based upon voluntary co-operation among mutually benefiting and exchanging partners. Capitalist economies measure up to the two basic criteria of a 'free private enterprise exchange economy': first, transactions are 'private', in the sense that the ultimate contracting parties are not governments or trade unions, but producing and consuming individuals; second, these individuals are effectively free to enter into, or to withdraw from, contractual exchanges with others. Capitalist economies (or employment societies) are systems of

production, exchange and consumption guided by market competition among contracting individuals.

3   Friedman maintains that freedom of the individual – 'the absence of coercion of a man [sic] by his fellow men' – is the single most important criterion for judging the degree of adequacy or 'goodness' of any society. In economic matters, as we would expect from the above arguments, freedom of the individual is best secured through a system of competitive 'free market' capitalism. Only a free enterprise exchange economy can ensure the liberty of producing and consuming individuals – their freedom to work for whom they choose, to invest when and where they like, to compete against others in business, and to consume according to their own personal preferences. What Friedman calls 'the basic problem' of all human societies, that of co-ordinating the producing and consuming activities of large numbers of individuals, cannot be solved by centrally organized government directives. Friedman's conviction that only free market economies can ensure the liberty of individuals leads him to draw a basic contrast between two kinds of arrangements for organizing economic activity. Soviet-type *command economies* tend to maximize the subordination of individuals to a concentrated centre of power; goods and services are allocated directly to them by the state, and most individuals have limited freedom to choose where and for whom they work. By contrast, competitive *market economies* – comprising money-based, relatively anonymous transactions, in which individuals can always exercise their freedom to enter or withdraw from any particular economic exchange – disperse power and responsibility and maximize the economic liberty of individuals. These market economies also ensure that individuals monitor their own performance and have an incentive to monitor it effectively. Thus, workers are highly motivated to work hard and efficiently for the employer of their choice. Investors have an incentive to risk their own property as well as to make the best and most profitable use of it. Consumers spending their own money have an incentive to spend it wisely. And so on.

4   Competitive market economies, Friedman says, ensure not only the economic liberty of individuals but also *political* freedom, that is, individuals' freedom from arbitrary and all-encompassing state power. Competitive capitalist systems in fact maximize political freedom, because they separate economic power from political power, thereby enabling the one to counterbalance or offset the other.

This conviction leads Friedman to reject Beveridge's social democratic belief in the necessity and desirability of increasing state regulation of the capitalist economy as a means of maximizing political freedom. Real political liberty, in Friedman's view, can be achieved only by allowing governments to supervise those matters (such as military defence and policing) which cannot be handled through the market at all; activities which the market can handle only very inefficiently and ineffectively ('natural monopolies', such as electricity provision, are a case in point); or transactions which would otherwise entail 'externalities' or 'neighbourhood effects', that is, great costs to groups other than those involved directly in market transactions. Friedman recalls Spencer's old maxim: the state in market capitalist society should as far as possible be *limited in scope* and biased openly in favour of market transactions. This does not mean that the *power* of the state should be limited. State power is essential both as a forum for determining and administering the rules of market competition as well as for filling its (few) gaps and limiting its (few) malfunctions. While political liberty depends upon maximizing the scope and power of market transactions, Friedman also concedes that the road to the free market can only be kept open by strong, well-armed bureaucratic states. A society organized along purely competitive market lines is impossible. Wherever possible, however, state power should be limited in favour of free market competition; state intervention is only ever justified to keep the market 'free'. In 'free' societies, in which the liberty of individuals is maximized, the state must be both powerful *and* limited in scope.

5 With these arguments for the strong state and the free market in hand, Friedman boldly condemns the social democratic vision of the full employment welfare state. Despite its good intentions, this vision is in reality a recipe for mass unemployment. Friedman insists that the full employment welfare state produces new economic crisis tendencies and, over the long term, worsening rates of unemployment; thereby it contradicts its promise to maintain the full employment of labour and capital.

His argument concerning unemployment is a central element of contemporary monetary and supply-side economics (see Chapters 6 and 7), and can be summarized briefly as follows. The noble objective of full employment cannot be achieved through welfare state means, Friedman insists, because state planning and regulation of the type advocated by Beveridge and Keynes interferes seriously with the market mechanisms for determining wages, prices, investment and the distribution of jobs. The growing role of government and the political difficulty of legislating higher taxes to finance ever larger government spending results in a fluctuating and rising rate of inflation. According to Friedman's (so-called monetarist) explanation, post-war governments have allowed the supply of money to grow more rapidly than the output of goods and services in the economy, and in so doing have produced, through their excessive and constantly increasing spending, sharp increases in the actual and anticipated rate of inflation.

This state-generated inflation generates uncertainty and confusion among capitalist investors and, therefore, a cautiousness or outright unwillingness to expand, enter into new ventures or employ new workers. Friedman consequently challenges the view (arising from the work of the economist A. W. Phillips) that there is a stable inverse relationship between the rate of unemployment and the rate of inflation (the 'Phillips curve'). Under welfare state conditions, on the contrary, the gradual weakening of market mechanisms results in growing unemployment *and* accelerating inflation.

The 'distortion' of the market price system by the state also perpetuates the life of unproductive as well as uncompetitive 'lame duck' enterprises and, therefore, leads to a maldistribution of paid workers among different industrial sectors. The profitability and competitiveness of enterprises are reduced, thereby increasing the long-term probability of plant closures and redundancies.[1] Furthermore, the growth of the state's social policy programmes reduces the costs to workers of being unemployed or, in effect, subsidizes people for not working in the labour market. State programmes eat away at the foundations of market competition. They discourage hard work, competitiveness and achievement in the labour market; and the more individuals are entitled to various public transfer payments, the more they are encouraged to become state-coddled layabouts, who float through life on a giant government mattress. This supplanting of the competitive individualism of the market by bureaucratic state collectivism in effect results in a type of 'voluntary' unemployment – cushioned by various social policy benefits, many individuals simply no longer deem it worthwhile to engage in (certain types of) waged and salaried work.

6   Generous and light-handed government policies towards trade unions have only exacerbated these causes of a long-term upward trend in the rate of unemployment. In Friedman's view, the substan-

tial increase in trade union power has greatly contributed to rising unemployment. Trade unions obstruct the free market mechanism and price their members out of jobs. By raising wages for *unionized* workers to 'artificial' levels, that is, to above market rates, unions effectively force companies to cut their wages bill by employing less labour. Consequently, some unionized workers lose their jobs (or, equivalently, other non-unionized workers are unable to find jobs in unionized industries because of closed-shop agreements). Workers so displaced find it difficult to find a job in non-unionized sectors of the economy because the state-provided cushion of transfer payments and minimum wages and conditions legislation prevent wages in these sectors from falling to the market level thereby encouraging workers to choose to go on the dole). Since wage levels are rendered inelastic in the non-unionized sector of the economy, employers are disinclined to hire more labour. Hence, the non-unionized sector has only a limited capacity to absorb workers displaced from the unionized sector. The overall result is a steady increase in the long-term, so-called 'natural' rate of unemployment, a trend only reinforced by the other welfare state 'distortions' of the market mechanism mentioned above.

7   According to Friedman, the full employment welfare state not only produces economic crisis tendencies by interfering with the market mechanism and aiding and abetting trade unions; it also erodes individual freedom and equality of opportunity. Slowly but surely, the capitalist economy becomes an appendage of centralized state power and, with that, individuals in the spheres of state and economy become pawns in the hands of those who control state power. Hardly any aspect of daily life – from the household to the workplace – is exempt from the increasing authority of politicians, state administrators and planners. The full employment welfare state, Friedman insists, 'has given birth to a large bureaucracy that shows tendencies of growing by what it feeds on, extending its scope from one area of our life to another'. The spread of state bureaucracy not only undermines the foundations of individual freedom from state tyranny, it also violates the principle of equality of individual opportunity, since free competition among individuals in the market is suffocated by a do-gooder New Class, comprising professional politicians, government bureaucrats and their policy-taking clients and beneficiaries.

8   It follows from this diagnosis of the present crisis of the full employment welfare state that Friedman is openly hostile to all proposed social democratic remedies for restoring full employment. Any economic crisis management strategy based upon higher government spending to create jobs, expansive monetary policy, state assistance to declining firms and industries, and protection against foreign competition, in his view, is bound to *deepen* the present unemployment crisis. What is rather required is a radically different strategy for reducing 'structural rigidities' which restrict the supply of goods and services within the economy – that is, altering its supply side. This means giving freer rein to market forces (in matters such as state-provided education, health and communications); diminishing state intervention in labour markets and capitalist enterprise; replacing the whole collection of welfare state programmes by a 'negative income tax' (discussed in Chapter 9); lifting restrictions on international trade and, in general, cutting back the size and scope of the public sector. (Friedman proposes legislation that would compulsorily require governments to limit carefully the growth of the money supply, to balance their budgets, and to limit their spending. These 'cut-backs' are necessary since, in his view, the excessively large welfare state has the objectionable effect of distorting the market price system and of 'crowding out' productive investment and, hence, the creation of 'real' jobs in profitable and competitive industries.) In order to stimulate investment and foster competition, company profits must also be boosted, by cutting company taxes and workers' real wages, by reducing production costs in various ways, and especially by curtailing trade union power. The present privileges of trade unions – their capacity to enforce closed shop agreements, to picket, to impose costs on employers and third parties – must be restricted, so as to create a more 'flexible', co-operative and geographically mobile workforce, as well as to protect the market 'liberties' of both individual workers and employers.

According to Friedman, these types of supply-side measures are urgently required to deal with the present unemployment crisis. Considered as an overall strategy for reducing unemployment, they amount to a phased withdrawal of state power from the economy and the gradual revival of 'free' market competition. Since the goals of full employment and the liberty and equality of opportunity for all individuals cannot be achieved through welfare state arrangements, the entrenched privileges of trade unions, politicians, welfare bureaucracies and their clients must be overcome. The 'tyranny of the status quo' must be broken – in favour of a strong, clearly differentiated state which respects and guarantees private economic freedom and the 'ingenuity and fertility' of the market.

Some difficulties

It is evident from this brief sketch that Friedman's arguments and political proposals, though hardly original, are highly provocative. It is also clear that some of Friedman's *diagnoses* of the present difficulties of the full employment welfare state are telling – most notably those which point to its excessively bureaucratic character, its interference with the market mechanism and its consequent structuring of capital–labour relations in a manner potentially disadvantageous to private capitalist firms (see Chapter 2). Despite these observations, there are serious difficulties with Friedman's proposed 'strong state, free market' strategy for reducing unemployment. Three of the most crucial difficulties – which we consider fatal to Friedman's overall proposals – are discussed below.

In the *first* place, there are serious weaknesses in Friedman's view that unemployment is merely a temporary expression of the excessive growth of state transfer payments and the 'rigidity' of market prices, and that they can be remedied by resuscitating market forces. The analysis *assumes* that while this 'liberation' of the market (or 'the ordeal by fire', as a British supporter of Friedman puts it)[2] is taking place, trade unions will willingly lay down their arms. Friedman also *assumes* that private capitalist firms will quickly and confidently occupy the new market territory opened up for them by making new investments and hiring new workers. Both these assumptions are dubious, but the second is especially problematic. Friedman seriously underestimates the way in which market competition typically generates uncertainty and 'holding back' among capitalist investors, who are nowadays very prone to ask: Should we wait a little longer before investing? Will this 'free market' strategy of the present government survive the coming elections? Or is this just another flash in the pan strategy? This type of uncertainty and lack of foresight is inherent in 'free markets', and is highlighted by the recent joke: How many free market liberals does it take to replace a light bulb? Answer: none, they leave it to market forces. Market uncertainty, as Keynes and Beveridge long ago emphasized, can snowball, reinforcing a general unwillingness among investors to expand or enter into new ventures. Friedman's 'free market' strategy for significantly reducing unemployment ignores this fundamental point that the liberation of market competition might well *increase* many investors' uncertainty or reticence to invest and, therefore, *deepen* the long-term unemployment trend. Indeed, in the current economic crisis, further disinvestment, investment in job-saving technologies, producing 'jobless growth' in manufacturing industry, or relocation of investment to the Third World,[3] are likely outcomes, and certainly consistent with the 'free' market privileges of private firms operating in a capitalist economy. Moreover, Friedman's remedy for unemployment – disconnecting what he takes to be the market's artificial life supports – is rather silent about the length of time required for significantly reducing unemployment. He does not take seriously the absurd possibility that the patient (i.e. the market) will die or be crippled severely before the cure can take effect. That this *is* a real possibility is suggested by a recent estimate of the rates of economic growth that would be required to achieve full employment levels (in Beveridge's sense of 'more jobs than men') by the mid 1990s (see Table 1). This estimate (dating from 1980, when levels of unemployment were considerably lower than at present) suggests that if technological changes resulted in increased levels of productivity comparable with the boom years 1951–73, the economic growth rates necessary for achieving full employment would amount to an average annual rate of approximately 6–7 per cent for OECD countries as a whole. With the exception of France, all of the national rates of required growth shown in Table 1 are higher than during the post-war boom years, 1951–73. Britain in particular would appear to be faced by a Herculean task, for the rate of economic growth it would require to restore employment would be higher than at any time since the years of the First World War.

The *second* flaw in Friedman's argument takes the form of a contradiction between his defence of the goal of maximizing individual

Table 1 *Estimated annual average growth rate of gross domestic product required to achieve full employment by 1994 (percentage figures)*

Japan	10.0	France	5.5
West Germany	6.2	USA	4.2
Italy	5.6	UK	3.2

Source: H. Shutt, *The Jobs Crisis: Increasing Unemployment in the Developed World*, Economist Intelligence Unit, Special Report, Number 85, 1980, p.63.

freedom of choice and his homilies on behalf of market capitalism. Friedman never tires of repeating his 'libertarian' demand: the boundaries between the state and the capitalist economy must be redrawn because comprehensive welfare state regulation destroys 'free markets' and thereby saps individual initiative and freedom of choice. He is silent, however, about the ways in which 'free markets' themselves frustrate or block individuals' liberties.

To begin with, Friedman conveniently forgets that, during the past three centuries, 'free markets' were created only through an enormous increase in new types of compulsory supervision of individuals' lives. To state, as Friedman does, that 'history suggests that capitalism is a necessary condition for political freedom' is to ignore the point, emphasized for instance in Karl Polanyi's classic work,[4] that not only new forms of compulsory (paid) work, but also the penitentiary, workhouse and asylum were vital conditions of the early modern growth of capitalist employment societies, and not simply isolated accidents on the modern highway of individual liberty through the market. Note also that Friedman's defence of free markets rules out the freedom of individuals and groups *not* to enter into market exchange processes. (Consider the case of local rural communities or of environmental groups who seek to prevent private corporations from mining or 'developing' their land as if it were a marketable commodity just like any other.) Furthermore, Friedman's scheme underestimates the enormous power of monopolistic business enterprises (e.g. ICI, Mitsubishi, Rank-Xerox, ITT) to establish the rules of market competition. Big business, or so Friedman replies, is relatively unimportant from the point of view of capitalist employment societies considered as a whole. But is this so? While there no doubt continues to be thousands of small businesses and many self-employed persons in most welfare capitalist countries, it is also evident that their economies are heavily dominated by large firms. Friedman's silence about this fact of 'organized capitalism' is unjustified – 'imperfect competition', as many twentieth-century economists have pointed out correctly, is a necessary outcome of market competition, in which competing firms are forced to strive to become monopolists in order to protect themselves against other competitors. It follows from this point that Friedman's ideology of freedom of individual market choice is just that: a justification of not only 'the individual' but also an apology for the power of big business to organize and *determine* individuals' choices concerning when, where and how much they work, what they consume and how they in general live.

Friedman's failure to appreciate the organized nature of modern capitalism also provides a clue, finally, as to why he turns a blind eye to the very typical case – a case emphasized correctly by Beveridge, among others – where certain individuals and groups are *forced* to retire hurt from the 'free' market game. Market competition has an inherent tendency to produce *unequal* outcomes among its currently unequal participants, and groups (such as part-time paid workers, the unemployed, welfare claimants and ethnic minorities) who are nowadays relatively poor and powerless would rightly be suspicious of Friedman's claim that only free markets can guarantee equality of opportunity and liberty. This tendency towards inequality is usually exacerbated by the fact that the invisible hand of 'free' market competition usually picks the pockets of those whom it has already rendered unemployed, poor and powerless. Friedman fails to recognize, indeed, denies openly that social inequalities, for instance between the employed and the unemployed, are typically *deepened* by market competition. Once individuals have been flung by the invisible hand of 'free' market forces into the ranks of the unemployed, they find it hard to make ends meet, let alone to compete with others for scarce waged or salaried jobs or for compensating work either in the so-called 'shadow' economy or in the household. Market competition leads not to greater liberty and equality of opportunity among individuals but, simply, to a process of *polarization* between the employed and the unemployed.[5]

A *third* difficulty concerns the explicit link which Friedman draws between the expansion of free markets and the extension of political freedom, that is, citizens' freedom from the arbitrary exercise of state power. Friedman often remarks that the tide is turning against the bureaucratic full employment welfare state, and that greater political liberty is on the horizon. This supposed link between free markets and political liberty is highly doubtful. Indeed, it may be asked (as should always be asked of *any* political thinker) whether the aims and methods of Friedman's proposals for reducing unemployment are compatible? In other words, is the *means* (the strong, independent state) of achieving the *goal* of maximizing individual liberty, within a market that guarantees full employment of labour and capital, in fact contradictory? This question is crucial, because in some countries – Chile and Turkey for example – establishing and maintaining a market economy requires nothing less than military dictatorship, secret police forces and even death squads. A property system not controlled fully or directly by the state is no doubt a necessary condition of political freedom, but it is certainly not a sufficient condition. Only *democratic* freedoms – which enable all citizens to meet, publish and decide freely how they wish to be governed – can ultimately ensure political liberty.

It is doubtful whether Friedman's proposals are consistent with political democracy in this sense. Indeed, the opposite conclusion is more plausible. The policy of restricting the welfare state in the direction of 'free' market capitalism would in practice require tough law and order responses against its various opponents in civil society. For instance, the strong state, free market strategy would evidently necessitate the abolition or considerable weakening of trade unions, their legal circumscription and forcible transformation into not much more than friendly societies charged with disciplining their members. It would also likely suppose the further weakening of open and accountable government and the drastic restriction of competition among political parties. While none of these outcomes would be consistent with Friedman's 'libertarian' vision, they would be likely to be required by it in practice. Friends of democratic liberty would, therefore, do well to resist the charm of Friedman's libertarian vision. His crusade to overcome the welfare state, reduce unemployment and to resurrect a 'healthy' market economy seems to be little more than a recipe for further job loss, growing polarization between the employed and unemployed and *increasing* state control over the lives of many of its citizens.

Notes

1 This claim finds some support in the highly influential diagnosis of the British economy presented by R. Bacon and W. Eltis in *Britain's Economic Problem: Too Few Producers* (London, 1976). According to the authors, successive governments of both political parties in Britain have eroded the competitiveness of the British economy by encouraging large numbers of workers to move out of private industry and into various 'unproductive' service occupations organized by the state. Civil servants, social workers, and other public service workers have become increasingly numerous; consequently, their growing requirements for consumer goods have had to be satisfied by declining numbers of 'productive' market sector workers. By transferring more and more jobs to the public sector, Bacon and Eltis argue, government uses up national resources and erodes the foundations of economic prosperity.

2 Patrick Minford, 'Trade unions destroy a million jobs', *The Journal of Economic Affairs*, **2** (January 1982), p. 73.

3 The lack of a well developed *international* perspective in Friedman's writings is quite striking, and further weakens his defence of free markets. Indeed, the new round of *internationalization* of capitalist investment presently taking place in the global economy (see the Introduction) makes a nonsense of the idea of a free market since, unlike capitalist investors, workers are scarcely mobile within national economies (they often *choose* not to alter their place of residence) and, excepting those who do migrate from one country to another, can hardly respond to market conditions world-wide.

4 Karl Polanyi, *Origins of Our Time. The Great Transformation* (London, 1944).

5 This is also the central and very important argument of R. E. Pahl, *Divisions of Labour* (Oxford, 1984). This study is a decisive antidote to Friedman's erroneous view that the poor do not work in the labour market because they are not poor enough (being supported by a soft cushion of welfare state supports), as well as an important corrective to the widespread but again mistaken assumption that, after being made unemployed, individuals 'get by' through engaging in compensating activity outside of official labour markets (a view defended by Richard Rose, *Getting By in Three Economies: The Resources of Official, Unofficial and Domestic Economies*, Centre for the Study of Public Policies, University of Strathclyde, 1983).

Further reading

Milton Friedman, *Inflation and Unemployment: The New Dimension of Politics* (London, 1977).

Milton Friedman, *Market or Plan?*, with a critical comment by Alec Nove (London, 1984).

Milton and Rose Friedman, *Capitalism and Freedom* (Chicago, 1962).

Milton and Rose Friedman, *Free to Choose*, (London, 1980).

Milton and Rose Friedman, *Tyranny of the Status Quo* (London, 1984), esp. ch. 6.

Andrew Gamble, 'The free economy and the strong state: the rise of the social market economy', in *The Socialist Register 1979*, edited by R. Miliband and J. Saville (London, 1979), pp. 1–25.

C. B. Macpherson, 'Elegant tombstones: a note on Friedman's freedom', in *Democratic Theory: Essays in Retrieval* (Oxford, 1973).

Murray Milgate and John Eatwell, 'Unemployment and the market mechanism', in *Keynes's Economics and the Theory of Value and Distribution*, edited by John Eatwell and Murray Milgate (London, 1983), pp. 260–80.

6 Populist Conservatism and jobless growth

The key contribution of Government in a free society is to do all it can to create a climate in which enterprise can flourish, above all by removing obstacles to the working of markets, especially the labour market. The Government's Medium Term Financial Strategy aims to set the growth of money demand that is consistent with declining inflation and declining unemployment. Boosting demand without the necessary improvements in the performance of the economy would only generate higher inflation. [Government White Paper, *Employment. The Challenge for the Nation*, March 1985]

The election of the Conservatives under Margaret Thatcher in 1979 was the specific moment in post-war British political history when Beveridge's vision of the full employment welfare state was summarily repudiated. Drawing on the diagnoses and prescriptions of Friedman and the new 'supply-side' economists, and adopting a political style which was overtly populist, the new Conservative government relegated full employment as its *primary* economic objective and called on those disenchanted with existing political arrangements and policies to join it in bringing about the restoration of 'sound money' and the 'free market'. This chapter identifies the main elements in the Thatcher governments' economic programme since 1979, demonstrates their affinity with the ideas discussed in the previous chapter, and points to the impact of these policies on contemporary Britain.

The conversion to free market Conservatism

Since Margaret Thatcher succeeded Edward Heath as party leader in 1975, the Conservatives have increasingly rejected the policies and political arrangements of the full employment welfare state which were the central features of the paternalistic 'One Nation'

Conservatism of Butler, Macmillan and Heath.[1] Instead, they have reverted to more traditional 'free market' policies which emphasize government's primary responsibilities for maintaining 'sound' finances and private 'enterprise' (that is, securing a 'strong state, free market').

Against the background of the Wilson governments' policies (Chapter 3), 'libertarian' elements in the party (notably Enoch Powell) argued for greater differentiation from Labour, and by the end of the late 1960s had gained substantial influence over party policy. The programme which the Conservatives put to the electorate in 1970 promised that a future Conservative government would 'disengage' government from industry and end nationalization, cut taxes and government expenditure, impose new restrictions on the trade unions and on immigration, and provide new incentives for saving. However, two years after Prime Minister Heath had boldly proclaimed the advent of a 'quiet revolution' which would 'change the course and the history of this nation', his government had reversed its course. Government spending was substantially increased, bankrupt private companies were bailed out with public money, controls over the money supply were relaxed, and wage and price controls introduced. The so-called U-turn of 1972 and the subsequent election defeats of February and October 1974 provided the impetus for a radical reappraisal of Conservative policy, and were the political setting against which Thatcher defeated Heath in the contest for the party leadership in 1975.

The intellectual leadership for the party's conversion to 'free market' Conservatism was provided by Sir Keith Joseph who (like Thatcher) had been a member of the Heath government. Conservatives, Joseph argued, had gone too far in compromising with socialism. They needed to espouse a more distinctive set of principles and policies which would not apologize for but rejoice in capitalism. In a series of publications – notably *Why Britain Needs A Social Market Economy* and *Stranded On The Middle Ground* – Joseph borrowed heavily from Friedman, Hayek and other liberal economists, whose ideas were popularized in Britain by the Institute of Economic Affairs, to elaborate his 'free market' vision.

According to Joseph, post-war Conservatives had too readily accepted the new power of government implicit in Macmillan's 'Middle Way' (Chapter 3). Rather than helping solve Britain's twin problems of high inflation and high unemployment, Joseph argued, Keynesian – or Beveridge-type – policies of demand management, high public expenditure and high taxation had actually caused them. By borrowing money from private banks to stimulate demand, governments had effectively encouraged inflation, because the amount of money in the economy had been allowed to grow much faster than productivity. Eventually, a lower level of materials and labour began to chase a larger amount of money with the result that prices rose. Here, Joseph explicitly endorsed Friedman's monetarist theory of inflation and, in so doing, explicitly condemned the policies of the Heath government (which had allowed the money supply to grow by 50 per cent in two years). According to the monetarists, inflation is not the fault of trade unions or businessmen. It is the fault of government for making too much money available in the economy. Governments' attempts to ensure high levels of employment by Keynesian methods simply enhance inflationary expectations leading to actual inflation and no additional jobs in the long run (since it is assumed firms and workers are already producing as much as markets demand). Governments must, therefore, squeeze inflation out of the economy by strictly controlling the money supply through high interest rates and drastic cuts in government borrowing.

However, Joseph warned on many occasions that 'monetarism is not enough' to keep inflation and unemployment down. There still remained the important questions of what to do about such detailed structural – or 'supply-side' – questions as wage and salary costs, productivity, geographical mobility of labour, the relationship between welfare benefits and people's willingness to accept available jobs. Here again, Joseph's 'solution' borrowed heavily from Friedman and the new liberal economists, as well as from the philosophical writings of Hayek.[2] Governments, Joseph argued, cannot accept responsibility for securing and maintaining full employment. Only 'people' (i.e. capital and labour) can do that by making their firms more competitive and by accepting lower wages and salaries. A strong state is needed, however, to help create these conditions. The state should function to enhance market competition by cutting direct taxation, encouraging greater labour mobility through lower welfare benefits and curtailing the powers of trade unions, and by facilitating lower wage settlements. These 'supply-side' policies are necessary since – Joseph argued – the 'natural' rate of unemployment has been rising, not because of a deficiency in demand (Keynes's and Beveridge's idea) but because of distortions in the economy which have reduced individuals' willingness to supply labour or firms' propensity to invest and, therefore, to supply goods or services.

Joseph's free market ideas never met with universal approval, even within the Conservative Party. His suggestion that the party should embrace wholesale the economic doctrines of Friedman, Hayek and the new liberal economists did not sit comfortably with the traditional Conservative emphases on pragmatism, flexibility and the maintenance of social solidarity.[3] Nevertheless, under the leadership of Margaret Thatcher, Joseph's intellectual vision was more and more translated into a package of powerful political themes which exploited growing popular disenchantment with the full employment welfare state. The party's manifesto for the 1979 general election (echoing Heath's programme in 1970) emphasized the need to redress the balance that 'had been increasingly tilted in favour of the state at the expense of the individual'. It also stressed the positive benefits of reducing popular expectations about what governments could and should do. Past governments had tried to do too much, the manifesto argued and, in so doing, had neglected priorities. A new Conservative government would concentrate on priorities and would work 'with the grain of human nature'. It would maintain strict control over the money supply, reduce personal taxation and the public sector borrowing requirement (the PSBR), cut public expenditure in virtually every area (except defence and law and order, and health), increase incentives to engage in paid work, reduce the size and scope of government, stress the private sector's role and transfer to it as much commercial and industrial activity as possible. As for wages, they would be entirely matters between companies and workers. There would be no formal wages policy. However, the manifesto warned, 'no one should or can protect them from the results of the agreements they make' and a Conservative government would introduce new measures to restrict picketing and to tax strikers' welfare benefits.

From vision to government policy

How the Conservatives' strong state, free market vision of British society has been translated into government policies since 1979, and the impact of those policies on unemployment and labour market conditions are the concerns of the remainder of this chapter. The following review of the Thatcher governments' employment policies is divided into three parts: the first is concerned with monetarism; the second with supply-side policies, including taxation, wages and labour market policies, restrictions on trade unions, and government job creation schemes; and the third with aid to industry.

Monetary restraint to reduce inflation

The control of inflation – not the maintenance of high levels of employment – was the first priority of the newly-elected Thatcher government in 1979. This objective was to be achieved not by implementing direct government controls over wages and prices, but by the government making a credible commitment to controlling inflation by stipulating strict targets for monetary growth, public expenditure and government borrowing in the expectation that inflationary pressures would be quickly dissipated without the need for a recession or even a deceleration of economic growth. This was following the so-called rational expectations theory of monetarism.

Consistent with this theory, Chancellor of the Exchequer Howe announced the government's 'Medium Term Financial Strategy' in the budget of March 1980. This strategy stipulated specific targets for the growth of the money supply, and government spending and borrowing over the next four years. By fiscal year 1983–4, the Chancellor anticipated, the annual growth in the money supply would be reduced from between a range of 7 to 11 per cent to between 4 and 8 per cent. Government spending over the same period would be reduced from 42 per cent of gross domestic product to under 40 per cent of GDP; and the PSBR – the difference between government revenue and expenditure – would be reduced from 3.75 per cent of GDP to 1.5 per cent by 1983–4, thus lowering inflation and preventing the 'crowding out' of private investment.

The conduct and effects of the Thatcher governments' monetarist policies were entirely predictable. In practice, the government found it extremely difficult to measure, let alone restrain the growth in the money supply. Moreover, far from reducing government involvement in the economy, the government's role was actually *increased*, although exercised in different ways. Targets were consistently exceeded, especially in 1980–1 and 1982–3, primarily because the government had also abolished exchange controls, and partly because firms had to borrow more from the banks simply to cope with the large increases in interest rates which the government had imposed. Government borrowing (except for 1982–3) was also faster than anticipated, as public expenditure on trade, industry,[4] unemployment insurance, and social security continued to rise as the economy declined into the worst slump in Britain since the 1930s.[5] Faced with extraordinarily high interest rates, and the failure of wage settlements to adjust instantaneously to slump conditions (as anticipated by Friedman and other free marketeers), firms began to experience serious liquidity problems which forced them to reduce production and employment levels.

Facing widespread unpopularity, the loss of a number of by-elections to the newly formed Social Democrat–Liberal Alliance, and a clamour for reflation from opposition parties, 'One Nation' Conservatives (dubbed 'wets'), employers and unions, Prime Minister Thatcher retorted that her government would make no U-turns. It would maintain its resolve and continue fighting the main 'enemy': inflation. Inflation was indeed reduced to 3.7 per cent in May 1983, but primarily because of the government's deflationary policy (forcing firms to reduce their stocks of goods and temporarily increasing the supply of goods in the economy) and a fortuitous decline in world commodity prices. The severe cost of achieving this objective, however, was borne by the swelling ranks of the unemployed.

From pure monetarism to supply-side

From late 1981, as unemployment rose to record levels, government policies increasingly reflected the influence of supply-side theory, which (following Say's Law) supposes that supply creates its own demand. According to supply-side theory (which is sometimes described as a branch of monetarism), governments should pursue policies which stimulate private savings and investment, rather than consumption. In this way, they can alleviate both economic stagnation – by creating jobs and spending power – and inflation – by increasing the production and supply of goods and services – to absorb the spending power. According to the version of this theory outlined by Conservative leaders since 1981 the Thatcher governments would reduce taxation (especially direct taxation); remove labour and capital market 'rigidities', including the restrictive practices of trade unions and business firms which forced up wages, and salaries and prices; encourage industrial restructuring through 'positive' financial assistance; 'improve' job training and lower social welfare benefits in order to increase incentives to engage in paid work and job training. Some of these policies were intended to have immediate effects, such as removing large numbers of people off the unemployed register. Others have been directed towards longer-term objectives, such as the development of a British 'enterprise culture'. In doing so, as the later discussion shows, these policies have also contrasted sharply with the 'strong state, free market' expounded by Friedman and Joseph.

Taxation

One of the most popular issues for the Conservatives in the 1979 general election, and one which helped them win that election, was their promise to lower direct taxation. In office, the Thatcher governments have altered the tax system in three important ways. First, marginal rates of direct taxation have been lowered across all income bands, but especially, the higher rates for wealthy people. Second, in order to compensate for the anticipated loss of revenue and avoid a higher budget deficit (cf. the American supply-side view of deficits in Chapter 7), indirect taxation has been increased substantially. Thus, in their first budget, the government increased VAT from 8 to 15 per cent. Subsequently, national insurance contributions and charges for public sector services (gas, water, electricity, and national health) have been increased substantially, not only to reduce their dependence on government subsidies, but actually to produce a surplus for the Exchequer. Third, the government has reduced business taxation, especially the national insurance surcharge and, under Chancellor of the Exchequer Lawson, increased corporation tax relief for the service industries at the cost of removing it for older manufacturing industry. Additional tax incentives have also been provided to encourage outside investment in new small businesses (e.g. the Business Start-Up Scheme, later renamed the Business Expansion Scheme, introduced in 1981).

Following Friedman and other market liberals, the government has argued that these changes will make those in paid work better off, and those looking for such work more inclined to accept lower paid jobs. Notwithstanding this dubious claim, the government's changes in personal taxation have had the effect of making the tax system less progressive and increasing the burden of direct and indirect taxation. The low paid in particular are now subject to even higher effective marginal tax rates,[6] while those on higher incomes have actually had their taxation reduced. At the same time, the overall burden of direct and indirect taxation (including national insurance contributions, but leaving aside rises in public sector charges) has also increased, from 34 per cent of GDP in 1978–9 to over 40 per cent in 1984–5.

Wage and labour market policies

A second set of the Thatcher governments' 'supply-side' policies was also designed to increase workers' incentives to accept paid work and to reduce production costs by lowering real wages, attacking trade unions' power, encouraging and then requiring teenagers' participation in government job schemes, and by abolishing restrictive government regulations.

Against the background (and ultimate breakdown) of Labour's troublesome 'Social Contract' policy, the Conservatives promised a return to free collective bargaining. Having dismantled Labour's formal pay policy, the new government relied initially on exhorting wage negotiators to understand the consequences of their actions. The implied threat was that if wage restraint was not forthcoming, unemployment would result, especially since the government had no intention of inflating the money supply. In the public sector, however, where the government itself was the employer, restrictive cash limits were imposed, with the result that wages (except those of the armed forces and the police) have dropped well behind those working in the private sector.

As unemployment and public concern rose in response to the government's deflationary policies, the Thatcher government began advancing the view common in the 1930s – and nowadays articulated by market liberal economists such as Friedman – that 'excessively high' real (not just nominal money) wages in the market sector were responsible for high levels of unemployment. According to this view (discussed in the previous chapter), workers are not only being priced out of employment by high government taxation; they – or their unions – also price themselves out of jobs by demanding inordinately high wages. In this instance, as in others, the government attempted to off-load the problem of unemployment on to workers themselves. In line with this argument, the government has sought to undermine the power of the trade unions, which it believes keep wages artificially high and distort the market for labour.

Workers' statutory rights have also been undermined by cuts in the budgets of such agencies as the wages and factory inspectorates which are responsible for enforcing minimum wage laws and health and safety conditions. This has resulted in worsening wages and conditions for adult workers, as well as significant increases in the employment of school children, contrary to the Employment of Children Act of 1973. In July 1985, the government signalled its intention to reform the wage councils which set minimum wage rates for about 2.7 million workers (about 80 per cent of whom are women who work part time) in shops, the clothing industry, hotels and catering, agriculture and other areas where pay is low (£63 ($82) and £72 ($94) per week) and where workers tend not to be unionized.

Restricting trade unions' power

Despite evidence of popular demands for restricting the power of the trade unions, the Thatcher government's initial approach to trade unions and industrial relations emphasized caution. This was primarily because it was anxious to avoid repeating the Heath government's failures in the early 1970s. However, there can be little doubt that the initial cautious approach was the first stage in a medium-term incremental strategy designed to reduce union influence in industrial bargaining. In essence, and with some exceptions,[7] this strategy eschewed the sort of heavy-handed state intervention embodied in the 1971 Industrial Relations Act and relied, instead, on a much more subtle (and successful) approach which placed responsibilities on employers to assert their 'right to manage', and on the trade unions to accept the consequences of their industrial actions.

In the first phase of this overall strategy, the government sought to attack workers' rights and union power at the margins. In 1979, claimants' rights against unfair dismissal and unions' rights to be notified of forthcoming redundancies were reduced. In the 1980 Employment Act, new restrictions were imposed on secondary picketing and new closed shops; and workers' rights regarding dismissal and maternity leave were further restricted. The 1980 Social Security Act also deemed strikers to have received strike pay from their unions and, accordingly, reduced their state benefit payments.

After Norman Tebbit (who earned notoriety by suggesting to delegates to a Conservative Party conference that the unemployed should 'get on their bikes' and look for a job) became Secretary of State for Employment in September 1981, the government's approach to trade unionism entered a second, more coercive phase. This phase increasingly took advantage of the new political opportunities offered by rising unemployment to weaken further workplace and union organization. A leaked memorandum from the Treasury to the Cabinet on 'Action to combat unemployment and improve the working of the labour market' argued that 'if the Government were to make fragmentation of labour markets part of its general drive and publicity, it is possible that progress could be made'. The document also discussed 'action to weaken the bargaining position of public-sector unions'. Indicative of this hardened approach, the Employment

Act of 1982 imposed further restrictions on the closed shop; removed some of the unions' immunities from legal action (including employers' claims for damages and courts' sequestration of union funds); prohibited commercial practices which require paid work to be done by union labour; and made so-called 'political strikes' illegal. Subsequent legislation sought to limit the actions of trade union leaders by providing for secret ballots for elections and compulsory ballots on strike action and unions' retention of political funds.

Within the public sector, the pressure on trade union powers and workers' rights has been supplemented by the government's imposition of cash limits and the appointment of aggressive henchmen (such as MacGregor at British Steel and the National Coal Board, Edwardes at British Leyland, and King at British Airways) with mandates to instil 'financial discipline' (invariably by shedding jobs), reduce subsidies in order to lower overall government expenditure and, in some instances, prepare industries – or parts of industries – for eventual 'privatization'.

Once again, an incremental strategy that takes account of political and economic conditions has been pursued. Care has been taken to limit the number of direct confrontations with powerful groups of public sector workers at any one time, and the government's restrictive trade union laws have been applied sparingly. Thus, the government declined a confrontation with the National Union of Mineworkers in 1981, agreeing instead to increase subsidies to the National Coal Board. Yet, when political and economic conditions appeared favourable, the Thatcher governments have shown little compunction in imposing their will on steel workers, civil servants, rail workers, teachers and, most recently, on the miners, in each case to force redundancies and reduce wages and conditions (and, in the case of the miners, at considerable cost to the Exchequer).[8] As a result, between 1979 and 1985, the National Coal Board has shed some 62,000 jobs, British Rail 34,000, British Shipbuilders 40,000, and British Steel 122,000. Cuts in public expenditure and privatizing of government agencies' ancilliary services (e.g. cleaning in the National Health Service) have also reduced pay and conditions and served the purpose of undermining the strength of public sector unions. Moreover, Thatcher and her loyalists have actively criticized trade unions' actions, especially in pursuing strikes. Typically, such criticisms have been overtly populist in appealing to workers not to follow the advice of their leaders, thereby placing their jobs in jeopardy by pricing themselves out of the labour market.

Job creation schemes

The view that unemployment was due, at least partly, to relatively high wages has also influenced the Thatcher governments' attitude to job creation programmes, particularly for teenagers. In their first flush of Friedmanite enthusiasm, when they were preoccupied with reducing inflation through lower government spending, the Conservatives cut £170 million from such programmes as STEP, YOP, TOPS (see Chapter 3), sacking the chairman of the Manpower Services Commission when he complained. They also shelved Labour's proposed Restructuring of Industry subsidy, and ended the Small Firms Employment Subsidy. However, when unemployment – particularly among teenagers – began to rise sharply in 1980 and 1981, the government reduced the number of jobless people on the unemployment register, attempted to influence wage rates among low-paid (young) workers, and sought to alter the priorities in existing educational and training systems in favour of what they called 'wealth-creation'. In line with the new policy, STEP was replaced by a national scheme – the Community Enterprise Programme (later, the Community Programme) – designed to provide places for young adult workers previously unemployed for long periods. Expenditure on YOP (later renamed the Youth Training Scheme) was increased significantly and three new job schemes were added: the Enterprise Allowance Scheme, which provides a wage subsidy for unemployed people who set up their own businesses; the Young Workers' Scheme, designed to encourage lower wages (necessary in the government's view to make British industry more competitive) by offering wage subsidies; and the Jobs Release Scheme, which encourages employers to divide existing full-time jobs into part-time jobs.

As a result of the huge expansion in these and other schemes (financed largely by the European Community's Social Fund), the Manpower Services Commission has become the country's largest employer. By December 1984, some 662,000 people were participating in these schemes, reducing the number of registered unemployed by some 475,000. In March 1985, the government extended its strategy one step further by making YTS places available to all school leavers. Shortly thereafter, 16–18 year olds were deprived of their right to supplementary social welfare benefits, despite evidence that, under the existing voluntary arrangements, one in three YTS places remained unfilled and that those who drop out from YTS are just as likely to find a job as those who finish their course. One of the clear effects of the YTS has been to reduce the wages of school leavers.[9]

Thus, in pursuing its strategy for lower real wages, the Thatcher government has effectively made state-sponsored vocational training compulsory for teenagers.

Financial assistance to restructure private industry

A third aspect of the Thatcher governments' 'supply-side' approach to the problem of mass unemployment reveals closer similarities with Keynesian practices, rather than a celebration of Friedman's 'strong state, free market' approach. Although the Thatcher governments have steadfastly resisted overtures from ailing private companies requesting financial aid in order to protect jobs, and have drastically reduced regional aid to promote private investment (as the monetarists recommend), they have continued policies which aim to encourage technological replacement and industrial restructuring in the private sector, and to direct government and foreign contracts to British companies.

Particularly since 1982, the government has offered substantial financial and technical assistance to private companies prepared to utilize innovations in micro-electronics, fibre optics, information and other high technologies. While these policies are quite consistent with supply-side theory (and, as discussed in Chapter 3, are most likely to result in further job losses by encouraging companies to centralize and rationalize their production), the government's attitude to foreign firms penetrating British markets and to financial support for British exporters is not. Mrs Thatcher's heart-on-the-sleeve patriotism has led to a number of contracts for military and computer hardware being awarded to British manufacturers over foreign competitors; to continued support for voluntary export restraint agreements with Japan (for cars and other products) and with other countries (for textiles); and, most recently, to the government providing 'soft' loans to exporters – all justified as protecting employment opportunities in Britain.

Arguing that Britain needs to cultivate an 'enterprise culture' similar to those of Japan or Singapore or the United States, and that future job growth will be generated more from small companies in the private sector, the Thatcher governments have also sought to encourage the creation of small businesses. The establishment of a Loan Guarantee Scheme and of 'enterprise zones' represent their private enterprise alternatives to previous governments' reliance on handing out large sums of public money to private industry. However, in comparison to similar programmes conducted by governments in the rest of western Europe, Japan and the United States, the scale of assistance offered by the Thatcher government is small. Even if the assistance was greater, it is extremely unlikely that the small business sector – despite its recent growth – will produce a sufficiently large number of jobs to replace the jobs lost in large-scale manufacturing industry since the 1960s.

The coherence of the Thatcher governments' programme

This review of the Thatcher governments' employment policies is admittedly selective, and yet it demonstrates that their approach to the unemployment problem cannot be described solely in terms of liberating the 'free market' through the strong state. Certainly, the governments' rhetoric speaks in terms of 'enlarging freedom of choice' and 'reducing the role of the state'; and certainly these governments have rejected state-imposed wages and prices policies in favour of workers and employers learning to understand the consequences of industrial bargaining. Moreover, in their 'resolute approach' to lowering inflation, to 'market rigidities', to industrial militancy and the market power of trade unions, to social unrest, to industrial inefficiency, as well as to alleged EEC excesses and Soviet and Argentinian aggression, the Thatcher governments have done much to promote a 'strong state' image. Thus, most (if not all) of the policy decisions in these areas have either *not* resulted in making government intervention less intrusive or have led to the development of new and more elaborate forms of intervention in areas where there was previously little or none. It is difficult to conclude, for instance, that the government's restrictive monetary policies have been any less elaborate or interfering than previous governments' wages and prices policies; or that high interest rates and a reduced PSBR have been any less oppressive on the unemployed, on social welfare recipients or on those still employed, especially in low wage jobs.

Having stressed the compatibility of the Thatcher governments' employment policies with the 'strong state, free market' model, it is equally important to stress both the incremental nature of their approach to inflation and unemployment and the elements of continuity with previous policies. No government can be expected in practice to comply exactly with a theoretical vision (such as that of Friedman) for restructuring contemporary employment societies. It would be misleading, therefore, to argue that the British Conservative

Party was converted wholesale to monetarism and supply-side economics. Rather, these economic theories offered a troubled Conservative Party a method of healing its divisions (following Thatcher's defeat of Heath for the party leadership), a winning political argument (in the context of considerable public disenchantment with the full employment welfare state), achieving electoral victories (following defeat in four out of the last five general elections), and a way of ensuring 'governing competence' [Bulpitt] (against the background of the shambles of Labour's 'Social Contract' policies). For the Conservatives (one of the most successful conservative parties in the world), even under Thatcher's astute leadership, politics is most importantly about gaining office, effectively implementing policies, and retaining office.

It is within this context of 'the politics of power' – and not only the 'strong state, free market' paradigm – that the coherence of the Thatcher governments' employment policies must be interpreted. Their incremental, cautious approach to policy innovation has often necessitated tailoring their ideological cloth to immediate political circumstances. Thus, the first Thatcher government – because the Cabinet was comprised of a substantial number of traditional 'One Nation' Conservatives – was initially intent on allowing the nationalized industries, employers and unions, and local authorities to act relatively autonomously from government, on condition that they accepted the consequences of their decisions.

When, however, the economic events of 1980 and 1981 showed this batch of policies to be inadeqate and to threaten the government's political appeal, it resorted to a second, less coherent and differently justified set of policies. Power became much more centralized in the hands of Thatcher and her 'strong state, free market' supporters (particularly after the Cabinet reshuffle of September 1981), and was exercised in a much more partisan manner. The government raised its own economic expectations (to achieve a zero inflation rate and a balanced budget) and, in the political climate which then existed, it found it remarkably easy (even before the Falklands War) to off-load its political responsibilities for inflation, unemployment, production, and so forth on to others: the world recession, unions and management, the EEC and the United States.

It was also within this second phase that supply-side policies (including tax 'giveaways') and privatization (to pay for the tax reductions) became much more important. The nationalized industries were required increasingly to behave as market sector corporations; and the trade unions were subjected to more and more legal restrictions, some of which, rather ironically, have helped revitalize grass-roots trade unionism. Furthermore, behind the rhetoric of 'the resolute approach' and the mouthing of monetarist/supply-side rhetoric, the government also relaxed its attitude to monetary and expenditure growth and to intervention in the exchange rate. When this happened – contrary to many observers – the government effectively performed a U-turn. Much to the annoyance of Friedman, it abandoned pure monetarism in favour of orthodox deflationary *fiscal* techniques to control inflation by using its control over the PSBR as its decisive yardstick.

On this reading, it is difficult to conclude that the Thatcher government has pursued one coherent employment policy strategy. Especially since 1982, the government's strategy has been different from its earlier approach and, to say the least, often confused. In response to rising public concern about unemployment, the government has shown a certain amount of flexibility (and continuity with the policies of previous governments) – notably in the areas of job creation, financial and technical assistance to state and private industry, protectionism, and even public expenditure, taxation, and monetary policy.

The limits of the Thatcher governments' policies

Despite this flexibility, the policies of the Thatcher governments have not provided a solution to the problem of rising mass unemployment in the mid 1980s. Indeed, the government has always relegated the post-war social democratic ideal of full male employment, choosing instead to concentrate on lowering inflation. It is hardly surprising therefore that between 1979 and February 1985 official unemployment rose by some 2 million to 3.3 million people, or 13.9 per cent of the labour force. (The independent Unemployment Unit, however, estimates an unemployed total of 3.7 million and a rate of 15 per cent based on the earlier basis of calculation.)[10] Furthermore, by mid 1985 the number of people who had been without a paid job for six months or more was 2 million, 60 per cent of all the unemployed; in mid 1979 it was 552,000, 40 per cent of the total.

Despite these trends, the Thatcher governments have argued that the foundations of economic recovery have been laid, such that Britain now has a leaner, fitter economy with which to compete in the harsh global trading conditions of the mid 1980s and 1990s. Is there a basis for this claim? And, what type of recovery will result?

Certainly, it is true that by the last quarter of 1984, output had recovered from the slump of 1980–1, but GDP was barely 4½ per cent higher than in 1979, despite the massive economic infusions from North Sea oil and gas. This, however, was mainly due to a consumer boom which the government's deflationary policies almost succeeded in choking off.

Other indicators of economic performance (aside from the dramatic increases in unemployment) also indicate that the government's claims are exaggerated. Since exchange controls were abolished in 1979, private investment abroad (mainly by banks and other financial institutions) has risen sharply (from £4.7 billion in 1978 to £11 billion in 1983). Over the same period, investment in domestic manufacturing industry has fallen by about one-third (from £7.5 billion in 1979 to £5.2 billion in 1984), despite the supposed boost to be provided by tax cuts. In consequence, according to OECD data for 1980, investment accounted for a lower share of income per head in Britain (14.7 per cent) than in any other industrial country except Portugal. The shortfall was particularly serious in the construction sector, which depends so much on public spending. There is no evidence to suggest that this pattern has changed since 1980 and, if anything, the government has reinforced this under-investment by cutting capital allowances against corporation tax, and by frittering away government revenue from North Sea oil and gas (over £40 billion since 1979) on tax cuts which have helped finance a consumer boom and have thereby encouraged an increase in imports. Following the devastation of much of the country's traditional manufacturing sector in the slump of 1980–1, the British economy is now, moreover, dominated more than ever by foreign-owned transnational corporations and, thus, highly vulnerable to capital flight and further job losses. For the first time ever, Britain has become a net importer of manufactured goods.

The government boasts that productivity has risen. Productive output per worker has indeed risen significantly (by 10.2 per cent in 1981, 3.5 per cent in 1982, 9.1 per cent in 1983, and by 2.6 per cent in 1984). However, this rise in productivity was more or less inevitable as employers in the public and market sectors reduced employment by closing marginal plants, while other less profitable firms went bankrupt. It does not necessarily represent a real improvement in plant, machinery or production techniques.

When all these indicators of economic performance are taken into account, Britain's economy may be said to be experiencing *jobless growth*. Encouraged by the Thatcher governments' policies, output and productivity have been rising, but so has unemployment. Indeed, as two economists have argued, 'the current productivity record of much of manufacturing industry is like the cricket team that improves its batting average by only playing its better batsmen!'[11] Chapter 3 referred to the onset of a process of *de-industrialization* in Britain. Clearly, since 1979 this process has been accelerated rather than reversed, with the consequence that total employment has declined sharply – from 23 million in June 1979 to 21.4 million in February 1985 (a fall of 7 per cent) – and in the manufacturing sector to the lowest point since the Industrial Revolution (from 7.1 million in mid 1979 to 5.4 million in mid 1985, a fall of 22 per cent).

Before 1979, the decline in manufacturing jobs was offset by the creation of some 2 million jobs in the service sector. Despite the Thatcher governments' attempts to stimulate employment in services and the hi-tech sectors, the number of hi-tech jobs has fallen and those in services have barely risen (by just over 100,000). Moreover, at the same time that the number of jobs in manufacturing and services has fallen, so the number of people seeking jobs has increased. By 1986, the work force is expected to have grown by over 1 million since 1975, as the combined effects of the 1960s 'baby boom', declining numbers of retiring workers, and increasing numbers of women in or seeking jobs (11 million compared with about 5.5 million in 1944) all increase the demand for full-time and part-time jobs.

There is nothing in the Thatcher governments' policies which can solve the present unemployment problem. This is evident in the government's feeble attempts to highlight the 342,000 new jobs which have been created since September 1983. Not only is this figure a very small percentage of the unemployed total, but 207,000 of it represents part-time jobs (mostly taken by women, and in many cases resulting from enforced loss of full-time jobs), the equivalent of only 45,000 full-time jobs. More importantly, in its rhetoric and policies, the government has actually encouraged jobless growth and, by implication, the development of a *dual society* (see Chapter 4). Some sections of the population (the employed, especially those in the 'wealth-creating' market sector with 'real' full-time jobs; the rich; and those living in the smaller Conservative-dominated towns of south-east England) are being privileged by the government's policies, while other groups (the part-time employed, the jobless and other social welfare recipients; those working in the state sector; those living in northern England, Wales and Scotland, and in the inner cities; and women and ethnic minorities) are losing ground. In order to ensure its viability, this divisive strategy has been coupled more and more with an overtly *populist* style of government, in which the government, claiming a popular mandate, creates disgruntled bodies of 'public opinion' – taxpayers, ratepayers, rank and file trade unionists, small shareholders, council (public) housing tenants – which it then disingeniously 'consults', over the heads of established forms of representation. (These forms of representation include local governments, para-state agencies or 'quangos', trade union leaders and business and professional associations.) The government thus aims to better legitimize the very policies which it has in the first place formulated.

The government's rhetoric that unemployment is essentially the fault and responsibility of individuals, not governments or business, well illustrates the logic – and negative social consequences[12] – of this approach. To date, this populist governing strategy has helped the Thatcher government sustain its popularity. The results of the 1983 general election provide some evidence that this dual formula can also be a successful electoral strategy. The second Thatcher government nevertheless appears to be politically vulnerable, as its own supporters in Parliament look enviously towards the advances in employment achieved by the Reagan administration (discussed in the next chapter), and as the Labour Party has (perhaps temporarily) suppressed its self-destructive tendencies. Whether the government's populist endorsement of jobless growth becomes a political liability will, therefore, depend as much upon the vagaries of electoral arithmetic, as upon the ability of its opponents to convince the electorate that there are other viable and better alternatives for dealing with mass unemployment.

Notes

1 The term 'One Nation' derives from the trilogy of 'Young England' novels written by Benjamin Disraeli, the founder of the modern Conservative Party and its leader in the 1860s and 1870s. In those novels, and particularly in *Sybil*, Disraeli argued that the duty of true Conservatives was to try to bridge the gap between Two Nations, the rich and the poor. They should work towards creating One Nation by upholding decency

and duty rather than stark commercial gain. As leading figures in the post-war Conservative Party, Butler, Macmillan, and Heath saw themselves as pragmatic successors to this ideological tradition and, accordingly, lent their support to the principles of the full employment welfare state.

2   The main principle underlying Hayek's most important political works – *The Road to Serfdom* (1944), *The Constitution of Liberty* (1957) and *Law, Legislation and Liberty* (1976) – is that it is not part of govern-ments' duty to seek to implement any specific social or economic goals such as justice, equality, full employment or some conception of 'the good life'. This is because one set of goals is no better than another and, in any case, the preferences, wishes, and interests of individuals are basically immutable. The only genuine public good is the provision of law and order: government must, therefore, facilitate individuals' pursuit of their own conception of good, free from coercion by others.

3   Thus, the party's two strategic documents published in Opposition – *The Right Approach* (1976) and *The Right Approach to the Economy* (1977) – confined themselves to setting out general Conservative principles in an attempt to unite the party, and particularly the shadow cabinet behind Thatcher.

4   On a number of occasions since 1979, the Thatcher governments have been forced to raise the external borrowing limits of various nationalized industries. As Secretary of State for Industry, Sir Keith Joseph was even obliged through fear of further increases in unemployment to suppress his Friedmanite inclinations. Government subsidies to such 'lame ducks' as British Steel, British Leyland and British Shipbuilders were extended. For example, in December 1982, the Cabinet was persuaded by the pros-pect of even higher levels of unemployment in Scotland to increase financial assistance to British Steel, in order to save the corporation's loss-making plant at Ravenscraig. Following BSC announcing another 1000 job losses in May 1983, the government increased its financial sup-port to the corporation by two-thirds.

5   A report from the House of Lords Select Committee on Unemployment in 1982 estimated the annual fiscal cost of a person being unemployed at £5000 in lost revenue and additional government expenditure. If the value of lost production was also considered, this figure would be much higher.

6   The Treasury and Civil Service Select Committee of the House of Commons has calculated, for instance, that 500,000 low-paid families in Britain pay marginal tax rates of 60 per cent or more. This 'poverty trap' has widened significantly since 1979.

7 Notably, the government's outright prohibition of trade union membership at the GCHQ intelligence gathering establishment at Cheltenham in 1983.

8 The independent Henley Centre for Forecasting calculated the cost of the 1984–5 miners' strike at £2.98 billion in lost production, higher oil use, extra policing and lost income from the miners, in order to achieve an annual saving of £250 million by the National Coal Board.

9 In February 1985, the weekly allowance for people on the YTS was £26.25 (about $35) compared with average weekly wages for 16–17 year olds of £60 ($78).

10 The difference arises from the government removing from the unemployment register about 200,000 women ineligible for unemployment benefit and 160,000 men over 59 who are no longer required to sign on in order to receive National Insurance credits.

11 Willem H. Buiter and Marcus H. Miller, 'The macroeconomic consequences of a change of regime in the U.K. under Mrs Thatcher', Centre for Labour Economics, London School of Economics, discussion paper no. 179 (November 1983), p. 76.

12 Since 1979, for example, the number of people living in poverty has increased from 11.5 million to 15 million, more than one in four of the population.

Further reading

Wyn Grant and Shiv Nath, *The Politics of Economic Policymaking* (London, 1984), ch. 7.

David Held, 'Power and legitimacy in contemporary Britain', in *State and Society in Contemporary Britain. A Critical Introduction*, edited by Gregor McLennan, David Held and Stuart Hall (Cambridge, 1984).

Bob Jessop, Kevin Bonnett, Simon Bromley and Tom Ling, 'Authoritarian populism, two nations and Thatcherism', *New Left Review*, no. 147 (September–October 1984).

Sir Keith Joseph, *Monetarism in Not Enough* (London, 1976).

Sir Keith Joseph, *Stranded on the Middle Ground? Reflections on Circumstances and Policies* (London, 1976).

7 Reagan's disguised Keynesianism

It will be my intention to curb the size and influence of the federal establishment . . . . It is not my intention to do away with government. It is rather to make it work – work with us – not over us; to stand by our side, not ride our back. Government can and must provide opportunity, not smother it.   [President Reagan's inaugural address, 20 January 1981]

In November 1980, Ronald Reagan was elected President of the United States on much the same 'strong state, free market' programme as the Thatcher government the previous year. Promising price stability, high employment and long-term economic growth, and employing the ideas of Friedman and other pro-market economists within a skilfully executed populist rhetoric, Reagan proposed massive tax cuts, deregulating American industry and reducing government expenditure on social welfare in order to release the energies of 'free enterprise America'. Four years later, Reagan was re-elected by huge electoral margins, having presided over his country's strongest economic recovery since 1950 which, in the space of just over two years, resulted in the creation of some 8.4 million new jobs. Many British politicians, including leading members of the Thatcher government, have pointed to the success of Reagan's policies and recommended them as the solution to the unemployment problem in Britain. This chapter outlines the circumstances which gave rise to the election of Reagan and the nature of his administration's economic policies, and assesses the impact of these policies on unemployment in the US. In so doing, the discussion identifies some crucial differences between Reagan's policies and those of the Thatcher governments, and suggests why they do not provide an appropriate solution to unemployment in western Europe, let alone in the United States.

The full employment welfare state

In 1980, the American economy was contracting following years of sluggish growth. Inflation was over 10 per cent, and unemployment was over 7 per cent. Reagan asked the American electorate during his presidential election campaign, 'Are you better off than you were 4 years ago?' The emphatic negative answer they (or at least 26 per cent of the electorate) gave him confirmed his belief that the basic cause of these stagflationary conditions and, therefore, the chief impediment to restoring non-inflationary economic growth and increased employment in the 1980s was previous administrations' Keynesian policies.

In the United States, a Keynesian consensus developed much later than in Britain. The Roosevelt administration had adopted Keynes's arguments to justify its economic experimentation in the mid 1930s. However, no Keynesian consensus was constructed until twenty-five years later, despite the wartime experience of full employment, the passage of the Employment Act in 1946,[1] and the massive increases, from the 1930s, in government spending particularly for military installations and hardware, public works (especially highways), housing and urban development and agriculture.

Kennedy was the first unabashed Keynesian President (1961-3) willing to declare a commitment, underpinned by planned deficit spending, to full male employment (defined as no more than 4 per cent unemployed). Following the country's third and worst slump since the Second World War and unemployment exceeding 5 million for the first time since the 1930s, Kennedy committed his Democratic administration to annual growth rates of 5 per cent in order to reduce unemployment. He opted to stimulate demand not, however, by increasing government spending (as advocated by Keynesians such as J. K. Galbraith), but through substantial tax cuts. Following Kennedy's assassination in 1963, and despite demands for increased public spending (to extend social welfare provision and, later, the escalating war in Vietnam), tax cuts remained the primary fiscal tool of President Johnson's administration (1963-8).

As a result of the stimulative effect of the Kennedy–Johnson tax reduction policies – and against the background of American hegemony in international trade, finance and technology, and stable commodity prices – the United States economy experienced the longest recorded period of peacetime expansion in its history. Between 1961 and 1968, real GNP increased by a remarkable 39 per cent, although unemployment levels remained stubbornly high (5.3 per cent between 1960 and 1965) until the Vietnam draft reduced the rate to below the desired 4 per cent after 1966. The remarkable performance of the American economy during the 1960s served to engender a new Keynesian orthodoxy committed to the pursuit of economic growth and to the notion that active government intervention was not just compatible with prosperity, but essential to it. The new Keynesian orthodoxy embraced not only the majority Democratic Party but also many leading Republicans (such as Nelson Rockefeller), the trade unions and almost the entire business community. In 1965 even Milton Friedman recognized that 'we are all Keynesians now' (but he doubted whether anybody still believed in all elements of Keynesian economics). This orthodoxy even extended into political attitudes towards government welfare provision. Indeed, whereas the New Deal had embraced government intervention cautiously as a temporary expedient, Kennedy's New Frontier and Johnson's Great Society exhibited an almost naive, technocratic faith in the ability of government, manned by the 'best and the brightest', to remedy poverty and cyclical and structural unemployment.

The decline of the Keynesian consensus

The effusive optimism which surrounded the creation of the full employment welfare state in the 1960s soon gave way to increasing pessimism and uncertainty. By the early 1970s, three crucial political problems in the American political economy became evident, preparing the ground for a shift in policy priorities of the type legitimized by Reagan's election in 1980. These problems included the decreasing ability of government to satisfy heightened popular expectations; the declining popularity of 'big government' due to its size, cost and increasingly bureaucratic form; and the increasing fragility of the New Deal coalition on which Kennedy and Johnson had depended for political support. Each of these problems became more pressing during the 1970s as traditional demand management policies proved increasingly inadequate for maintaining high employment and price stability.

1   As in Britain (see Chapter 3), the American full employment welfare state of the 1960s and 1970s led directly to a heightening of popular expectations and political conflict. Stimulated by policymakers' optimism that most problems were capable of governmental

solutions, new social movements – blacks and other racial minorities, women, poor people, the young and elderly, anti-war protesters, environmentalists and consumers – became increasingly active politically. The new public interest groups which they formed demanded that government should not only respond to the demands of older groups such as trade unions, farmers and business, but also to their interests and values as well.

2 Partly as a result of this extension and intensification of political conflict, the size, cost and functions of the federal government increased dramatically. In particular, public spending on income maintenance programmes, job creation and training, housing and community development, and investment in natural resources, industry, education, health and social services rose substantially (from 36 per cent to 60 per cent of federal budget outlays between 1960 and 1977). The number of government agencies and the regulatory and redistributive functions of the federal government were also considerably expanded. In the late 1960s and early 1970s, the American economy began to 'stagflate' (high unemployment and inflation), persuading President Nixon (1968–74) – in the face of congressional opposition to expenditure cuts – to pursue an expansionary fiscal policy, bailing out some major companies and substantially increasing government spending on job creation and training, while seeking to control inflation through wage and price controls. Opposition to wage and price controls mounted, while inflation and unemployment continued to rise. Keynesian demand management solutions and the assumed inverse relationship between inflation and unemployment (the so-called Phillips curve) were treated with increasing scepticism and hostility.

3 The expansion of state welfare provision in the 1960s and 1970s and the new policy impasses posed by stagflation increased the fragility of the dominant political coalition. Since the 1930s, American politics had evolved around the New Deal coalition, based on the Democratic Party and including the trade unions, some farmers, the big city political machines of the north and east dominated by the various ethnic groups who had migrated there in the first decades of the century and, belatedly, a significant portion of big business. By the late 1960s, business support for the full employment welfare state – which had been assiduously courted by the Kennedy and Johnson administrations – had begun to wane. Business (and to a lesser extent the labour unions) complained increasingly about the

level and extent of 'social regulatory' policies (e.g. environmental, consumer protection, health and safety and civil rights legislation) introduced in response to the demands of the new social movements. Trade unions also found their heightened wage expectations increasingly subject to restrictive wage and price controls, particularly during the Nixon and Carter administrations.[2] As early as 1968, finally, mounting public concern over 'big government' was an important theme in Nixon's appeal to the 'silent majority' – a body of people supposedly passed over by the Kennedy–Johnson concern with disadvantaged groups – and in George Wallace's third party movement.

Reagan's programme: supply-siders and monetarists

During the 1980 presidential election campaign, Reagan successfully exploited these problems, especially the declining legitimacy of the full employment welfare state, and promised to end what he called 'big government's stifling of initiative'. Rejecting both Keynesian and traditionally conservative routes (resting on tight credit and balanced budgets), the Reagan administration launched its economic programme with two politically convenient (and, in part, contradictory) economic theories that had hitherto been on the periphery of American conservative thinking. Both theories espoused the advantages of relying upon free market mechanisms, and were descended lineally from the ideas of Friedman. One was a new form of *monetarism*, which emphasized the importance of 'rational expectations'; the other was *supply-side economics*. How, and with what effect, these theories have been translated into public policies since 1981 are the primary concerns of the following sections.

Monetarism

Monetarists within the Reagan administration argued that the only way to achieve high levels of employment without inflation was by maintaining strict control over the money supply. Drawing on the ideas of Friedman, they perceived the stagflation of the 1970s as the direct result of misguided Keynesian attempts to manipulate aggregate economic demand through periodic changes in monetary and fiscal policy. According to the rational expectations theory of monetarism which they endorsed, inflationary expectations of workers and businesses would be quickly reduced once government or the monetary authorities made clear their intention not to expand the money supply in order to bail out companies or to provide jobs for the unemployed.

On assuming office in 1981, Reagan immediately endorsed the Federal Reserve Board's restrictive monetary policy as being consistent with this rational expectations strategy.[3] After a brief honeymoon, however, Reagan followed in the footsteps of every recent President and began criticizing the Fed for reducing the money supply at too fast a rate, thus preventing the Treasury from financing an increasing budget deficit brought about by the $750 billion in foregone revenues given away in tax cuts in 1981. Despite the administration's protests, the high interest rate policy was not relaxed and, in the context of worsening international conditions, the economy moved into sharp recession in 1981–2. Interest rates and unemployment rose to their highest levels since the Second World War, and until 1982 the dollar became grossly undervalued. Under congressional and popular pressure to stimulate demand, the Fed and the administration again refused to relax the restrictive policy.

The recession of 1981–2 was the largest single factor explaining a fall in inflation in the United States from 12.4 per cent in 1980 to 3.8 per cent in 1983. As in Britain, however, the social and economic costs of this fall were enormous. Between July 1981 and January 1983, unemployment rose to 10.8 per cent of the workforce (the highest level since the 1930s), production worth an estimated $654 billion was permanently lost, and those in paid work lost billions of dollars in lost income through shorter working hours or lower wages. Even as the economy recovered in 1983 and 1984, real interest rates remained high, forcing up businesses' borrowing costs and discouraging investment. The dollar also became more and more over-valued as mobile international capital moved into the US to take advantage of high interest rates, making American goods and services more expensive in international markets, and subjecting American industries – such as motor vehicles and steel – to even more intense foreign competition.

Supply-side policies

The second theory underpinning Reagan's programme was supply-side economics. Supply siders (Laffer, Gilder and Wanniski being the most famous)[4] made four crucially important and (in the context of

America's stagflating economy of the 1970s) increasingly plausible (although intellectually unfashionable)arguments: (1) that rising tax rates discourage and distort work effort and market patterns of saving and investment; (2) that cuts in marginal tax rates – even to the extent of producing a budget deficit to which they are indifferent – are much more effective than government spending (which they abhor) in increasing employment and investment (since the cost of labour to firms is reduced and savings increase, and because in the long-run increased output actually raises government's total tax receipts); (3) that the paraphenalia of government regulation (identified with Johnson's Great Society, the environmentalist, safety and consumerist movements of the 1960s and 1970s) is an unnecessary and expensive burden on the American economy, increasing firms' costs, thereby constituting a disincentive to employ and produce; and (4) that social welfare benefits, such as Aid to Families with Dependent Children, food stamps and unemployment insurance, act as disincentives to work. As employed by the Reagan administrations, elements of supply-side theory were evident in at least four important policy areas: budgetary policy (including tax reductions and government spending); deregulation; wage and labour market policies; and government job creation schemes.

Budgetary policy
The first Reagan administration proposed to reduce and reorder federal government spending and taxation so as to balance the federal budget by 1984. Reagan's spending priorities involved reducing funding for social programmes, business subsidies and federal aid to state and local government, and increasing military expenditure. The reductions in social spending were to be effected in three ways: by abolishing some programmes (including public service employment, community service, and the Work Incentive programme); by reducing welfare entitlements and benefits (including those for low-income housing; the Special Supplementing Feeding Program for Women, Infants and Children (WIC); Aid to Families with Dependent Children (AFDC); Medicaid; food stamps; compensatory and vocational education; and general employment and training); and by cutting entitlements and benefits for (contributory) social security programmes, such as Medicare and Old Aged, Survivors and Disability Insurance, and unemployment insurance. In 1981, Congress agreed to most of these changes (amounting to projected

funding reductions of $140 billion) but, except for Social Security, has since acceded to few further requests for reductions, especially on welfare programmes. Nevertheless, between 1981 and 1985, federal expenditure on unemployment insurance was cut by 17 per cent, AFDC and food stamps by 14 per cent, and child nutrition programmes by 28 per cent. Even larger cuts were made in business subsidies (except to farmers), in spending on the environment, transportation and community and regional development, and in grants to state and local government.

While social and other non-military spending has been reduced, spending on military hardware has risen sharply under the Reagan administrations, rising from $150 billion in 1980 to an estimated $310 billion in 1986. As a result, military spending now comprises 32 per cent of the federal budget (compared with 26 per cent in 1981); 30 per cent of the military budget (2.0 per cent of GNP) is now spent on military procurement compared with 22 per cent (1.2 per cent of GNP) in 1981.

Since 1981, the administration has also sponsored three significant changes in *taxation* policy. First, the overall level of federal revenue from taxation has been reduced – from 20.8 per cent of GNP in 1981 to an expected level of 18.7 per cent in 1985. Second, by cutting the tax liabilities of all income groups by the same percentage, by lowering marginal tax rates on unearned income, by eroding the tax advantages for those on low incomes, and by increasing more regressive federal social insurance and excise taxes, the tax burden on the rich has been reduced and that on the poor has increased.[5] Third, business taxation has been reduced through more generous capital depreciation provisions, particularly for business plant and equipment (dubbed 'productive' investment) as against housing and consumer durables (dubbed 'unproductive' investment). Reagan's new tax plan, announced in early 1985, proposed drastic changes in corporate taxation. These were designed to remove numerous tax provisions favouring heavy manufacturing industries, while reducing the tax burden for hi-tech, service and consumer goods industries with high wage bills.

As a result of these federal spending and taxation policies – which have enjoyed substantial congressional support – the growth of budget expenditures and revenues has been reduced. However, because spending (resulting from increased military expenditure) has continued to rise faster than revenue from taxation, the budget deficit has increased dramatically, prompting harsh criticism from monetarist critics such as Milton and Rose Friedman.[6]

Deregulation

In 1981, Reagan became the first American President to rank 'deregulation' among his highest priorities. Since many changes could be implemented without new legislation (which majority Democrats in the House of Representatives were sure to oppose), administrative 'deregulation' began immediately and vigorously. Particular attention was directed towards environmental, safety and health protection agencies, whose policies, it was argued, were absorbing costs which would otherwise flow to 'productive' investments, thus creating job opportunities. The budgets of these agencies were sharply reduced;[7] regulatory enforcement standards were relaxed; legal actions against previous violators of regulations were dismissed; and officials sympathetic to Reagan's demands for regulatory 'relief' were appointed to these agencies. Subsequently, a number of these administrative actions and policies were challenged successfully in the courts, while others were reversed by Congress. Reagan disbanded his much celebrated Task Force on Regulatory Relief in August 1983.

Wages and labour market policies

The Reagan administrations have also sought to influence wages and labour market conditions. The severe monetary restraint of 1981, and the recession and job losses it produced, had the effect of drastically reducing worker militancy, especially in the highly unionized manufacturing sector, further weakening the American labour movement (which now represents only 18 per cent of the paid workforce). Many of the most successful unions in the 1950s and 1960s – the Steelworkers, the Auto Workers, the Machinists – found themselves locked into rapidly declining industries. In conditions of sustained mass unemployment, growing competition from low-wage, non-union firms from within the United States and from abroad, and 'deregulation' – notably of trucking, airlines (which predated the Reagan administration) and buses – job security declined.[8] With these changes, the strike weapon was curtailed severely and union wage rates, industry-wide master contracts and work rules were undermined. In some instances, (e.g. the Greyhound bus company), trade unions were forced to allow companies to operate 'two-tier' wage structures paying the old, higher rates to existing workers and inferior rates to new employees. Reagan's crushing of the strike by air traffic controllers in his first year of office also sent out a clear message to public sector trade unions and the public that the administration was prepared to go to almost any length to stifle union militancy.

Job creation schemes

Throughout the recession of 1981–2, the Reagan administration withstood congressional pressures for government job schemes – dubbed 'make-work' jobs by Reagan. Indeed, one of the first casualties of the 1981 budget cuts were funds for public service employment under the Comprehensive Employment and Training Act, which at the time was providing some 325,000 jobs. Once the recession began to abate, however, Reagan acceded to congressional demands in December 1982 and (much to the annoyance of his administration's monetarists, as well as Friedman) approved a jobs bill, raising petrol tax in order to spend $5 billion on highways and bridges. However, more reflective of Reagan's supply-side prejudices were his proposals to relieve structural unemployment, which he recognized would still remain after the cyclical recovery. He identified three groups of structurally-unemployed workers in need of help: the long-term unemployed; workers displaced by the decline of certain industries and trades; and untrained young workers. His Employment Act of 1983 called for a job voucher system,[9] the creation of enterprise zones (dubbed 'slum free enterprise zones' by Friedman), and a 'youth employment opportunity wage' (which the Congress refused to accept) allowing employers to pay sub-minimum wages to young workers during the summer months. Like the Thatcher government in Britain, the Reagan administration has also provided for displaced adult workers and teenagers by establishing job training programmes controlled by private industry councils (on which a majority of seats are held by local business representatives). Faced with increased import penetration of American markets, due partly to an overvalued dollar, the administration has also given additional financial assistance to the Chrysler Corporation, and supported various protectionist measures – notably for cars and motorcycles, steel, lumber and textiles – in order to preserve employment. As a result, the share of US manufacturing industry protected by non-tariff barriers has increased from 20 to 30 per cent since 1980.

The inconsistencies of the Reagan programme

It is clear from this brief review of the Reagan administrations' policies that the reduction of unemployment is viewed as a residual goal, one that is seen to depend upon higher economic growth through increased private investment and lower inflation. However, while the administration repudiates the policies and political arrangements for the full employment welfare state and celebrates the 'free' market, it clearly does not anticipate a weak role for the state or complete reliance on the 'free' market in matters of economic policy. In the administration's view, the state must take responsibility for price stability by restraining monetary growth. It must also adopt a direct and positive role in reallocating economic and social priorities in the market by redistributing income towards private capital (through cuts in taxation and social welfare spending) and by removing regulatory constraints. Through this *'strong state' strategy legitimated by 'free market' ideology*, the Reagan administration claims that everyone will benefit from the increased income and employment opportunities flowing from renewed economic growth. Essentially this is a type of 'trickle down' policy, whereby even those in the middle and at the bottom will benefit from the increased savings and investment of those at the top.

The conduct of employment policies since 1981 has, however, revealed a number of significant policy inconsistencies within the Reagan administrations' strategy, and these have led to some changes in policy. The most obvious inconsistency in the early months was that between monetarist and supply-side policies. The monetarists believed that the key to high employment and economic growth was price stability through restrictive monetary growth. This, however, was not the view of the supply siders. They rejected the monetarist idea that government can or should maintain strict control over the money supply. They argued instead that the money supply tends to adapt to the demand for money and is not, therefore, susceptible to control. In consequence of this conflict between monetarists and supply siders, the expansionary impact of the tax cuts (and the substantial increases in military and social spending) of 1981 was dampened by the deflationary effect of the Fed's tight monetary policy. While the latter was designed to reduce inflation, it made credit increasingly scarce and expensive and cut off funds to the very private sector Reagan was trying to encourage. Subsequently the dollar became so grossly overvalued (due to high interest rates) that American industry found itself facing foreign competitors enjoying significant price advantages in the short term, as well as extra margins in the longer term with which to enhance their investment in research and development and pose future challenges to America's technological leadership.

A second inconsistency – concerning the budget deficit – also resulted from tension between monetarists and supply siders. In 1981, both monetarists and supply siders within the administration argued – from rather different theoretical bases – that a large budget deficit would result from the proposed tax cuts and increases in military expenditure. Monetarists following Friedman's advice insisted that if adequate social spending cuts were achieved, the budget could be balanced by 1984. Supply siders, however, expected the deficit to rise in the short term but did not see this as the primary concern, since additional tax revenues would offset at least part of it and increased savings rates would help finance it, both increases resulting from higher economic growth. After just nine months, the supply siders began losing the argument within the administration. The deficit continued to grow (and interest rates remained high), sucking in savings from all around the world instead of increasing American savings rates. In the face of growing opposition from monetarists within the administration, from Congress and Wall Street, the supply-side tax cuts were delayed and compromised. In their place was installed a *mélange* of contradictory policies, in which greater emphasis was placed on balancing the budget through further spending cuts and tax reforms.

Supply side policies? Or disguised Keynesianism?

Despite these deep-seated tensions in their policies, the Reagan administrations – in contrast to Thatcher's governments in Britain – have been successful in reducing the (seasonally adjusted) level of registered unemployment from over 12 million or 10.8 per cent of the civilian population in December 1982 to 8.1 million or 7.1 per cent in November 1984, as 8.4 million new (mostly full-time) jobs were created during 1983 and 1984.

Reagan's explanation for this growth in employment is typically populist. He argues that 'hard work and risk-taking has given birth to an American Renaissance. Born in the safe harbor of freedom, economic growth gathered force, and rolled out in a rising tide that has reached distant shores . . .'. A less partisan verdict would conclude that the American economy has recovered as a result of the Reagan administrations boosting demand through large scale government spending, massive tax cuts and looser monetary policy. In striking contrast to Thatcher's Britain, Reagan's America has spent its way out of recession. Reagan's monetarist/supply-side policies are a sort of disguised Keynesianism in that they acknowledge that tax cuts and (by virtue of their indifference to budget deficits) government spending can stimulate economic growth. As the earlier discussion of the employment policies of President Kennedy (a self-confessed Keynesian) demonstrated, tax cuts are a standard Keynesian means of increasing economic demand and have frequently been combined with large budget deficits. Thus, the irony in Reagan's case is that, against his best intentions he has pursued a bold (Keynesian) programme of tax cuts and increased government spending in order to produce a $200 billion budget deficit as a cure for 11 per cent unemployment. This much seems clear. What is less certain, however, is whether Reagan's disguised Keynesian solution offers a viable and/or desirable strategy for relieving contemporary unemployment in the United States. This doubt is fuelled considerably when three major difficulties associated with Reagan's strategy are considered closely.

Social injustice

The Reagan administrations' policies have incurred extremely high social costs, further encouraging the development of a *dual* or 'split-level' economy. The spending and tax policies which they have pursued have discriminated explicitly against the poor and the less well-off in favour of the already well-off – a point openly conceded in a now-famous interview with Reagan's former Budget Director, David Stockman. In 1984, the *Wall Street Journal* reported that budgetary cuts were taking $390 from the typical household earning under $10,000 (just below the poverty line) and giving an average of $8720 to those already earning over $80,000. According to most measures, the middle class has done little better than maintain its position during Reagan's administration, despite the 23 per cent cut in taxes. Salaries of chief executives, however, have increased some 40 per cent over this period, further concentrating wealth among the top 2 per cent of better-off families. At the other end of the social scale, and as a result of cuts in unemployment insurance coverage and increases in structural unemployment, over 70 per cent of the unemployed (5.7 million people) did not receive unemployment benefits (although, in cases of near destitution, and depending on state regulations, they remained eligible for food stamps, Medicaid, Aid for Families of Dependent Children and other benefits). The number of Americans living in poverty has also increased from 29.3 million in 1980 to 35.3 million in 1983, thus reverting to the levels of the early 1960s (before

Johnson's Great Society legislation). The impact of the recession and cuts in social spending on black and Hispanic minorities and households headed by women was especially severe.

As the administration has reordered economic priorities and as American business has embarked upon new competitive strategies directed towards accelerating the centralization and rationalization of production, *geographic* and *sectoral* disparities have also sharpened significantly. Already prosperous regions and industrial sectors have prospered further, while others in decline have been condemned to stagnation. The recession of 1981–2 affected growth areas of the country, such as the 'Sunbelt' (the west and south-west) and New England, much less than the poorer, and in some instances, economically stagnant states in the south and mid-west. The deep recession in the auto industry, for instance, had by early 1983 increased unemployment in Michigan to 16.5 per cent. Even after two years of economic recovery and a national unemployment rate just above 7 per cent, wide regional disparities persist.[10] These disparities have been exacerbated by the administration's tax and spending policies. In 1982, for instance, the sunbelt states of the west and south-west received almost two-thirds (of which California and Texas accrued half) of the total net flow of federal money. Moreover, among the seven states which shared half of all new prime government military contracts in 1982, only one had unemployment levels above the national average.[11]

High spending and budget deficits

The Reagan administrations' policies have also caused some severe economic problems. By 1985, the budget deficit will have risen from $60 billion in 1980 to a projected $218 billion (6.1 per cent of GNP). Apart from imposing severe costs on other countries (notably Third World countries, which have to find an additional $3.5 billion every time American interest rates rise by 1 per cent), such large budget deficits accumulate so much national debt and so alter the country's fiscal system that economic recoveries will no longer generate sufficient revenues quickly enough to eliminate past deficits. Indeed, assuming no new recessions, the Congressional Budget Office has estimated that the cumulative deficit during the years 1986–8 will be just below $800 billion. With projected structural deficits of this size and a growing share of the taxpayer's dollar going to pay for the interest on the debt, there must be grave doubts whether Reagan or his successors will be able to spend their way out of future (perhaps worse) recessions, particularly since personal income taxes are now indexed for inflation. The large deficits and high interest rates have also resulted in the dollar becoming overvalued (making US exports more expensive and imports cheaper) and the United States developing an enormous balance of trade deficit with the rest of the world. Indeed, for the first time since 1914, the US has become a net debtor nation – currently the world's largest, behind Brazil and Mexico – with little immediate prospect of this position being reversed. With the overvalued dollar, American markets have been flooded by cheap foreign cars, steel, textiles and even hi-tech imports, and as a result even more jobs in these industries have been lost, leading to demands for protectionism. Finally, although Reagan's deficit spending on military procurement has undoubtedly stimulated output and employment,[12] it may also have distorted investment and employment patterns, thereby damaging America's long-term productive and competitive capacity.

Growing structural unemployment

Even allowing for these immediate social and economic costs, there is a third, and much more serious problem with Reagan's policies. Reagan's disguised Keynesian policies have only succeeded in reducing *cyclical* unemployment, in the sense that the jobless total has adjusted to a new level of cyclical demand. Since the late 1960s, the United States has experienced four major recessions. With the single exception of the one in 1979–80, the official unemployment rate has not only risen to new and higher levels at the depth of each successive recession, but when the economy recovered the rate remained higher than in the previous recovery. The pattern of recession and recovery has thus produced a 'rachet effect'.* Not only has there been a long-term tendency for unemployment to rise, but also an increase in the length of time people remain unemployed during each recession, and a declining proportion of job vacancies to the number of people unemployed.

---

* Unemployment rose from 3.4 per cent in March 1969 to 6.1 per cent in December 1970; then from 4.6 per cent in October 1973 to 9.0 per cent in May 1975; and, finally, from 5.7 per cent in July 1977 to 7.8 per cent in July 1980.

Part of the explanation for this growing structural problem is the growing *supply* of workers. During most of the post-war period, the American labour force grew at a faster pace than in most other OECD countries, as a rising number of women (encouraged by economic necessity, the women's movement and anti-discrimination legislation implemented during the 1960s and 1970s), young people (born in the baby boom of the late 1940s and 1950s), and formerly self-employed or unpaid agricultural workers entered the paid labour force.[13] Although the pace of growth has slowed in the 1980s (because of the lower birth rates in the 1960s), the American labour force is still growing. Another 6.6 million workers (representing a 6.2 per cent increase) have entered the labour market since 1980.

The other explanation for growing structural unemployment concerns the lower level of *demand* for labour. As the United States has had to contend with increased competition from Japan and western Europe, as well as from Third World countries,[14] and as markets and technologies changed at a faster pace, industrial production has become more centralized and 'rationalized', leading to job loss and 'deskilling'. As a result, during the late 1960s and 1970s, America's economic hegemony was eroded as a process of *deindustrialization* was set in train. The country's basic industrial capacity in manufacturing began to decline both numerically, and in terms of its importance to the overall economy. Whereas, for example, 24.5 per cent of the civilian workforce was employed in manufacturing industry in 1950, by 1980 the share had dropped to 19 per cent (a 1.1 per cent fall between 1950 and 1970, but a 4.4 per cent drop between 1970 and 1980). Under the Reagan administration, the manufacturing sector's share of employment has fallen a further 1.8 per cent since 1980 and, according to US Department of Labor estimates, this decline is expected to continue at least until the end of the century.

The way out of unemployment?

These three difficulties – social justice, chronic budget deficits and growing structural unemployment – are usually minimized by defenders of Reagan's strategy, who point to the rapid growth of job opportunities in the high-technology manufacturing and service industries. The evidence for their faith in the job-creating potential of these industries appears much less convincing.

Hi-tech jobs

Because of their recent rapid growth, hi-tech jobs have been identified as a potential direct and indirect source of large numbers of future jobs. According to a report by the US Department of Labor, however, only between 1.0 and 4.6 million new jobs will be created in this sector between 1982 and 1995. Although this figure represents an increase of between 32 and 39 per cent over the period, these jobs will represent only between 4.3 and 16 per cent of all jobs in the economy. [15] Moreover, certain industries which grew rapidly in the 1970s, including those producing computers and data processing, and office and accounting machines, will grow at a slower rate in the 1980s and early 1990s, partly as a result of increased foreign competition resulting from Reagan's high interest rate policies. Furthermore, two US Congress studies have predicted that up to 4 million production jobs – a quarter of the factory workforce – could be lost in robots by 1990, while only 800,000 jobs will be created in producing these labour-saving machines.

Service jobs

As doubts have been raised about the future ability of manufacturing industry to create sufficient jobs in the future, attention has been directed increasingly towards the more labour-intensive service sector which, since 1970, has provided 84 per cent of net new jobs and currently accounts for about 70 per cent of GNP. From 1960 to 1984, almost 40 million new jobs were created in the service sector, compared with just over 4 million in manufacturing. The hopes invested in the service sector's capacity to ensure higher rates of employment seem inflated, however.

Not only will services need to create two or three jobs for every manufacturing job lost, but jobs are being created in this sector at a decreasing pace, as increasing use of new technology reduces employment opportunities and, as in manufacturing, encourages the export of service jobs. [16] Also, a report from the House of Representatives' Committee on Banking, Finance and Urban Affairs in 1984 concluded that service employment to date has not been very successful either in reabsorbing workers displaced from the manufacturing sector or in providing strong and adequate income-earning opportunites for the mass of available workers. The report pointed out additionally that many of the new service jobs (in such areas as retailing, restaurants and hotels) are poorly paid, and that the sophisticated information technology characteristic of many service industries holds the potential for deskilling the nature of work for a large portion of our workforce. There is little overlap between the job requirements of many service industries, and the skill and wage levels of the large number of displaced workers in the manufacturing sector.

Since women, minorities, older workers and part-time workers comprise a larger proportion of the workforce in services than in manufacturing, such a development will have important negative consequences for the traditionally well-paid, male workers in manufacturing industry.

These limits upon the potential growth of the hi-tech manufacturing and service industries are part of the growing structural crisis in the American economy. This crisis – growing numbers of workers, reduced demand for their labour, heightened foreign competition, industrial centralization and 'rationalization' and changing markets and technologies – raises serious doubts about the Reagan administration's populist claim to have stimulated an American Renaissance. This crisis is also prompting demands from policy-makers and political commentators in the United States for government to pursue a new corporatist-type industrial policy, which redirects investment to declining 'sunset' and/or emerging 'sunrise' industries (usually the hi-tech industries).[17] In Britain, such calls can also be heard. As outlined by the British Labour Party, they are associated with social democratic demands for industrial democracy and state planning. It is these proposals to which we now turn in the next chapter.

Notes

1 Congress approved the Employment Act of 1946, but this included no formal commitment to full employment, only a lengthy, tortuous, and highly qualified 'Declaration of Policy' that, other things being equal, the federal government would do its best to find jobs for those who wanted them, so long as other national objectives were not compromised.

2 As in Britain, conditions of high employment in the 1960s enabled strong unions to gain substantial wage increases, since employers remained confident that continually high levels of demand would allow them to continue to bear increased costs. Between 1965 and 1973, real wages in the United States rose by almost 40 per cent.

3 The Federal Reserve Board, which is an independent agency of the federal government, had been committed to bringing down inflation by

gradually reducing monetary growth through high interest rates since the appointment of Paul Volcker (by President Carter) in 1979.

4 Arthur Laffer, 'Supply-side economics', *Financial Analysts Journal* (September–October 1981); George Gilder, *Wealth and Poverty* (New York, 1981); Jude Wanniski, *The Way the World Works* (New York, 1978). The theory was popularized by Wanniski as an editorial writer for the *Wall Street Journal* and by Republican Congressman Jack Kemp of New York.

5 As a result of these changes, the bottom 40 per cent of families in 1984 were paying proportionately more of their income in taxes, with most of the increased burden falling on the poorest 20 per cent of families; at the same time, the top 60 per cent were paying disproportionately less of their income in taxes (Palmer and Sawhill, 1982).

6 Milton and Rose Friedman, *Tyranny of the Status Quo* (London, 1984).

7 Between 1980 and 1982, for example, the Environmental Protection Agency's budget for its air and water quality, hazardous waste, and toxic substance programmes (which represent most of the EPA's regulatory activities) was reduced by almost two-thirds. Between 1981 and 1984, the number of full-time employees in these four major programmes fell by 30 per cent.

8 Faced with increased competition from non-unionized commuter airlines as a result of 'deregulation', Continental Airlines, for instance, invoked chapter 11 of the US Bankruptcy Act, went into voluntary bankruptcy, sacked its entire workforce and then re-hired only those workers it wanted (4200 instead of the original 12,000). Between 1978 and 1982, 20 per cent of workers in the trucking industry lost their jobs at least partly as a result of deregulation.

9 Under the voucher plan, workers could elect to receive vouchers to the value of half their supplemental weekly benefits for double the benefit period in place of the full value of the vouchers for the normal period. The purpose of the proposal was to encourage the employment of the long-term unemployed, since vouchers could be submitted to an employer who would receive tax relief to the value of the vouchers.

10 Unemployment rates in states such as Ohio, Michigan and Indiana (in the mid-west) and Alabama, Mississippi, West Virginia and Louisiana (in the south) remain in double figures, whereas those in states such as Massachusetts, New Jersey and Texas are nearer to 6 per cent.

11 John L. Palmer and Isabel V. Sawhill (eds), *The Reagan Experiment. An Examination of Economic and Social Policies under the Reagan Administration* (Washington, DC, 1982).

12 By 1982–3, the increases in military spending sanctioned in 1981 had already led to an increase in real military purchases of roughly 10 per cent ($15 billion) annually. As a result, industrial production for military use increased substantially, even during the recession when other industries were declining. However, because the industries which produce military hardware are now more capital-intensive than previously, the effect on unemployment is much less.

13 Between 1951 and 1984, the civilian labour force (over 16 years of age) almost doubled, from 62.0 million to 113.5 million. Most of this increase (47 per cent) occurred between 1970 and 1980. Between 1951 and 1984, the number of women in the labour market increased 161 per cent, from 19 million (34.6 per cent of all adult women) to 49.7 million (53.6 per cent).

14 The US share of the world product (GNP) fell from 34 per cent in 1950 to 25 per cent in 1974 while those of Japan and Third World countries (mostly oil-producers) increased. America's share of world trade also fell from 18.4 per cent in 1950 to 13.4 per cent in 1977. Between 1965 and 1977, the share of manufactured imports from the Third World into the United States increased from 15 to 24 per cent.

15 Richard W. Riche *et al.*, 'High technology today and tomorrow: a small slice of the employment pie', *Monthly Labor Review*, **106** no.11 (November 1983), pp. 50–8. The wide range in this estimate reflects different assumptions about probable rates of economic growth.

16 American Airlines, for instance, employs 225 women keypunch operators in Bridgetown, Barbados to key in information from their flight coupons. The data is then transmitted to the company's computer in Tulsa, Oklahoma for analysis via satellite and telephone.

17 See, for example, Felix Rohatyn, 'The coming emergency and what can be done about it' and 'Reconstructing America', *New York Review of Books*. (4 December 1980 and 5 March 1981); Kevin Phillips, *Staying on Top. The Business Case for a National Industrial Strategy* (New York, 1984). Less authoritarian variants on these strategies include Robert Reich, *The Next American Frontier* (New York, 1984); and Lester Thurow, *The Zero-Sum Society* (New York, 1980). On these options, see James O'Connor, *Accumulation Crisis* (New York, 1984) p. 242ff.

Further reading

Gar Alperovitz and Jeff Faux, *Rebuilding America. A Blueprint for the New Economy* (New York, 1984), chs 1–4.

Teresa Amott, 'The politics of Reaganonomics', in *Free Market Conservatism. A Critique of Theory and Practice*, edited by Edward Nell (London, 1984).

Barry Bluestone and Bennett Harrison, *The Deindustrialization of America* (New York, 1982).

S. M. Miller and Donald Tomaskovic-Devey, *Recapitalizing America. Alternatives to the Corporate Distortion of National Policy* (London, 1983), chs 7–9.

John E. Schwartz, *America's Hidden Success. A Reassessment of Twenty Years of Public Policy* (New York, 1984), esp. ch. 4.

8 Labour's nostalgia for full employment

Our aim is to create full employment for all sections of the community, including women and ethnic minorities, in all parts of the country – including in our most depressed regions and inner city and rural areas .... We completely reject the pessimism of those who point to the world recession, and to the introduction of new technology, and claim that no government – not even a Labour Government committed to socialist policies – can provide jobs for all its people. [*Labour's Programme 1982*]

Since its electoral defeat in 1979, the British Labour Party has sought to devise a new package of employment policies which both addresses the worsening problem of mass unemployment and provides a distinct alternative to Thatcher's populist Conservatism. In considering Labour's alternatives, this chapter has two important purposes. First, it seeks to compare Labour's policies with the three competing political views on employment outlined in previous chapters. It does this by giving particular emphasis to the question of whether these policies represent – as party policy-makers claim – an entirely *new* response to mass unemployment in the 1980s, or whether they are better viewed as an attempt to reinstate a revised version of Beveridge's original vision of the full employment welfare state. Second, this chapter assesses the viability of Labour's objective of full employment of all adult persons.

Labour's expansive vision of full employment

There can be no doubt about Labour's commitment to full employment. Echoing Beveridge's call in 1944 to 'will the end' and 'will the means' to achieve and maintain full employment, Labour's policy documents assert boldly that:

Britain has the ingenuity and resources to restore full employment *and* produce the goods and services of the future. There is no reason why we cannot design and produce the goods and services that will be needed in the 1990s. All that is lacking is the political will to make it possible. [*A Future That Works*, 1984]

Paid work should be made available to all those who seek it, and, according to *Labour's Programme 1982*, a future Labour government would be committed to reducing unemployment to under 1 million within five years of assuming office.

The Labour Party appears to have few qualms about its previous post-war commitment to Beveridge's vision of the full employment welfare state. It endorses his call (discussed in Chapter 2) for greater equality of opportunity, for stimulating growth within the market sector, for state planning and co-ordination of private capital 'under democratic control', and for a gradual restoration of a full employment programme through constitutional means. However, Labour's commitment to restoring full employment is not only to be understood as a return to the *status quo ante* based on Beveridge's original vision. While recognizing some of the limitations of that vision, the party nevertheless wants to extend it, so as to ensure full employment for men *and* women *and* ethnic minorities in all parts of the country and, as well, to demonstrate a new (if vaguely defined) concern for the *quality* as well as the quantity of work. Thus, work should not only be safe and fairly paid, but should be 'fulfilling' (rather than monotonous) and 'organised to meet the differing needs of workers, especially those combining paid work with child care' [*Labour's Programme 1982*]. Furthermore, Labour is committed to reducing working hours (to thirty-five hours a week) and to shortening working life and, even more ambitiously, the party declares its support for 'look[ing] behind the labour market and paid work, to the unpaid work done in the home'. In other words, in contrast to Beveridge, Labour recognizes the need to take account of both the *formal* labour market and the *informal* sector, where other types of (presently unpaid) work are performed. Referring to the current disparity between men's and women's share of housework and child care, Labour asserts the need to reject the concept of the male breadwinner (which is seen to perpetuate female dependency), and urges that responsibility for child care should be shared equally between women and men. Finally, Labour looks forward to 'a society in which the balance between work

and leisure (including educational activities) is radically changed and
people can choose to have more free time for their own activities'.

Beyond Beveridge

This revised and expanded vision of a more egalitarian, full employment society is supplemented by a diagnosis of the sources of contemporary mass unemployment. This diagnosis is wholly Keynesian,
reflecting in many ways the views of the Cambridge school of
economists (discussed in Chapter 2). The contemporary unemployment crisis is seen as due primarily to demand deficiency: the
Thatcher governments have deliberately taken spending power out of
the economy through cuts in public expenditure, increases in taxation, high interest rates and (until 1984) high exchange rates.
Labour's proposed alternative solution is *reflation*: to induce higher
levels of demand through lower taxation and, most importantly,
through massive public investment designed to stimulate job-creating
economic growth in both the public and private sectors. To pay for
this huge fiscal stimulus, a future Labour government would borrow
money 'from people who choose not to spend it – private savers'.

Labour's policy-makers argue, however, that reinstating
Keynesian demand management policies will not be enough to restore
full employment. A future Labour government would need to embark
upon a major new exercise in *economic planning* which goes further
than Beveridge's original recommendation by tightly controlling the
logic of the market through political (i.e. state) directives. Behind
newly erected protective barriers (import and exchange controls),
private capital would be nationalized or redirected to serve national
interests (such as full employment and greater social justice) through
an extensive new planning framework covering four different levels of
economic decision-making: national, sectoral, regional and
individual enterprises.

At the national level, a new Department of Economic and Industrial Planning and a National Planning Council (or restructured
National Economic Development Council) are advocated to initiate
'rolling' five-year plans for creating conditions of full employment.
These two institutions would become central to government
economic policy and provide the national focus for planning. As such,
they would be concerned with the overall management of the
economy (through policies for public expenditure, taxation, interest
and exchange rates), and would be charged with ensuring that govern-

ment economic policy, particularly the return to full employment, would not be deflected by the sort of short-term crises which have characterized post-war economic policies (see Chapter 3). The new planning department would also sponsor a new National Investment Bank, a restructured National Enterprise Board and a Price Commission.

According to the Labour Party documents, each yearly planning cycle would begin with a national collective bargaining exercise among trade unions, employers and government – a National Economic Assessment (NEA) – which would be concerned to assess the economy's growth prospects, reconcile conflicting claims on economic resources, personal consumption, public and private investment, public services and the balance of trade. The NEA would be responsible for agreeing overall national priorities and, if necessary, making changes to existing five-year plans. Labour's document *Economic Planning and Industrial Democracy* states:

To be comprehensive such an assessment will have to cover the share of the national income going to profits, to earnings from employment, to rents, to social benefits and to other incomes. The assessment should also take a view on the movement in costs and prices which will support and sustain expansion and be compatible with economic and social objectives.

Industrial sectors considered vital to both the co-ordination of economic recovery and industrial regeneration would be subject to planning through Economic Development Councils (EDCs) and Sector Working Parties (SWPs). Following wide consultation with unions and management in the relevant industrial sector, and taking into account the special needs of particular regions and regional competition, the planning deparment would publish proposals which would then be put to the National Planning Council for discussion, before the Cabinet Committee for Economic Planning considers and the government publishes its five-year 'rolling' plan. Such plans would be subject to annual review following the annual NEA, and would be concerned to direct growth and new jobs to those areas which needed them most.

Following the Japanese model of state industrial planning operated by MITI (the Ministry of International Trade and Industry), the newly empowered planning department would also be required to negotiate development plans with leading companies in particular industrial sectors on a wide range of planning objectives. Agreed plans would include vital business activities such as purchasing policy, import penetration in their industries, investment plans, the introduction of new technologies, pricing, job training, as well as industrial relations. Companies' participation in these plans, the Labour Party proposes, would be ensured by making future government financial assistance (ranging from cash aid and investment grants to credit access from the National Development Bank and training assistance from the Manpower Services Commission) conditional on their co-operation. The proposed Price Commission would also be vested with discretionary powers to allow or refuse price increases which would be subject to development plans being agreed. A future Labour government would also develop reserve powers, enabling it to issue directives to companies on a variety of industrial matters. A Labour government would also invest in individual companies or purchase them outright (through either the National Investment Bank or the National Enterprise Board); ensure that capital assistance to large companies would only be available through the planning system; exercise discretionary control over corporate purchasing policy; and, finally, provide trade protection for companies and industries through import and exchange controls.

Labour also intends public enterprise to play a new pivotal role in its goal of restoring full employment through a coherent planning framework. However, it is argued that this commitment does not only involve extensions of state ownership and renationalization of many companies denationalized by the Conservatives; it also involves developing novel forms of public ownership. Deeply conscious of the popular image of socialism as bureaucratic, Labour wants to encourage 'social ownership' of property through a number of different routes. First, individual companies initially owned by the state would rapidly be converted to common property through extensions of industrial democracy, thereafter competing directly with private sector companies. Second, 'municipal socialism' along the lines of the Enterprise Boards sponsored by the Greater London and West Midlands County Councils would be encouraged through a network of regional enterprise boards.[1] These would be financed by local authorities and private sector pension funds. Local authorities' powers to invest in and draw up planning agreements with local industry would also be enlarged. Finally, Labour wants to provide further encouragement to consumers' and workers' co-operatives by making available additional technical and managerial assistance through the Co-operative Development Agency and the Industrial Common Ownership Act. Financial assistance would be offered through new tax concessions, and by providing new incentives for firms to convert to co-operatives [*Labour's Charter for Co-ops*]. Most radically, perhaps, Labour has tentatively endorsed the Swedish Social Democratic Labour Party's concept of a *wage-earner investment fund*, which would be run by regional boards with trade union members forming the majority, and would derive its funds from special profit taxes, payroll levies and workers' contractual savings (i.e. savings resulting from collective bargaining at national, sectoral, regional or company level). The purpose of these funds would be to create 'capital without the capitalist' and, thereby, ensure beneficial re-investment in industry, greater worker participation and a more equitable distribution of social wealth.[2]

Labour's policy-makers view the introduction of these new planning mechanisms as a means of extending democracy in the labour market. 'For democratic planning to work', Labour argues in *Partners in Rebuilding Britain*, 'we must build on the commitment to the future on the part of working people and management .... [S]tatutory underpinning of [rights] will provide a catalyst for workers' involvement in decision making at all levels of the economy.' Planning negotiations between a Labour government and leading companies would involve not only Sector Planning Groups and trade unions, but new legislation would go much further than Beveridge by strengthening the hand of labour against capital by providing workers with new rights of influence and participation in important company decisions. These would include rights for trade union representatives to receive information about their companies affairs (involving changes in the Companies Acts); rights to be consulted in advance on such matters as corporate finance and investment, productivity, wages, salaries and conditions of service; and rights to representation through Joint Union Committees up to and including 50 per cent membership of boards of management. Armed with these new rights, Labour envisages that workers would be able to influence their company's policies and also ensure their participation in agreed development plans [*Economic Planning and Industrial Democracy*]. In exchange for these new rights, the Labour Party emphasizes, the trade unions are expected to exercise their traditional disciplinary role in industrial relations. They 'will have the responsibility with employers to ensure that industrial relations arrangements contribute to economic reconstruction and that any disputes are conducted with proper regard for the interests of the community and in accordance with TUC guidelines'.

Clearly, Labour's proposals for creating full employment reveal important continuities with the policies pursued by previous Labour governments. In its endorsement of economic planning and the NEA, for instance, Labour has committed itself once again to the whole paraphenalia of tripartite or 'corporatist'-type governing structures so characteristic of certain phases of previous Labour (and Conservative) governments (see Chapter 3). There are, however, some new and important qualitative changes within those broad parameters. The simple equation between 'public' and 'state' enterprise and the long-standing Labour assumption that economic planning has to be of the highly centralized state variety are rejected in favour of more democratic, flexible, decentralized and open-ended commitments which are a long way from the 'revisionist' statist socialism of Crosland and Gaitskell in the 1950s. Equally, Labour's new concept of industrial democracy – greater democratic participation of workers at the workplace – is some distance removed from its traditional equations with trade union leaders consulting with Labour ministers in Downing Street or Whitehall. Finally, Labour's definition of full employment is positively expansive, when compared with the models of the disciplinary state, the strong state, free market, or even the social democratic vision of Beveridge. Employment rights would be extended to hitherto excluded interests, notably women and ethnic minorities; attention would also be directed towards the nature of paid work (as well as its quantity), to the need to reduce work-time (to thirty-five hours per week and by reducing the age for retirement) and to expand leisure by extending opportunities for education and training.

The viability of Labour's full employment commitment

Virtually all of Labour's current proposals for achieving a more egalitarian and democratic full employment society show some sense of a recognition on the part of party policy-makers of the immensity of their task. Indeed, following Labour's disastrous defeat in 1983 and the election of the Kinnock–Hattersley leadership, party policy-makers have placed great emphasis on 'selling' their policies to a sceptical electorate through a professionally-managed media campaign – 'Labour's Jobs and Industry Campaign' – which seeks to persuade the public that Labour has practical policies to tackle unemployment, rebuild the economy and to 'increase public understanding of the responsibility governments have for unemployment'. In spite of these publicity efforts, there are a number of reasons why one should doubt Labour's (indeed, any British government's) ability to achieve their 'full employment' objectives. These are: that the Treasury and the City will retain decisive influence over short-term monetary and fiscal policy; that the elaborate planning framework envisaged would be likely to heighten expectations which could not be satisfied; that it would enhance the size and role of the bureaucratic state, and would once again depend on the difficult task of securing a political accord between government, private capital and labour; and that Labour's remedy does not adequately address the process of deindustrialization which the British economy has been experiencing over the last twenty or so years.

It is clear that Labour's policy-makers are acutely aware that many of their proposals have been tried (albeit in less elaborate and diluted form) by previous Labour governments, and that these efforts failed to produce the desired results. Thus, the joint Labour Party–TUC document, *Economic Planning and Industrial Democracy*, is at pains to stress the contrasts between the party's new planning commitments and the failures of the Wilson and Wilson–Callaghan governments. It argues that the failures of the National Plan of 1965 were basically institutional: the Wilson government's Department of Economic Affairs was never allowed to play the central role in economic policy-making envisaged for the proposed Department of Economic and Industrial Planning, because controls over public expenditure and other macro-economic matters were not incorporated into the planning framework. 'Mistaken macro-economic judgements, about for example the exchange rate, undermined the DEA', *Economic Planning and Industrial Democracy* argues, 'and these judgements reflected Treasury priorities.' Moreover, the Plan failed to exercise influence over the behaviour of individual companies. The failures of the Wilson–Callaghan government's industrial strategy, introduced in 1975, are also blamed on the 'absence of a coherent planning framework' and the lack of adequate powers to influence corporate decisions, as well as on unsympathetic civil servants and the vague prescriptions for worker and trade union participation.

Certainly, these factors were important in accounting for previous Labour governments' failures, and they undoubtedly point to the need for a directive rather than indicative planning system. However, even if such a powerful planning apparatus was introduced successfully, it would be difficult if not impossible to marginalize effectively Treasury (and City) control over the instruments of *short-term* economic policy. If, as a consequence, short-term Treasury influence was not reduced, a National Planning Council or Department of Economic and Industrial Planning could not operate effectively in the *long term*.

Moreover, even if Britain's first directive planning system were to be introduced by the next Labour government, the problems of post-war economic policy (detailed in Chapter 3) would remain, possibly exacerbated by both the introduction of the new planning system itself and the absence of wage controls. The discussion in Chapter 3 demonstrated that political commitments to the full employment welfare state, particularly when made by newly elected Labour governments, tend to inflate popular expectations for improved economic well-being which ultimately, when they cannot be met, lead to governments taking steps to restrain demands, thereby enhancing the state's (unpopular) control over economic life. Labour's current proposals for full employment seem likely to refuel these old problems by increasing the power of trade unions over capital, resulting in renewed political unpopularity and ultimately preventing a future Labour government from achieving its full employment objectives. Not only would the raised economic expectations of white male workers need to be accommodated but, within Labour's extended definition of full employment, also those of women, ethnic minorities and other groups. In the process of Labour trying to reach full employment, the old conflicts between men and women ('a woman's place is in the home') and between ethnic groupings could well be rekindled, resulting in new and potentially explosive tensions within Labour's traditionally fragile political coalition.

The successful realization of Labour's objectives would also depend crucially upon the successful reconstruction of tripartite or corporatist-type forums in which economic planning and industrial democracy could be practised. Labour's full employment policies charge these forums with nothing less than the determination and reconciliation of national economic priorities. However, previous post-war experience demonstrates their inherent fragility, due primarily to trade unions' unwillingness or inability to ensure their members' compliance, and private capital's unwillingness to accept any significant degree of state control over their investment and employment plans. Labour nevertheless proposes to give workers and their trade unions effective veto power – a 'new positive role' – over planning decisions, so as to force private capital into planning agreements with the state. These are surely arrangements fraught with considerable difficulties. What, for instance, are Labour's contingency plans in the event of trade union representatives not agreeing to forgo wage increases within the National Economic Assessment in order to allow higher investment for new jobs? What will happen should private capital refuse to suppress its market strategies and surrender its management prerogatives in favour of Labour government–union priorities? Will the central bureaucracy in the planning department and the national council be able to cope with the administrative burdens of planning for many industrial sectors, even if a Labour government could restrict the power of private capital? What of the likely inflationary consequences of the Labour government's heavy borrowing and lack of enforceable means of controlling wages?[3]

Recent events in Sweden suggest that even greater political difficulties can be anticipated should Labour seek to implement the wage earner investment fund principle. To date, there have been few practical experiments in this field. If trade unions' previous attitudes to pension fund investment are any guide, one can anticipate reticence if not outright opposition to such a plan. Hitherto, British trade union leaders (Arthur Scargill of the National Union of Mineworkers being an exception) have refused to use their pension funds' power to influence investment, confining their unions' activities instead to traditional collective bargaining and national economic policy negotiations with government. To introduce such a plan, therefore, a Labour government would need to overcome these past trade union prejudices. In such an eventuality, Labour would also need to devise mechanisms by which interest rates could be determined outside traditional capital and credit markets, as well as fair criteria for allocating funds, and methods with which to monitor investments. All these requirements would generate significant political difficulties.

Labour's response to these doubts about the viability of its programme have been twofold: first, to assert that although the policies may be similar to those of previous governments, Labour's *political will* will be stronger, strong enough in fact to overcome most difficulties and to achieve the return to full employment; and second, that Labour will not promise too much too quickly. *A Future That Works* argues that a 'decade of Tory devastation, the loss of oil revenues and the impact of technological change all mean that the task in 1988 [the expected date of the next general election] will be far harder than it would have been had we been elected in 1983'. This perception, coupled with many voters' refusal to believe Labour's

1983 general election promises for restoring full employment, persuaded party leaders to dampen expectations about what a future Labour government would be able to achieve. Thus, Labour has subsequently abandoned its previous commitment to reduce unemployment to under 1 million within five years. And, recently, party leaders have recognized that it will not be possible to renationalize many of the industries and firms denationalized by the Thatcher governments.

Stripped to its bare essentials, nevertheless, the major premise of Labour's policies is that full employment can be achieved and sustained. In the context of the contemporary global political economy, however, the proposition that the 'golden age' of full employment can be restored through political will and careful planning must be doubted. Chapter 3 identified four vital characteristics of that past era of full male employment: free trade policies in international commerce and finance; national governments' adoption of Keynesian demand-stimulus policies; a combination of good luck and governmental policies which ensured low inflation; and a reservoir of growth and technological possibilities which west European (and Japanese) economies could exploit. As the discussion in that chapter also pointed out, these special conditions of the 1950s, 1960s and early 1970s are not repeatable, due to the fact that all western economies have been undergoing a process of *deindustrialization*, which in the 1970s has been accelerating.

The British economy has by no means escaped the negative consequences of deindustrialization. Since 1966, the number of workers employed in British manufacturing industry has declined from 9.2 million in 1966 to 5.4 million in December 1984. This represents a net job loss of 40.9 per cent (3.75 million workers). About 1.84 million manufacturing jobs – 49 per cent of the post 1966 losses – have been lost since 1979 alone. By 1984, only 26 per cent of the working population was employed in manufacturing industry compared with 31 per cent in 1979. Furthermore, in many industries which were once pivotal to British manufacturing, the losses have been greatest. Employment in metal manufacturing and engineering, for instance, has fallen by one-third since 1979, compared with one-fifth for all manufacturing industry.

It is well known that Britain needs to export goods and services to pay for vital imports of food and raw materials. Since the 1970s, however, the historical trade surplus in manufacturing has been declining steadily as foreign competitors have penetrated further into

British markets. Since 1982, the country has become a net importer of manufactured goods for the first time since the Industrial Revolution. The Chief Economic Adviser to the Treasury has expressed the view that this will be a *permanent* (i.e. irreversible) change. Import penetration in the manufacturing sector (measured as the ratio of the value of imports to gross domestic output) has increased dramatically since the 1970s, especially in vehicles, clothing and footwear, instrument and electrical engineering, and textiles. Transnational manufacturing companies – including 'British' companies like I C I, Dunlop, and B S R – which account for most imports and exports, conduct ever increasing proportions of their business elsewhere.[4]

While it is true that other employment societies, such as the United States, have also been undergoing similar structural decline, no other country has experienced decline on the same scale as Britain. Indeed, Labour's own documents repeatedly make this point [*Working Together For Britain*]. Nevertheless, not all blame for this industrial decline can be laid at the door of the Thatcher governments, although Labour is certainly right to argue – as the discussion in Chapter 6 noted – that their deflationary policies have exacerbated this process. But for Labour to claim that the process of deindustrialization can be reversed is naive, indicating a lamentable nostalgia for a bygone past. Can the imposition of import and exchange controls proposed by the Labour Party single-handedly reverse the effects of the new international division of labour, that is, the export of jobs to low-wage economies in South America and Asia or the flight of capital to these Third World areas, as well as to other E E C countries and the United States? Faced with exchange controls, what is to stop other transnational companies from transferring their labour-intensive stages of production to Hong Kong or some other 'factory state'? How could import or exchange controls regulate the type of paid work being offered by private firms? Common Market controls already provide strong incentives for companies to establish plants in Britain, but all too frequently their main purpose is to assemble parts that have been manufactured elsewhere. Indeed, ironically, existing import controls, such as the Multi-Fibre Arrangements (which limit increases in textiles imports), tend to protect more foreign jobs (in the sweatshops of Hong Kong, India, South Korea and Taiwan) than British jobs –because the British textile industry is so small – while costing the consumer countless millions in higher prices.

The Labour Party is not only relying on an unrealistic expansion of manufacturing jobs but also on an improbable view of the likely levels of growth in the private *services* sector. The party takes comfort from the fact that since 1976 the numbers of full-time jobs in such service industries as banking, finance, insurance, and hotels and catering have risen. However, the rate of job growth in these sectors has actually been decelerating over this period, while the service sector's contribution to the balance of payments (in terms of invisible service sector earnings) has been declining even faster than that of the manufacturing industry.[5] It is unlikely, therefore, that service jobs will be able to offset the decline in manufacturing; and, as in the manufacturing sector, there is likely to be a heightened trend towards 'British' companies, especially in financial services, expanding their foreign rather than their domestic activities. Indeed, in the contemporary era of global telecommunications and computer technology, there is really little need for transnational companies in these industries to maintain their costly facilities in Britain, especially considering that they can locate their facilities nearer to more productive markets in continental Europe and the United States.

One should also treat cautiously the Keynesian assumption in Labour's programme that increased public investment, especially in hi-tech innovation, would lead to wholesale reductions in unemployment. The effect in the long term could be the opposite. In November 1982, Labour's 'Alternative Budget' proposed a £9 billion reflation requiring £5.5 billion in additional borrowing [*Programme for Recovery*]. Labour's 'Alternative Budget' in March 1985 proposed a £3.5 billion reflation. Whichever figures are used, the effect of reflation on jobs is likely to be very modest. According to the TUC's estimates, a £24 billion reflation over five years is likely to produce only 500,000 new jobs. Furthermore, such reflationary measures would probably have other unintended negative effects, notably on inflation, wage increases, the balance of payments, government borrowing, as well as on the natural environment (see Chapter 4). Should other major economies not reflate at the same time, a future Labour government in Britain would face the problems President Mitterrand has faced in France. Moreover, should the United States maintain its current budget deficits with their accompanying high interest rates, a British government would be hard pressed to compete for funds in international credit and capital markets.

Faced with these familiar problems associated with Keynesian policies, a Labour government would be likely to be obliged to opt for the type of deflationary policies which were so characteristic of previous Labour and Conservative administrations. Indeed, it must be emphasized that demand management or Keynesian policies of the type proposed by Labour can only deal with small deviations from full employment, such as those which occurred in the era of full male employment during the 1950s and 1960s. In an economy undergoing deindustrialization, their effect would be minimal and, as Chapter 3 indicated, such policies might actually inhibit vital structural and technological changes. In the long term, new government-directed 'investment in new technologies' for the purposes of modernization and increased productivity might also have the opposite effect of their intentions.[6] They might increase efficiency and productivity and, in so doing, enhance the prospects of further job *losses*.

Fundamentally, Labour's programme for a return to full employ ment rests on the highly speculative and unconvincing premise that markedly faster economic growth is possible. Most economic estimates deny this possibility (see Chapter 2).[7] In the foreseeable future, further deindustrialization is likely in Britain. Prevailing international conditions suggest that richer employment societies (if they want to stay rich) will be required to abandon their traditional manufacturing and other heavy industry to poorer, newly industrializing countries. In the long term, the richer employment societies will not be able to make up for this loss through additional growth in the service sector.

Most of the discussion in this chapter has been concerned with the viability of Labour's programme. It is, however, equally legitimate to ask whether Labour's proposals are *desirable*. Despite the party's new expansive rhetoric, Labour's plans to reinstate its corporatist-type political arrangements (at a time when at least 3 million people will be unemployed) will probably perpetuate the 'dualization' of British society. The proposals anticipate extending new industrial democratic rights to union members in paid work and, yet, no such rights or benefits are specified for the unemployed, the part-time employed, the non-unionized and their families, as well as pensioners and other marginal social groups. Indeed, should a future Labour government experience the sort of economic and financial difficulties which this chapter has predicted, it would be sorely tempted to accommodate the demands of the most economically powerful groups, who would then enjoy privileged access to governing structures at the expense of weaker and more marginal social groups, including those dependent on state welfare. Arguably, therefore, Labour's proposals would have the unintended effect of reinforcing the 'dualized' nature of contemporary Britain.

These normative questions, as well as the earlier doubts about the viability of Labour's programme, point to the need for contemporary employment societies – in which there is less demand for labour yet more people seeking entry into the labour market and increasing numbers of part-time workers – to invent new mechanisms for deciding not only who obtains paid work and how such work in the formal sector is divided up, but also how work in the informal and household sectors is allocated and rewarded. Notwithstanding recent vague intimations from Labour's leaders, these pressing issues are largely ignored in Labour's documents. In the final chapter, some of these silences are addressed through an examination of the utopian socialist proposals of the French social critic, André Gorz.

Notes

1   The Greater London Enterprise Board was established by the Labour-controlled Greater London Council in 1982 as an agency run by local government which could invest in and provide technical assistance to *commercially viable* businesses, many of which are worker-owned. In providing assistance, GLEB discriminated positively in favour of women and ethnic minorities. During its first year of operation, it claimed to have saved or developed some 2000 jobs.

2   Some further considerations of the wage-earner investment fund include W. Korpi, *The Working Class in Welfare Capitalism* (London, 1978) pp. 327–34; Kristina Ahlén, 'Sweden Introduces Employee Ownership', *Political Quarterly*, **56**, no.2. (April–June 1985), pp. 186–93; Rudolf Meidner, *Employee Investment Funds: An Approach to Collective Capital Formation* (London, 1978). GLEB's officials view present deindustrialization in Britain as indicative of a crisis of restructuring of production in the global capitalist economy (compare the discussion of the new international division of labour in the Introduction). In contrast to the earlier twentieth-century model of capitalist production (the production of standardized goods; assembly line manufacturing; semi-skilled workers), the new phase of capitalist production is seen to be based on 'flexible specialization', involving new technologies, greater reliance upon part-time employment, sub-contracting and franchising, non-unionized workers and new patterns of global investment and production. The negative effects of this present restructuring process, it is argued, requires an 'alternative approach' based on popular democratic planning and 'socially useful' production at all levels of the economy.

3   Some economists have recognized these problems. One proposal is that governments make binding agreements with the trade unions to the effect

that they will only agree to implement certain policies once the trade unions have delivered on their agreements. See, for example, Mario Nuti, 'Beyond the market and beyond planning', *Socialist Register*, forthcoming (1985). On proposals to control private capital, see for instance Gareth Locksley and Richard Minns, 'Pension Funds – The key to economic management' *The Guardian*, 3 April 1985.

4   ICI currently derives 75 per cent of its income from outside Britain. Since 1979, the company has maintained its level of employment abroad but cut its British workforce by one-third. Dunlop currently derives over 95 per cent of its profits from Africa, Asia and Australasia compared with just 30 per cent in 1972. BSR, which employs over 95 per cent of its workforce outside Britain, moved its headquarters from the West Midlands to Hong Kong in 1984.

5   Between 1979 and 1983, for instance, Britain's share of world trade in private transactions of 'invisibles' fell from 9.6 per cent to 8.5 per cent.

6   See Jonathan Gershung, 'New technology – what new jobs', *Industrial Relations Journal* (autumn 1985), pp. 74–84.

7   One study has calculated that manufacturing output would have to grow by some 5 per cent a year throughout the remainder of the 1980s for unemployment to be reduced to 1 million; see I. Begg and J. Rhodes, 'Will British industry recover?', *Cambridge Economic Policy Review*, **8** no.2 (April 1982).

Further reading

Ian Benson and John Lloyd, *New Technology and Industrial Change. The Impact of the Scientific-Technical Revolution on Labour and Industry* (London, 1983), ch. 9.

Bill Jordan, *Mass Unemployment and the Future of Britain* (Oxford, 1982).

Labour's Jobs and Industry Campaign, *Labour: Working Together for Britain* (London, 1985).

The Labour Party, *Labour's Programme 1982* (London, 1982), pt A.

The Labour Party, *A Future That Works. Statement to Annual Conference 1984 by the National Executive Committee* (London, 1984).

The Labour Party, *Labour's Charter for Co-ops* (London, 1985).

TUC-Labour Party Liaison Committee, *Economic Planning and Industrial Democracy. The Framework for Full Employment*, Report to the 1982 TUC Congress and Labour Party Conference (London, 1982).

TUC-Labour Party Liaison Committee, *Partners in Rebuilding Britain* (London, 1983).

9 Beyond the employment society

Keynes is dead.   [André Gorz]

In the introduction to this book, the idea of the employment society was introduced and explained. Modern societies were described as employment societies in that, unlike all other past and present societies, paid work performed within a labour market (itself institutionally separated off from the state and work performed in households mainly by women) has come to play a crucial role in shaping the whole of life within these societies. This was our way of describing the emergence of *capitalist* economies – 'modes of production' in which a great deal of work (housework, informal 'shadow work', and state sector labour are the main exceptions) is a commodity, bought and sold on the market along with other commodities. We pointed out that capitalist economies rarely provided enough paid labour for the adult, male population – the main exception was the three decades after the Second World War – and that, accordingly, 'unemployment' has been a chronic feature of these economies from their beginning.

Criticism of unemployment – the often traumatic experience of being out of paid employment – began to develop during the early nineteenth century. We indicated that what was new about the proposals for full employment – an ideal invented during the nineteenth century – was the claim that capitalist economies could be reformed through state regulation so as to provide jobs for all adult men. We traced the origins and development of the full employment welfare state, giving particular emphasis to the events of the 1920s and 1930s which made possible the political triumph of the type of full employment welfare state vision popularized by Beveridge, Keynes and others. And, finally, we showed how, during the past two decades, rising unemployment has helped generate a new and often bitter controversy among social democrats, free market liberals and advocates of the disciplinary state about how 'full employment' can again be *restored*.

Through the course of this book, doubts have been raised about the feasibility and, indeed, the desirability of 'restoring' full male employment. In particular, we argued that the conditions that made possible full male employment after 1945 in countries such as Britain and the United States are not repeatable, and that, consequently, there is an urgent need in the present period for new and unorthodox political ideas and strategies for remedying the present unemployment crisis. It is therefore pertinent to conclude this book with a consideration of some utopian socialist views on unemployment and the future of paid work. For in sharp contrast to the three other views considered in earlier chapters, the utopian socialist tradition, since its inception in the early decades of the nineteenth century, has always questioned modern employment societies' fetishism of paid labour and, in order to solve the problem of unemployment, called for its reduction or outright abolition.

Paul Lafargue's *The Right to be Lazy* (completed in 1883 in a French prison by the Cuban-born, classics-trained, vagabond son-in-law of Karl Marx) was one of the most influential early utopian socialist tracts in favour of limiting paid work. The appearance of *The Right to be Lazy* in the early 1880s was by no means coincidental, for this was precisely the period in which the demand to eliminate unemployment became a central theme in the European workers' movement (see Chapter 1). Lafargue's pamphlet, an important contribution in efforts to establish 1 May as World Labour Day, bitterly attacks this trade union demand for the 'right to work'. In his view, the call for the right to work is symptomatic of a strange delusion possessing the working classes of employment societies: the 'furious passion for work'. Betraying their better instincts, workers fall in love with paid employment and capitulate to the brutal and physically and morally exhausting logic of market capitalist production and exchange: 'Work, work, proletarians, to increase social wealth and your individual poverty; work, work, in order that becoming poorer, you may have more reason to work and become miserable. Such is the inexorable law of capitalist production.' The modern capitalist system spreads to the four corners of the earth, says Lafargue, and in so doing reduces working men, women and children everywhere to machine-like slaves. They are supposed to work constantly (note Lafargue's misleading assumption that 'work' in employment societies is synonymous with paid work), without decent health, pleasures, holidays, or liberties of any kind. The modern factory in this sense resembles a house of correction, in which the working classes are imprisoned, condemned to twelve or more hours of toil per day.

Lafargue views the habits of the capitalist class as parasitic, as the other side of the coin of this compulsory labour of capitalist economies. In order to maintain demand for the goods produced through paid labour, and therefore to maintain the system of paid labour itself, this capitalist class wallows in a life of forced and prudish entertainment, fat unproductiveness and belching over-consumption. In opposition to this absurd and lop-sided state of affairs, Lafargue proposes the abolition ('peaceably if we may, forcibly if we must') of waged and salaried labour, as well as the class system itself. He recommends a three hour working day for all (supervised by the state), the rest of the day and night being reserved for leisure, feasting and love-making. Modern machinery is viewed as making all this possible. Whatever compulsory work needed to be done would become a beneficial exercise to the human body, a mere supplement to the pleasures of idleness. Quoting with approval the German Enlightenment thinker, Lessing, he demands, 'Let us be lazy in everything, except in loving and drinking, except in being lazy.'

Amidst the recent breakdown of consensus about the full employment welfare state, nineteenth-century utopian socialist proposals for reducing and redistributing paid work have begun to reappear in the political arena. André Gorz's *Farewell to the Working Class* (1980) and *Paths to Paradise* (1983) are among the most important and influential socialist contributions to the contemporary debate about full employment. These are deliberately 'utopian' books. They rely upon the standard utopian technique of pointing to a future radically different from the present, and they do this by making *exaggerated* arguments which serve as standards against which present reality can be measured and judged as *inadequate*. The picture of the future presented by these books is also sketchy and inexact, and this too is a mark of their utopianism. Just as Lafargue's utopian island of loving and drinking and laziness is shrouded in fog, so Gorz's utopian socialism is often lacking in clarity and definition. Gorz, therefore, does not pretend to have answered all of the many questions his books raise. He is rather concerned to mount an attack on what he describes as the prevailing nostalgic and unimaginative attachment, especially on the left, to the goal of restoring full employment.[1] Five themes in Gorz's utopian socialist argument are of special relevance to our contention that the experience of full male employment is unrepeatable and that, therefore, there is presently a great need for unorthodox political proposals for equitably redistributing and reducing paid work.

1   According to Gorz, political programmes based on the vision of maintaining or restoring the full employment welfare state are now exhausted. A society based on mass unemployment is coming into being before our very eyes; waged and salaried work is being abolished by the widespread introduction into the workplace of micro-electronic and telecommunications systems. In each of the leading industrialized countries of western Europe, he argues, independent economic forecasts suggest that during the next decade automation ('the robot revolution') will eliminate up to 4–5 million full-time jobs. Unless there is a sharp reduction in the number of working hours as well as radical changes in the form and purpose of paid productive activity, unemployment levels of 30–50 per cent by the end of the century seem not altogether unlikely.

Gorz could greatly strengthen his case against full male employment by examining the other, non-technological factors responsible for the present unemployment crisis discussed in earlier chapters of this book. He does not consider, for instance, the crucial significance of changes in the international monetary and trading systems, the emerging new international division of labour, and the political problems and social conflicts generated by the welfare state; nor does he take into account the likely continuing expansion of the labour supply due to demographic and social factors (such as the baby-boom of the late 1950s and early 1960s, and the re-entry of increasing numbers of women into full-time or part-time employment). Gorz instead emphasizes the revolutionary consequences of automation for the full employment welfare state. In both the industrial and service sectors of the economy, the increasing utilization of micro-electronics is no longer creating but *destroying* jobs. This new technology revolutionizes the means of producing both material goods and non-material services; in all types of manufacturing and office employment, more goods and services can be produced with less investment, raw materials (especially energy) and waged and salaried labour. From hereon, Gorz concludes, the employment societies will experience 'jobless growth'; reflation through new investment, whether public or private, cannot be expected to create vast numbers of new jobs. Restoring full employment through accelerating quantitative economic growth is no longer a realistic goal.

2   The present long wave of rapid technological change not only generates mass unemployment; according to Gorz, it also radically alters the socio-economic class structure of the employment societies. Under pressure from quickening technological change, the workers' movement in particular loses whatever unity it once enjoyed. Not the capitalist system, but 'the working class' is disintegrating. It becomes subdivided into three distinct strata. First, there is an aristocracy of 'tenured workers'. Concerned to protect its own jobs and resist automation, this stratum forms the backbone of the trade union movement. Threatened by the advance of automation, this traditional working class is becoming little more than a privileged minority of full-time waged workers. (In Britain, to mention one indicator in support of Gorz's claim, more than 5.5 million full-time jobs have been lost since the mid 1960s in manufacturing industry, the traditional heartland of this stratum.) The political identity of this aristocracy of industrial labour is heavily shaped by its commitment to paid work; it is in this sense a complement or 'replica' of capital, a group no longer capable of becoming an agent of radical social and political change. The second social stratum produced by the break-up of the working class is the growing mass of permanently unemployed. This group cannot be considered a 'reserve army' in Marx's sense for, as things stand, it is unlikely ever to re-enter the labour market. The mass of permanently unemployed find that there is little or no paid work available. The unemployed thereby become trapped in a vicious and ever expanding circle of poverty and idleness; they find that living on the dole is no holiday. Finally, there is a third stratum of the population, 'temporary workers', which is as it were trapped between the permanently unemployed and the aristocracy of tenured workers. This stratum of temporary workers is rapidly growing in the present period,[2] and it is employed in the least skilled and often most unsatisfying jobs. It has no job security and no definite class identity; it is engaged in casual, contracted, temporary and part-time employment. This stratum is frequently 'over-qualified' for the jobs it finds; unable to identify with 'the job', it endures paid work in order to earn a little money on which to exist. In the not too distant future, says Gorz, many jobs presently filled by temporary workers will be eliminated by automation.

3   Gorz uses the term 'non-class of non-workers' (or 'disaffected non-workers') to refer to the latter two strata of permanently unemployed and temporary workers.* Despite its present heterogeneity and lack of organization, this non-class of non-workers is likely to succeed the old and decaying industrial working-class movement as the most powerful opponent of the capitalist system. This is because this non-class of non-workers shares the following social and psychological characteristics. (1) It is allergic to paid work. It experiences employment as an externally imposed obligation, and this is a correct perception, says Gorz. We are witnessing the final stage in the historic decline of the polyvalent skilled worker. Paid work is no longer the worker's own activity; whether in the factory or office, work has become a passive, programmed activity subordinated totally to machines and machine-like organizations which squeeze out any scope for personal initiative. The present technological revolution only accelerates this deskilling and alienating trend. (2) Unlike the skilled workers of the age of industrial capitalism, the non-class of non-workers does not take pride in whatever employment it finds. Nor does this non-class acknowledge the actual or potential power paid work confers on workers. It therefore does not seek to appropriate collectively work and its tools; it simply is not interested in workers' control of production or class-based politics. For this non-class, it is no longer a question of finding freedom *within* paid work, but of *rejecting* work in order to act freely *outside* the labour market.

---

* The term 'non-class of non-workers' is misleading because it gives the false impression that the permanently unemployed and temporary workers do not engage in types of work in the household and the informal economy. Following Lafargue, Gorz supposes that in employment societies work is synonymous with paid work, thereby forgetting that employment is merely *one*, albeit crucial form of work. Gorz's failure to discuss unpaid work (such as that performed in households, mainly by women) sometimes produces implicitly sexist conclusions in his writings. (In *Paths to Paradise*, for instance, he completely ignores the gendered work patterns of the era of full male employment, instead insisting that 'there can no longer be full-time waged work for all, and waged work cannot remain the centre of gravity or even the central activity in our lives'.) His silence about unpaid forms of work also tempts him into highly romanticized accounts of life outside the sphere of the labour market (as in the following passage from *Farewell to the Working Class*: 'Non-economic activities are the very fabric of life itself. They encompass everything which is done, not for money, but out of friendship, love, compassion, concern; or for the satisfaction, pleasure and joy derived from the activities themselves and from their end results').

(3) Although the non-class of non-workers is a fragmented and composite group, it is generally suspicious of established institutions (such as corporations, trade unions, political parties and state institutions). It experiences the whole of the existing capitalist system as 'something external, akin to a spectacle or show'. It has no single god or religion and, in sharp contrast to the workers' movement of the nineteenth century, has no sense of historical mission.

Considered together, or so Gorz argues, these three characteristics of the non-class of non-workers endow it with great potential power to transform the existing capitalist system. However, this is not to underestimate the political difficulties facing this non-class. While its greatest strength lies in its reluctance to pose political problems in traditional ways – it is no longer in love with the idea of paid work or 'full employment', for instance – it presently suffers from a general lack of social and political consciousness. Until it develops this self-awareness –Gorz clearly sees his own writings as a contribution to this development– it stands in danger of remaining socially powerless and politically marginal.

4 According to Gorz, the present economic crisis – accelerating automation, job loss and the growth of an impoverished non-class of non-workers – confronts employment societies with a fundamental political choice. This concerns whether the full employment welfare state will be superseded by *either* an authoritarian state-regulated capitalism ('living-dead capitalism'), in which full-time jobs will be scarce and most of the population will be segregated, regimented and reduced to powerlessness by various state-administered programmes, *or* by a democratic and post-capitalist society which equitably reduces socially necessary work to a minimum so as to maximize each person's 'free use of time'. Gorz has no doubt that only the second option is desirable and, in the long run, feasible. In his view it is high time that the old utopian socialist demand (which the contemporary trade union movement seems largely to have forgotten or ignored) be renewed: work less for pay, live more! The vision of a post-employment society must now be central to socialist politics. In the words of Gorz:

Let us work less so that we all may work and do more things by ourselves in our free time. Socially useful labour, distributed among all those willing and able to work, will thus cease to be anyone's exclusive or leading activity. Instead, people's major occupation may be one or a number of self-defined activities, carried out not for money but for the interest, pleasure or benefit involved.

This demand to work less does *not* imply the right to 'rest more'. Gorz rejects calls (those of Lafargue, for instance) for more 'leisure'; he observes, correctly, that the enormous post-war growth of the manipulative 'leisure industry' paralyses the anti-capitalist and democratic potential of such calls. The demand to be employed less implies the right to 'live more'. It implies the right to do things that money cannot buy – and even to do some of the things that money presently *can* buy.[3] A politics of free time, Gorz argues, must aim at achieving a democratic 'civil society' freed from the dominating imperatives of employment – in other words, developing a sphere of life regulated not by state institutions and/or by capitalist corporations and trade unions, but by networks of self-governing, small-scale institutions (such as non-patriarchal households, neighbourhood centres, rural community associations, repair and DIY shops, producers' and consumers' cooperatives, libraries, and places to make films or to record and play music) whose individual members consider each other as equals and exercise their unique productive powers in their own free time.

5   Gorz insists that a multi-centred and self-governing civil society which maximized the free use of time could never do without state institutions (such as legislatures, civil administration, law courts, the police). Contrary to many previous utopian socialists, centralized state institutions as we know them could not be abolished or somehow made to wither away slowly. Gorz offers four overlapping reasons for this heresy. First, 'socially necessary' work (performed, say, by bus drivers, engineers, computer technicians and garbage collectors) cannot be eliminated once and for all; if it is to be shared equitably, performed efficiently and effectively and considerably reduced in quantity (Gorz suggests socially necessary work in this sense could be reduced to a mere two hours a day, ten hours a week, or fifteen weeks a year), it would have to be planned, and planning requires centrally co-ordinated state institutions. Second, Gorz observes that many of the tools (e.g. telephones, video machines, bicycles, computers) which would enable individuals and groups to live freely within civil society *could* be produced at the level of small, self-governing groups equipped with the latest information technologies; however, this would sometimes be inefficient and time-consuming, and so, in order radically to shorten the quantity of time given over to socially necessary work, these particular tools would often be better produced within large-scale, centrally-organized state institutions. Third, Gorz insists that socialists (and other political

actors) who call for the abolition of the state dream the impossible; conflicts among different individuals and groups are unlikely to disappear, and future socialist society will therefore always require some mechanisms of conflict resolution, for which certain types of state institutions (such as courts of law) are uniquely suited. What is more, socialists who call for the abolition of state institutions nearly always defend 'socialist morality' – by insisting that each individual and group should identify with, and embrace, the whole social order. This morality, Gorz observes correctly, is antipathetic to individual and group liberty, and may even have totalitarian implications. Finally, Gorz points out that state institutions are not always a damper upon liberty. For example, the existence of a police force – whose strictly defined and politically controlled functions need not be performed, as they are today, as a full-time career – makes it unnecessary for each individual to internalize a whole system of law and order. Similarly, the existence of a state-enforced traffic code makes it unnecessary to engage in tedious negotiations with every other road user at every intersection. These examples make it clear, or so Gorz argues, that certain state institutions may in fact be *enabling*, in the sense that they actually facilitate individuals' and groups' freedom in civil society.

Beyond utopia

Gorz's attempt to revive, redefine and popularize the old utopian socialist criticism of paid labour is only summarized briefly here. These five themes nevertheless illustrate the main outlines of his very stimulating and quite justified attack on the present political consensus about the need to restore full employment.

These themes also indicate that the terms 'civil society' and 'the state' occupy a central place in Gorz's polemic. The distinction between *civil society* (a non-state realm of voluntary co-operation among equal individuals and groups who have been released from the pressures of socially necessary work) and *the state* (a sphere of compulsory, hierarchical institutions necessary for the efficient and effective servicing and co-ordination of civil society) is fundamental to Gorz's definition of socialism. Also fundamental to this vision, consequently, is the distinction between the 'self-determined' activity of civil society (Gorz prefers not to speak of this as work) and compulsory (if unwaged) work within the state sector. These distinctions lead Gorz to insist that socialism will not be equivalent (as it was for Lafargue and many nineteenth-century socialists) to harmonious social co-operation without government, law and police. And, contrary to market liberals like Spencer and Friedman (Chapter 4), socialism, he says, will not be equivalent to a Soviet-type regime which suffocates civil society under a canopy of state bureaucracy, red tape, party propaganda, secret police, centralized planning and compulsory work. Gorz rather insists that socialism means a type of society in which socially necessary work has been minimized and distributed equally by making the state sector as small, and the sphere of civil society as large, as possible. Socialism will be a type of *post-employment* society in which individual citizens will enjoy a maximum of free time, as well as determine, through periodic involvement in political activity, the broad guidelines and instruments of a centralized state planning system necessary for the survival and free development of civil society.

It should be evident from this sketch that Gorz's vision of a future socialist society is weakened by a number of untreated gaps and questionable claims within his overall argument. One weakness arises from his unstated assumption that socialism could be constructed within a specifically national context – despite evidence that the new international division of labour, changes in the global monetary and trading systems and superpower strategies would all loom large as obstructive factors in any single employment society's attempt to make a transition to socialism in Gorz's sense. A further weakness arises from Gorz's belief (to be found also in Braverman's well known account of the twentieth-century degradation of work)[4] that paid work has already become a passive and meaningless activity programmed from above, and that, for reasons of technical efficiency and effectiveness, this condition would persist in the state-organized sector of socially necessary production in a future socialist society. This belief clearly exaggerates the degree of de-skilling, worker powerlessness and loss of work motivation in present-day employment societies; more importantly, it underestimates the ways in which future state planning of socially necessary production could *not* function rationally without active work-place democracy.*

---

* The most highly mechanized organizations – of the type envisaged by Gorz for minimizing the aggregate quantity of socially necessary work – are often high-risk systems and cannot operate automatically, that is, without active human input. Human skill, improvization and collective judgements are required to prevent them from regularly malfunctioning in unexpected and dangerous ways (as at the nuclear power plant at Three-Mile Island in the United States). In addition, the latest

Gorz's vision of a future socialist society also suffers from a certain vagueness and lack of detail. It is not so easy, however, to criticize Gorz for not providing a detailed picture of the future. To point to his disregard, say, of the necessary future role of market mechanisms or of the likely persistence of 'work shyness' under socialism is illegitimate, for this is only to describe his *utopian* way of thinking. Gorz constantly emphasizes that we must dare to ask questions about the present unemployment crisis which cannot be answered easily. His utopia is in this sense a deliberate provocation: it questions and rejects the apparently 'natural' ideal of full employment so as to stimulate political discussion about the future of paid work.

In our view, Gorz's utopianism is the greatest strength of his writings. It is indeed 'realistic' thinking about unemployment and paid work which in the present period is rapidly becoming unrealistic. Gorz is therefore right to point to the need for bold and impudent political claims, which can help throw light on our present circumstances, showing just how unimaginative are the prevailing public policies and political proposals for managing the present unemployment crisis. Gorz's proposals nevertheless raise many questions about *political strategy*, that is, questions about which social and political *means* could facilitate his envisaged *goal* of a state-protected civil society based on the free use of time. Three sets of strategic questions are especially important, and illustrate the overall thesis of this book that not only new political visions but *also* new political strategies for reducing and redistributing waged and salaried work must be made a central theme of contemporary politics.

1   *Is the 'non-class of non-workers' as allergic to paid work as Gorz claims, and is it capable of acting as a co-ordinated social movement in defence of free time?* Past experience suggests that the non-class of non-workers is unlikely to develop a common political

---

machine systems (such as robots and computers) produce unstructured and open-ended problems which can only be solved by those who work with them. Finally, these new technologies' remarkable capacity to flexibly alter both the flow of work and the types of products can be maximized only through collective human decisions at the point of production. For further discussion of these points, see Charles Perrow, *Normal Accidents. Living with High-Risk Technologies* (New York 1984); Larry Hirschhorn, *Beyond Mechanization: Work and Technology in a Post-Industrial Age* (London 1984); and Mike Cooley, *Architect or Bee? The Human/Technology Relationship* (Slough 1983).

identity, as Gorz anticipates. If anything the opposite will be true: unemployment has mostly depoliticizing and humiliating effects upon those who experience it. This was a clear lesson of the 1930s. As Middlemas explains, during that decade the unemployed found it extremely difficult to sustain membership of any social or political organizations through which they could define and defend their interests: 'The loss of workplace or union as a focus for activity, the onset of apathy, disorientation, undernourishment, combined with a lower level of political education, geographical fragmentation and incompatibility between stratified groups of unemployed workers, all militated against the creation of a mass movement *from below.*'⁵ Little has changed since that time. The 'non-class of non-workers' typically finds itself isolated, deserted for the time being by trade unions, the main political parties and the employed majority. Under these circumstances, it is not surprising that the non-class develops not an allergy, but a passion to engage in paid work. Gorz wishes away these obstacles to the non-class of non-workers overcoming its own powerlessness by itself. He thereby fails to recognize the need for developing a strategy of solidarity between the non-class of non-workers and trade unions and reform-oriented political parties. Gorz instead falls back upon the very questionable (Marxian) idea of a single revolutionary group which is presently passing through a vale of tears *en route* to a mountain paradise of freedom. In view of the highly differentiated character of temporary workers and the permanently unemployed, Gorz's belief that there is presently developing a single revolutionary subject must be rejected. The prospects for a society based upon more free time depend not upon theoretical assumptions about a (potentially) homogeneous political subject, but instead upon the development in practice of solidarity between the non-class of non-workers and various other groups within civil society and the state. A solidarity of those in favour of freedom from employment cannot rest upon *ascribed* common interests (as it does in Gorz's analysis). It must instead begin with the difficult political problem of how to build co-operation among groups – the unemployed, the part-time employed, social movements and left-wing political parties – who would in turn respect each other's right to articulate their differences of opinion. Solidarity in this sense would not assume some 'essential shared interest' of the participants. It would instead be based upon a shared awareness among the various social and political groups that their needs are equally frustrated by mass unemployment, that a return to full employment is impossible, and that the reduction and equitable redistribution of paid work is therefore essential.

Developing this solidarity will not be easy. As we have shown in earlier chapters of this book, major political parties, including those on the left, remain deeply imbued with the ethos of full employment. In addition, a politics of free time is understandably developing at only a slow pace among trade unions. Under conditions of deindustrialization and declining (or new types of) investment, trade unions cannot easily press demands for the reduction and redistribution of paid work. When firms close or migrate to other countries, for instance, militancy is more likely to *encourage* rather than prevent disinvestment. The shift towards 'jobless growth' based on highly capital-intensive investment also undermines the power of trade unions, who find it difficult to guarantee employment for their remaining members, let alone to support the unemployed and part-time employed. During the past five years or so, a push towards a standard thirty-five-hour week has been clearly identifiable among British and other west European trade unions; schemes for a thirty-two-hour week (e.g. the 'broad strategy' of the National Communications Workers' Union in Britain) are also increasingly common in wage and salary bargaining. While this suggests that the stratum of 'tenured workers' is not completely addicted to paid work, as Gorz claims, a more radical commitment to reducing and redistributing paid work – say, to a maximum twenty-four-hour/three-day week – nevertheless seems a long way off, even though it is clearly an essential condition of developing a viable and popular politics of free time.

2   The second type of strategic question prompted by Gorz's vision follows directly from this point. *Given that the demand to 'Work less, live more!' is desirable, which types of policies geared to reducing and redistributing paid work could best help make it a reality for all people?* Gorz's discussion of the reduction of paid work is notably unclear about these specific policies. This is unfortunate, since there are serious difficulties in formulating viable policies for guaranteeing that those people who are able and willing to engage in paid work have the right to such work, but for fewer hours, thereby spreading paid work and its benefits more equitably throughout civil society. There are several possible types of policies. The main ones are summarized below. Each has its difficulties although, depending on where and when they are utilized, they may be reduced or offset by combining two or more types of policies:

a Reducing basic weekly hours. A normal thirty-five-hour paid working week is given priority by trade union organizations in a number of employment societies. Some trade unions are already claiming an even shorter working week: for example, the British National Union of Bank Employees is claiming a twenty-eight-hour week spread over four days, already having enforced the thirty-five-hour week. Estimates of the number of jobs that might be preserved/created by a shorter paid working week differ greatly. According to a model designed by the German Institute for Economic Research in Berlin, an overall reduction of five hours in the paid working week in West Germany could lead to the creation of approximately 1 million new jobs within five years.[6] Others contest this estimate, pointing to the dismal failure of the Mitterrand government's legislated reductions in work time to provide even short-term relief from growing mass unemployment in France.[7] Regardless of which of these differing estimates is valid, it is clear that a reduction of basic weekly hours alone will not be a panacea for unemployment in the short term. Partly this is due to doubts as to whether employers will in fact create even part-time jobs to make up for the reductions in working time; employers' attempts to replace their labour requirements through automation and/or to compensate for the reduction of working time through productivity gains are more probable. And in the past, reductions of paid working time have been partly offset by employers' attempts to increase overtime working. This would clearly be counter-productive.

b Reducing overtime. The equitable expansion of freedom from employment clearly requires substantial cuts in overtime. Many paid workers, especially manual and service workers, still work long hours in the labour market. A sample survey conducted in 1977 in EEC countries indicated that average weekly hours for male employees in agriculture exceeded fifty hours in Britain and forty-five hours in seven other countries. In manufacturing industry they exceeded forty-two hours in three countries, one being Britain. In the service trades, they exceeded forty-three hours in France, and forty-two hours in two other countries.[8]

If overtime hours could be parcelled into full-time job units, and if employers could be pressured to fill those jobs, this could absorb significant numbers of unemployed workers. The problems in discouraging overtime are however considerable. Employers usually oppose attempts to reduce overtime, on the grounds that it increases their costs of hiring and training new employees. Overtime is also a vital element of the weekly earnings of many in low-paid industries, and any attempt compulsorily to reduce overtime would fall hardest on such low-paid workers. As things stand presently, few full-time workers would be prepared to accept a permanent loss in their overtime pay in order to provide waged or salaried work for the unemployed – unless, perhaps, their basic pay level was raised by a proportionate amount.

c Voluntary part-time employment.   The proportion of full-time paid workers who are interested in working shorter hours is much higher than is commonly supposed. According to a number of recent surveys, a majority of full-time employees would prefer to work less in the labour market, even if they thereby earned less.[9] Many workers want to be employed, say, five to six hours a week less, but do not wish to cut their working hours from forty to twenty hours a week. If this desire for voluntary part-time employment (preferably without a corresponding reduction in earnings) could be met, it might possibly have a modest impact upon overall unemployment figures. However, employers are reluctant to hire new workers due to the alleged costs of training. In addition, trade unions are deeply sceptical about voluntary part-time working arrangements. They suspect, correctly, that many part-time jobs are not secure, that the work is presently undergoing intensification (e.g. through speed-ups), and that part-time employees are usually discriminated against in such matters as promotion and entitlements. Trade unions also tend to assume that part-time workers will not support collective trade union policy, by strike action if need be. The conclusion drawn by many trade unions – that voluntary part-time employment undermines trade union solidarity and plays into the hands of employers – is arguably premature, however. Trade unions have barely begun to explore the possibilities of supplementing their collective strategies by bargaining vigorously in defence of the growing numbers of part-time employees (most of them women), and by demanding that every individual full-time employee be entitled to a right to work part-time *without* loss of entitlements or promotion opportunities.

d Early voluntary retirement.   As an alternative to altering hours of employment, action could be taken to reduce the size of the labour market, by considerably reducing the age of (voluntary) retirement, for example. The fight for a more meaningful and youthful existence at the end of one's employed life, instead of simply 'going into retirement' (or being forced there through compulsory redundancy), could create new jobs. The costs of this strategy are however considerable, not only in terms of increased pensions, but also through the possible loss of tax and national insurance contributions to state budgets. Many employees would also be reluctant to retire on their present pensions, preferring instead to achieve higher incomes by remaining within the labour market. If alternative forms of self-chosen work outside of the labour market were made more attractive, however, this reluctance to retire early from employment might be reduced greatly.

In view of the difficulties mentioned in this list of policy options, it is clear that an effective and equitable overall strategy for reducing paid working hours requires a *combination* of these partial strategies. Ways must also be found of co-ordinating these strategies at the plant, office, local, regional and even international levels through state reforms from above and radical social initiatives from below. This would help prevent the present serious discrepancies of working conditions from developing further, and might even help to reverse them. It would also help counter the reactionary initiatives of conservative politicians and employers, who more and more present the so-called 'flexibility' of working hours – voluntary forms of part-time employment which are in practice poorly paid and often compulsory – as an individual solution to the *collective* problem of equitably reducing paid working time.

3   *Finally, does not Gorz's overall vision of a post-employment society suppose the need for a transitional strategy that guarantees a social wage be paid to all adult citizens? If so, are there not serious political obstacles to the popularizing and successful implementation of this social wage?* Popularizing and implementing a guaranteed social wage is arguably one of the most crucial conditions of success of a policy of reducing and redistributing paid work, although Gorz gives it – and especially the barriers to its acceptance – insufficient emphasis. The basic principle of the social wage, first developed during the 1920s in Europe, and revived during the 1960s, is simple: every adult citizen would be paid by the state a weekly or monthly income, adequate for subsistence, on no other condition than that except proof of citizenship. Assuming that paid work could not be abolished at a stroke (as Gorz sometimes implies), those citizens wishing to earn extra income from paid employment could do so,

although those earnings would be taxed; those persons caring for children, as well as those persons unfit for employment, such as the frail elderly and the disabled, would be entitled to a supplement in order to protect their incomes from falling behind the able-bodied or those without dependent children. The cost of operating the social wage system would be paid for by a single tax upon incomes deriving from employment and/or upon employers' profits deriving from the rapidly expanding productivity and output associated with the present wave of 'jobless growth'. The collection of taxes and their redistribution in the form of a social wage would be administered by a single state agency. Since the present jungle of state payments (e.g. unemployment and social security benefits, students grants, child allowances) and tax allowances would be combined into one computerized system, considerable savings on administrative costs would result.

Contrary to what is often thought, the social wage system would not have socially regressive consequences. It would instead guarantee all individuals the right *not* to engage in employment, and would at the same time distribute more equally to everyone the wealth created by society as a whole. Provided with an adequate social wage, individuals would no longer be forced to sell their capacity to work in the labour market; the right to an income (and therefore the choice between different ways of life) would be separated fully from the possession of a job. Individuals could more freely choose how much time they wished to spend either in employment or in other activities in civil society, including work in the household and informal economy. A guaranteed social wage would also effectively weaken the undemocratic power of surveillance of welfare state bureaucracies over many claimants: all citizens would be *entitled* to the social wage regardless of their employment or social status. In addition, a guaranteed social wage for all individuals would finally terminate the present system of 'the family wage' (whereby *men* are alleged by state and private employers to be the sole 'breadwinners' of households) as well as the financial dependence of women upon men within households. For the first time under modern conditions, all women would be treated as equals of men in civil society. The social wage to which all women, regardless of their marital status, would be entitled automatically would make it possible for them to escape their present financial dependence upon men, and to move much more freely between the realms of paid and unpaid work.

In *Paths to Paradise*, Gorz considers for the first time the need for a guaranteed social income for life. When linked with the demand for reducing and redistributing paid labour, he observes rightly, the guarantee of a social wage could greatly enhance all individuals' liberty to choose different ways of life within civil society. Gorz fails to consider, however, the very serious strategic obstacles working against the acceptance of the social wage principle, especially among trade unions and socialist political parties. Within the latter, for instance, there is presently a deep hostility to the social wage principle. Partly this is due to a simple reaction against the appropriation of the principle by anti-socialists, especially market liberals.[10] There are further serious objections to the idea of a social wage, raised especially by trade unions. Under conditions of mass unemployment and a deepening 'dualization' of employment societies, public sector trade unions do not respond warmly to social wage proposals that would inevitably involve the elimination of jobs in the social policy bureaucracies of the state. Private sector trade unions also object to social wage proposals on the grounds that they would weaken trade unions' power to defend their members' livelihoods. If all citizens were entitled to a subsistence wage, these trade unions argue, collective bargaining would inevitably be confined to the matter of supplementary income derived from employment, thereby adding to the present difficulties trade unions encounter in preserving solidarity and attracting new members.

This trade union and political party opposition to the idea of the social wage is understandable, and yet troubling for Gorz's thesis. It is symptomatic of an irony – that the present labour movement is committed strongly to defending full-time paid work, whereas, as in the nineteenth-century campaigns for Sunday rest, the ten-hour day and the prohibition of child labour, large sections of the labour movement struggled *against* paid work – that will only be resolved and overcome in practice if creative strategies ensuring solidarity among the employed, unemployed and part-time employed can be invented and popularized.

After full employment

These three types of strategic questions and problems prompted by Gorz's analysis remain unresolved in his writings. As a confessed utopian, Gorz rightly does not apologize for these strategic weaknesses and gaps in his vision. This commitment to bold conjectures is nevertheless both the greatest strength – and a major source of weakness in his case. Sooner or later – better sooner than later – the utopian socialist vision of moving beyond the full employment welfare state will have to confront and resolve hard political questions concerning *how* this vision can be achieved in practice. The development of a *viable* socialism – workable and popular strategies for reducing and equitably redistributing paid work – is surely a necessary precondition of successfully defeating the inequitable, nostalgic and self-contradictory social democratic, market liberal and disciplinary state strategies for 'returning' to 'full employment'. Questions concerning ends *and* means must become central to contemporary socialist politics. For perhaps the most telling counter-argument with which socialists must deal in the debate about mass unemployment is the oft-heard charge that the political and social costs of reducing and redistributing work are too high; that is, that the socialist *goal* (of maximizing the freedom and equality of all individuals by abolishing their compulsory dependence upon employment) is contradicted by the lack of clarity about the *means* to be relied upon in achieving this goal.

This argument against the very idea of socialism is especially troubling in the present period, when the political project called socialism is losing its energy and direction. Today, 'socialism' means for most people either the dismal reality of state-dominated Soviet-type regimes, which no longer command much respect among western publics; or it refers to rhetorical or vague assurances (such as those of Gorz) that it is a radically different, and better society that bears little or no resemblance to the present-day realities of employment societies. The present unemployment crisis potentially provides the socialist tradition with a once-in-a-lifetime opportunity of breaking out of this impasse. If socialists are to seize this historic opportunity, they will not only have to convince others publicly that a new ideal is needed to replace the undesirable and unrepeatable, and therefore obsolete ideal of full male employment. Socialists will also have to resolve an equally formidable problem: that of inventing viable strategies for ending the tyranny of paid work, thereby making *possible* a post-employment society which maximizes individuals' choice of whether, or how much, they work for pay.

Notes

1 Consider, as just one further example of this nostalgia discussed in the previous chapter, the following passage from a recent booklet issued by the Communist Party of Britain, Marxist-Leninist, *Unemployment* (London, 1984), p. 15: 'No labour movement today can claim to be moving in the direction of socialism if it does not have as the first inscrip-

tion on its banner "an end to unemployment – we *will* work". No amount of alternative plans for coping with new technology can act as a substitute for the struggle in the workplace to safeguard jobs.'

2 This trend appears to be more long-standing than Gorz supposes. According to R. E. Pahl, *Divisions of Labour* (Oxford, 1984), p. 335, between the 'full employment' years of 1960 and 1980, the number of full-time employees in Britain fell by over 2 million, whereas that of part-time employees doubled to 4.4 million, of whom 3.8 million were women. According to other estimates, only 5 per cent of paid workers in 1951 had part-time employment in Britain, compared with 21 per cent today, most of these being located in the service sector. Consistent with this trend, the work force of British companies such as Sainsbury and Marks and Spencer is now over 60 per cent part-time, and employers in general talk more and more of the need for greater 'flexibility' in their labour requirements.

3 According to Gorz, extensive urbanization, the dominance of capitalist consumerism and the growth of state-directed services such as health and education have together resulted in a collapse of traditional networks of mutual aid as well as a general decline in individuals' capacity for self-reliance. He claims that this decline of mutual aid and self-reliance is a major source of unfreedom in employment societies, and that it is likely to be strengthened by the new long wave of information technology-based accumulation. He consequently argues against this bureaucratizing trend, and for a renewal of popular know-how and self-reliance in matters of health, housing, food consumption and child care. If implemented, this recommendation would undoubtedly lead to an *expansion* of the quantity of unpaid work performed by individuals outside the formal labour market.

4 Harry Braverman, *Labor and Monopoly Capital* (New York, 1974).

5 Keith Middlemas, 'Unemployment: the past and future of a political problem', in *Unemployment*, edited by Bernard Crick (London, 1981), p. 141.

6 Fritz Vilmar, 'Reduction in working hours – a way to full employment?', in *The Future of Work: Challenge and Opportunity*, edited by Gabriel Fragnière (Maastricht, 1984), p. 78.

7 F. Walz, 'Shorter working hours and their impact on overall employment', *Swiss Bank Corporation Economic and Financial Prospects*, **1** (February/March 1984), p. 5; Rolande Cuvillier, *The Reduction of Working Time* (Geneva, 1984).

8 *Eurostat: Labour Force Sample Survey, 1977* (Brussels, 1978), table 21, p. 31. According to a British TUC report, only 35 per cent of manual workers do not work overtime. The real average for those who do is

therefore approximately ten hours per week, in other words, a working week of about fifty hours (European Trade Union Confederation Campaign for Reduced Working Time, *TUC Progress Report No. 1*, November 1979, p. 9).

9 OECD, *Labour Supply Growth Constraints and Work Sharing* (Paris, 1982).

10 Friedman's proposed 'negative income tax' (mentioned in Chapter 4) is an example of this; another version is sketched in Keith Roberts, *Automation, Unemployment and the Distribution of Income* (Maastricht, 1982). In the hands of advocates of the 'strong state, free market' strategy, the social wage principle is understood as a mechanism for simplifying social policy arrangements as well as for improving the mobility of paid labour and generating greater 'flexibility' (read: reduction) of wages and salaries. The social policy institutions of the state, it is said, could be run more efficiently and cost effectively. Above all, the market mechanism could be rejuvenated. The state's provision of a guaranteed subsistence income to citizens would allow employees to adjust to the demands of employers. Old industries presently in decline and new enterprises, especially those linked to the new micro-electronics and telecommunications technologies, would be able to reduce their wages and salaries bill by paying workers less. Job-sharing and part-time employment, especially in poorly paid and insecure jobs, would also be likely to increase; supported by a subsistence income, and offered the option of a part-time job, the presently unemployed would have an incentive to enter the labour market in order to supplement their state-provided income with earned wages.

Further reading

Gabriel Fragnière (ed.), *The Future of Work: Challenge and Opportunity* (Maastricht, 1984).
André Gorz, *Ecology as Politics* (Boston, 1980).
André Gorz, *Farewell to the Working Class. An Essay on Post-Industrial Socialism* (London, 1982).
André Gorz, *Paths to Paradise. On the Liberation From Work* (London, 1985).
Bill Jordan, *Mass Unemployment and the Future of Britain* (Oxford, 1982).
Bill Jordan, 'The social wage: a right for all', *New Society*, **26** (April 1984), pp. 143–4.
Alec Nove, *The Economics of Feasible Socialism* (London, 1983).
J. Richardson and R. Henning (eds), *Unemployment: Policy Responses of Western Democracies* (London, 1984).

Bibliography

Wolfgang Abendroth, *A Short History of the European Working Class*, London: New Left Books, 1972.

Derek H. Aldcroft, *The Inter-War Economy; Britain 1919–1939*, London: Batsford, 1970.

Gar Alperovitz and Jeff Faux, *Rebuilding America. A Blueprint for the New Economy*, New York: Pantheon, 1984.

P. D. Anthony, *The Ideology of Work*, London: Tavistock Publications 1977.

Nixon Apple, 'The rise and fall of full employment capitalism', *Studies in Political Economy*, 4, autumn 1980, pp. 5–39.

Hannah Arendt, *The Human Condition*, London, 1958.

R. Bacon and W. Eltis, *Britain's Economic Problem: Too Few Producers*, London: Macmillan, 1976.

Laura Balbo, 'The Servicing Work of Women and the Capitalist State', *Political Power and Social Theory*, 3, 1982, pp. 251–70.

Richard J. Barnet and Ronald E. Muller, *Global Reach. The Power of the Multinational Corporations*, London: 1975.

Jean Baudrillard, *The Mirror of Production*, St Louis: Telos Press, 1975.

Jonathan Beecher and Richard Bienvenu (eds.), *The Utopian Vision of Charles Fourier*, Boston: Beacon Press, 1972.

Samuel H. Beer, *Modern British Politics. A Study of Parties and Pressure Groups*, London: Faber and Faber, 1965

I. Begg and J. Rhodes, 'Will British industry recover?', *Cambridge Economic Policy Review*, 8 no. 2, April 1982.

William Beveridge, *Unemployment: A Problem of Industry*, London: George Allen & Unwin 1909.

William Beveridge, *Full Employment in a Free Society*, London: George Allen and Unwin, 1944.

Michael Bleaney, 'Conservative economic strategy', in Stuart Hall and Martin Jacques (eds.), *The Politics of Thatcherism*, London: Lawrence and Wishart, 1983.

Fred L. Block, *The Origins of International Economic Disorder. A Study of United States International Monetary Policy From World War II to the Present*, Berkeley and London: University of California Press, 1978.

Barry Bluestone, Bennett Harrison and Lucy Gorham, *Storm Clouds on the Horizon. Labour Market Crisis and Industrial Policy*, Brookline, Massachusetts: Economic Education Project, May 1984.

Alan Booth, 'The "Keynesian Revolution" in economic policy-making', *The Economic History Review*, second series, **XXXVI** no. 1, February 1983, pp. 103–23.

Alan E. Booth and Sean Glynn, 'Unemployment in the interwar period: a multiple problem', *Journal of Contemporary History*, **10** no. 4, October 1975, pp. 611–36.

Fernand Braudel, *Afterthoughts on Material Civilization and Capitalism*, Baltimore and London, 1977.

Harry Braverman, *Labor and Monopoly Capital*, New York: Monthly Review Press 1974.

Samuel Brittan, *The Treasury Under the Tories*, Harmondsworth: Penguin, 1964.

Samuel Brittan, *The Economic Consequences of Democracy*, London: Temple Smith, 1977.

Willem H. Buiter and Marcus H. Miller, 'Monetary policy and international competitiveness: the problems of adjustment', in W. A. Eltis and P. J. N. Sinclair (eds.), *The Money Supply and the Exchange Rate*, Oxford: Oxford University Press, 1981.

Willem H. Buiter and Marcus H. Miller, 'The Thatcher experiment: the first two years', *Brookings Papers on Economic Activity*, **2**, 1981, pp. 315–79.

Willem H. Buiter and Marcus H. Miller, 'The macroeconomic consequences of a change of regime in the UK under Mrs. Thatcher', London: Centre for Labour Economics, London School of Economics, discussion paper no. 179, November 1983

Jim Bulpitt, 'The discipline of the new democracy: Mrs. Thatcher's domestic statecraft', Paper presented to the annual conference of the Political Studies Association of the United Kingdom, University of Manchester, April 1985.

Louie Burghes and Ruth Lister, *Unemployment: Who Pays the Price?*, London: Child Poverty Action Group, 1981.

Tom R. Burns *et al.* (eds.), *Work and Power*, London: Sage Publications, 1979.

Craig Calhoun, *The Question of Class Struggle*, Oxford: Basil Blackwell, 1983.

Stephen Castles, *Here for Good. Western Europe's New Ethnic Minorities*, London: Pluto Press, 1984.

Alan Cawson, *Corporatism and Welfare. Social Policy and State Intervention in Britain*, London: Heinemann 1983.

James W. Ceasar, 'The theory of governance of the Reagan administration', in Lester M. Salamon and Michael S. Lund (eds.), *The Reagan Presidency and the Governing of America*, Washington, DC: The Urban Institute Press, 1984.

J. D. Chambers, *The Workshop of the World*, London, 1961.

Edwin H. Clark, *Reagonomics and the Environment: An Evaluation*, in Norman J. Vig and Michael E. Kraft (eds.), *Environmental Policy in the 1980s. Reagan's New Agenda*, Washington, DC: Congressional Quarterly Press, 1984, pp. 341–58.

Mike Cooley, *Architect or Bee? The Human/Technology Relationship*, Slough: Langley Technical Services, 1983.

J. Cornwall, 'Modern capitalism and the trend towards deindustrialisation', *Journal of Economic Issues*, **XIV** no. 2, June 1980, pp. 275–89.

Bernard Crick (ed.), *Unemployment*, London, 1981.

Francis Cripps and Terry Ward, 'Government policies, European recession and problems of recovery', *Cambridge Journal of Economics*, **7**, 1983, pp. 85–99.

Rolande Cuvillier, *The Reduction of Working Time*, Geneva, 1984.

David Dickson, *Alternative Technology and the Politics of Technical Change*, Glasgow: Fontana, 1974.

J. C. R. Dow, *The Management of the British Economy, 1945–60*, Cambridge: Cambridge University Press, 1970.

Hans Peter Dreitzel, 'Some reflection on the misery of the work ethic', in J. W. Freiberg (ed.), *Critical Sociology: European Perspectives*, New York and London, 1979.

George C. Eads and Michael Fix (eds.), *Relief or Reform? Reagan's Regulatory Dilemma*, Washington, DC: The Urban Institute, 1984.

John Eatwell, 'The long-period theory of employment', *Cambridge Journal of Economics*, **7** nos. 3/4, September–December 1983.

John Eatwell and Murray Milgate (eds.), *Keynes's Economics and the Theory of Value and Distribution*, London, 1983.

The Ecology Party, *Working for a Future*, London: The Ecology Party, 1983.

Richard Edwards, *Contested Terrain: The Transformation of the Workplace in the Twentieth Century*, London: Heinemann 1979.

Ferenc Fehér *et al.*, *Dictatorship over Needs*, Oxford, Basil Blackwell, 1983.

Tom Forester (ed.), *The Information Technology Revolution*, Oxford: Basil Blackwell, 1985.

Gabriel Fragnière (ed.), *The Future of Work: Challenge and Opportunity*, Maastricht, 1984.

Andre Gunder Frank, *Crisis in the World Economy*, London: Heineman, 1980.

Andre Gunder Frank, *Reflections on the World Economic Crisis* London: Hutchinson, 1981.

Milton Friedman, *Inflation and Unemployment. The New Dimension of Politics*, London: The Institute of Economic Affairs, 1977.

Milton Friedman, *Market or Plan?*, with a critical comment by Alec Nove, London, 1984.

Milton and Rose Friedman, *Capitalism and Freedom*, Chicago and London: University of Chicago Press, 1962.

Milton and Rose Friedman, *Free to Choose*, London: Secker and Warburg, 1980.

Milton and Rose Friedman, *Tyranny of the Status Quo*, London: Secker and Warburg, 1984.

Folker Fröbel *et al.*, *The New International Division of Labour*, Cambridge: Cambridge University Press, 1980.

Andrew Gamble, *The Conservative Nation*, London: Routledge and Kegan Paul, 1974.

Andrew Gamble, 'The free market and the strong state', in Ralph Miliband and J. Saville (eds.), *The Socialist Register*, London: Merlin Press, 1978.

W. R. Garside, 'The failure of the radical alternative: public works, deficit finance and British interwar unemployment', *Journal of European Economic History*, **13**, 1984.

Anthony Giddens and Gavin Mackenzie (eds.), *Social Class and the Division of Labour: Essays in Honour of Ilya Neustadt*, Cambridge: Cambridge University Press 1983.

Herbert Gintis and Samuel Bowles, 'The welfare state and long-term economic growth: Marxian, neoclassical and Keynesian approaches', *American Economics Association Papers and Proceedings*, **72** no. 2, May 1982, pp. 341–5.

Sean Glynn and P. G. A. Howells, 'Unemployment in the 1930s: the "Keynesian Solution" reconsidered', *Australian Economic History Review*, **XX** no. 1, 1980, pp. 28–45.

Maurice Godelier, 'Work and its representations: a research proposal', *History Workshop*, **10**, 1980, pp. 164–74.

André Gorz, *Strategy for Labor. A Radical Proposal*, Boston: Beacon Press, 1968.

André Gorz (ed.), *The Division of Labour: The Labour Process and Class – Struggle in Modern Capitalism*, Brighton: Harvester, 1978.

André Gorz, *Ecology as Politics*, Boston: South End Press, 1980.

André Gorz, *Farewell to the Working Class*, London: Pluto Press, 1982.

André Gorz, *Paths to Paradise*, London: Pluto, 1984.

W. H. Greenleaf, *The British Political Tradition. Volume 1. The Rise of Collectivism*, London and New York: Methuen, 1983.

William Greider, 'The education of David Stockman', *The Atlantic Monthly*, **248** no. 12, December 1981.

Charles Handy, *The Future of Work*, Oxford: Basil Blackwell, 1984.

B. Hansen and W. W. Snyder, *Fiscal Policy in Seven Countries, 1955–1965*, Paris: OECD, March 1969.

Miklós Haraszti, *A Worker in a Worker's State*, Harmondsworth: Penguin, 1981.

Candee S. Harris, 'The magnitude of job loss from plant closings and the generation of replacement jobs: some recent evidence', *Annals of the American Academy of Political and Social Science*, **475**, September 1984, pp. 15–27.

José Harris, *Unemployment and Politics. A Study in English Social Policy, 1886–1914*, Oxford: Oxford University Press, 1982.

Kevin Hawkins, *Unemployment*, Second Edition, Harmondsworth: Penguin, 1984.

Friedrich A. Hayek, *1980s Unemployment and the Unions*, London: The Institute of Economic Affairs, 1984.

Hazel Henderson, *Creating Alternative Futures: The End of Economics*, New York: Berkley Windover Books, 1978.

Fred Hirsch, *Social Limits to Growth*, London, 1978.

Fred Hirsch and John H. Goldthorpe, *The Political Economy of Inflation*, Oxford: Basil Blackwell, 1978.

Larry Hirschhorn, *Beyond Mechanization: Work and Technology in a Post-Industrial Age*, London, 1984.

Geoff Hodgson, *The Democratic Economy*, Harmondsworth: Penguin Books, 1984.

Bill Jordan, *Freedom and the Welfare State*, London: 1975.

Bill Jordan, *Mass Unemployment and the Future of Britain*, Oxford, 1982.

Bill Jordan, 'The social wage: a right for all', *New Society*, **26**, April 1984, pp. 143–4.

George Joseph, *Women at Work. The British Experience*, London: Philip Allan, 1983.

Michael Kalecki, 'Political aspects of full employment', *Political Quarterly*, no. 3, 1943.

John Keane, *Public Life and Late Capitalism*, Cambridge: Cambridge University Press, 1984.

William Keegan, *Mrs Thatcher's Economic Experiment*, London: Allen Lane, 1984.

Robert Keohane, *After Hegemony: Co-operation and Discord in the World Political Economy*, Princeton: Princeton University Press, 1984.

Walter Korpi, *The Working Class in Welfare Capitalism*, London: Routledge & Kegan Paul, 1978.

Walter Korpi, *The Democratic Class Struggle*, London: Routledge & Kegan Paul, 1983.

Krishan Kumar, 'Unemployment as a problem in the development of industrial societies: the English experience', *The Sociological Review*, **32** no. 2, May 1984, pp. 185–233.

Krishan Kumar, 'The social culture of work: work, employment and unemployment as ways of life', *New Universities Quarterly*, winter 1979, pp. 5–28.

R. Layard, D. Metcalf and S. J. Nickell, 'The effect of collective bargaining on absolute and relative wages', *British Journal of Industrial Relations*, **XVI** no. 4, November 1978, pp. 287–302.

Jacques Le Goff, *Time, Work and Culture in the Middle Ages*, London, 1984.

William Leiss, *The Limits to Satisfaction. An Essay on the Problem of Needs and Commodities,* Toronto and Buffalo: University of Toronto Press, 1975.

Charles Lindblom, 'The market as prison', *The Journal of Politics*, **44**, 1982, pp. 324–36.

Alain Lipietz, 'Towards global Fordism?', *New Left Review*, no. 132, March–April 1982.

Theodore J. Lowi, 'Ronald Reagan – revolutionary?', in Lester M. Salamon and Michael S. Lund (eds.), *The Reagan Presidency and the Governing of America*, Washington, DC: The Urban Institute Press, 1984.

C. B. Macpherson, 'Elegant tombstones: a note on Friedman's freedom', in *Democratic Theory: Essays in Retrieval*, Oxford: Oxford University Press 1973.

Angus Maddison, *Phases of Capitalist Development*, Oxford: Oxford University Press, 1982.

Ira C. Magaziner and Robert B. Reich, *Minding America's Business*, New York: Harcourt Brace and Jovanovich, 1982.

Peter Manley and Derek Sawbridge, 'Women at work', *Lloyds Bank Review*, no. 135, January 1980, pp. 29–40.

Andrew Martin, 'The dynamics of change in a Keynesian political economy: the Swedish case and its implications', in Colin Crouch (ed.), *State and Economy in Contemporary Capitalism*, London: Croom Helm, 1979.

Andrew Martin and George Ross, 'European trade unions and the economic crisis: perceptions and strategies', *West European Politics*, **3**, January 1980.

Doreen Massey and Richard Meegan, *The Anatomy of Job Loss*, London: Pluto Press, 1982.

R. C. O. Matthews, 'Why has Britain had full employment since the war?', *Economic Journal*, **LXXVIII** no. 3, September 1968, pp. 555–69.

Paul McCracken *et al.*, *Towards Full Employment and Price Stability*, Paris: OECD, 1977.

Patrick Minford, 'Trade unions destroy a million jobs', *The Journal of Economic Affairs*, **2** no. 2, January 1982, pp. 73–9.

Patrick Minford, *Unemployment: cause and cure*, Oxford: Basil Blackwell, 1984.

Ramesh Mishra, *The Welfare State in Crisis*, Brighton: Harvester, 1984.

Margaret Mitchell, 'The effects of unemployment on the social condition of women and children in the 1930s', *History Workshop*, **19**, spring 1985, pp. 105–27.

D. E. Moggridge, *Keynes*, Glasgow: Fontana, 1976.

Jeremy Moon, 'The responses of British governments to unemployment', in Jeremy Richardson and Roger Henning (eds.), *Unemployment: Policy Responses in Western Democracies*, London: Sage, 1984.

Kenneth O. Morgan, *Labour in Power: 1945–51*, Oxford: Oxford University Press, 1984.

S. J. Nickell, 'Wages and unemployment: a general framework', *Economic Journal*, **92** no. 1, March 1982, pp. 51–5.

S. J. Nickell, 'The determinants of equilibrium unemployment in Britain', *Economic Journal*, **92** no. 3, September 1982, pp. 555–75.

Alec Nove, *The Economics of Feasible Socialism*, London: George Allen and Unwin, 1983.

James O'Connor, *Accumulation Crisis*, New York: Basil Blackwell, 1984.

Claus Offe, *Contradictions of the Welfare State*, edited John Keane, London: Hutchinson, 1984.

Claus Offe, *Disorganized Capitalism*, edited John Keane, Cambridge: Polity Press, 1985.

Ray E. Pahl, *Divisions of Labour*, Oxford: Basil Blackwell, 1984.

John L. Palmer and Isabel V. Sawhill (eds.), *The Reagan Experiment. An Examination of Economic and Social Policies under the Reagan Administration*, Washington, DC: The Urban Institute, 1982.

John L. Palmer and Isabel V. Sawhill (eds.), *The Reagan Record. An Assessment of America's Changing Domestic Priorities*, Cambridge, Mass.: Ballinger Publishing Company, 1984.

G. C. Peden, 'Sir Richard Hopkins and the "Keynesian Revolution" in employment policy, 1929–1945', *The Economic History Review*, second series, **XXXVI** no. 3, 1983, pp. 281–96.

G. C. Peden, 'The "Treasury View" on public works and employment in the interwar period', *The Economic History Review*, second series, **XXXVII** no. 2, May 1984, pp. 167–81.

Henry Pelling, *The Labour Governments, 1945–51*, London: Macmillan, 1984.

Charles Perrow, *Normal Accidents. Living with High-Risk Technologies*, New York, 1984.

Valerie A. Personik, 'The job outlook through 1995: industry output and employment projections', *Monthly Labor Review*, **106** no. 11, November 1983, pp. 24–36.

Ben Pimlott, *Hugh Dalton*, London: Jonathan Cape, 1985.

Ivy Pinchbeck, *Women Workers and the Industrial Revolution, 1750–1850*, London: Virago, 1981.

Karl Polanyi, *Origins of Our Time: The Great Transformation*, London, 1944.

Programme For Recovery. A Statement by the Shadow Chancellor and Labour's Treasury Team, London: The Labour Party, 23 November 1982.

Adam Przeworski and Michael Wallerstein, 'The structure of class conflict in democratic capitalist societies', *The American Political Science Review*, **76**, no. 2, June 1982.

J. Rada, *The Impact of Micro-Electronics*, Geneva: International Labour Organization, 1980.

Robert B. Reich, *The Next American Frontier*, New York: Penguin, 1984.

Vernon Richards (ed.), *Why Work?*, London: Freedom Press, 1983.

J. Richardson and R. Henning (eds.), *Unemployment: Policy Responses of Western Democracies*, London: 1984.

Richard W. Riche, Daniel E. Hecker and John U. Burgan, 'High technology today and tomorrow: a small slice of the employment pie', *Monthly Labor Review*, **106** no. 11, November 1983, pp. 50–8.

Peter Riddell, *The Thatcher Government*, Oxford: Martin Robertson, 1983.

Denise Riley, 'The free mothers: protonatalism and working mothers in industry at the end of the last war in Britain', *History Workshop*, **11**, spring 1981, pp. 59–118.

Keith Roberts, *Automation, Unemployment and the Distribution of Income*, Maastricht, 1982.

Paul Craig Roberts, *The Supply-Side Revolution: An Insider's Account of Policymaking in Washington*, Cambridge, Mass.: Harvard University Press, 1984.

James Robertson, *The Sane Alternative*, Wolverhampton, 1983.

Joan Robinson, *Contributions to Modern Economics*, Oxford: Basil Blackwell, 1973.

Richard Rose, *Getting By in Three Economies: The Resources of Official, Unofficial and Domestic Economies*, Glasgow, 1983.

Charles F. Sabel, *Work and Politics: Division of Labour in Industry*, Cambridge: Cambridge University Press, 1982.

Marshall Sahlins, *Stone-Age Economics*, London, 1974.

R. Samuel, 'Workshop of the world: steam power and hand technology in mid-Victorian Britain', *History Workshop*, no. 3, spring 1977, pp. 6–72.

Philippe C. Schmitter and Gerhard Lehmbruch (eds.), *Trends Toward Corporatist Intermediation*, London: Sage, 1979.

Philippe C. Schmitter and Gerhard Lehmbruch (eds.), *Patterns of Corporatist Policy Making*, London: Sage, 1982.

Maurice Scott, with Robert A. Laslett, *Can We Get Back To Full Employment?*, London: Macmillan, 1978.

William Sewell, *Work and Revolution in France: The Language of Labor From the Old Regime to 1848*, Cambridge: Cambridge University Press, 1980.

Brian Showler and Adrian Sinfield (eds.), *The Workless State*, Oxford: Martin Robertson, 1981.

Robert Skidelsky, *Politicians and the Slump. The Labour Government of 1929–31*, London: Macmillan, 1967.

Robert Skidelsky, 'The decline of Keynesian politics', in Colin Crouch (ed.), *State and Economy in Contemporary Capitalism*, London: Croom Helm, 1979.

Robert Skidelsky, 'Keynes and the Treasury view: the case for and against an active unemployment policy, 1920–1939', in W. J. Mommsen (ed.), *The Emergence of the Welfare State in Britain and Germany, 1850–1950*, London: Croom Helm, 1981.

Social Democratic Party, *Economic Policy*, London, 1984.

Gareth Stedman Jones, *Languages of Class: Studies in English Working Class History 1832–1982*, Cambridge: Cambridge University Press, 1983.

Peter Steinfels, *The Neo-Conservatives. The Men Who Are Changing America's Politics*, New York: Simon and Schuster, 1980.

Michael Stewart, *Keynes and After*, Harmondsworth: Penguin Books, 1967.

Bruce Stokes, 'Beaming jobs overseas', *National Journal*, 27 July 1985, pp. 1726–31.

Charles F. Stone and Isabel V. Sawhill, *Economic Policy in the Reagan Years*, Washington, DC: The Urban Institute Press, 1984.

Paul Stoneman, Niklaus Blattner and Olivier Pastre, 'Major findings and policy responses to the impact of information technologies on productivity and employment' in *Micro-electronics, Robotics and Jobs*, Paris: OECD, 1982.

T. Thomas, 'Aggregate demand in the United Kingdom 1918–45', in Roderick Floud and Donald McClosky (eds.), *The Economic History of Britain since 1700*, vol. 2, Cambridge: Cambridge University Press, 1981.

E. P. Thompson, *The Making of the English Working Class*, Harmondsworth: Penguin, 1972.

E. P. Thompson, 'Time, work discipline and industrial capitalism', *Past and Present*, no. 38, 1967, pp. 56–97.

Grahame Thompson, '"Rolling Back" the state? economic intervention 1975–82', in Gregor McLennan, David Held and Stuart Hall (eds.), *State and Society in Contemporary Britain. A Critical Introduction*, Cambridge: Polity Press, 1984.

Jenny Thornley, *Workers' Cooperatives. Jobs and Dreams*, London: Heinemann, 1981.

J. D. Tomlinson, 'Unemployment and government policy between the wars: a note', *Journal of Contemporary History*, **13** no. 1, January 1978, pp. 65–78.

Alain Touraine, *The Voice and the Eye. An Analysis of Social Movements*, Cambridge: Cambridge University Press, 1981.

TUC Women's Advisory Committee, *Women in the Labour Market*, London: TUC, March 1983.

US Congress, Joint Economic Committee, Subcommittee on Economic Goals and Intergovernmental Policy, Hearing, *The Impact of Robotics on Employment*, 98th Congress, First Session, 18 March 1983.

US Congress, House Committee on Banking, Finance and Urban Affairs, Subcommittee on Economic Stablization, *Service Industries: The Changing Shape of the American Economy*, 98th Congress, Second Session, November 1984.

Hilary Wainwright and Dave Elliott, *The Lucas Plan. A New Trade Unionism in the Making?*, London and New York: Allison and Buslay, 1982.

F. Walz, 'Shorter working hours and their impact on overall employment', *Swiss Bank Corporation Economic and Financial Prospects*, **1**, February/March, 1984.

Donald Winch, *Economics and Policy. A Historical Study*, London: Hodder and Stoughton, 1969.

William Winpisinger, Fred Block *et al.*, 'Growth and employment', *Socialist Review*, nos. 75–6, May–August 1984, pp. 9–40.

Alan Wolfe, *America's Impasse. The Rise and Fall of the Politics of Growth*, New York: Pantheon, 1981.

David A. Wolfe, 'Mercantilism, Liberalism and Keynesianism: Changing forms of state intervention in capitalist economies', *Canadian Journal of Political and Social Theory*, **5** nos. 1–2, winter–spring 1981, pp. 69–96.

Index

Amery, Leo   32
anti-nuclear groups   86
Attlee, Clement   54, 55, 57; Attlee
   government   55–7

balance of payments problems   47,
   56, 63, 66, 67, 68, 156; in the
   United States   137
Baldwin, Stanley   32
Bank of England   35; *see also*
   monetary policy
Beaverbrook, Lord   32
Beveridge, William   17, 23, 41,
   53, 54, 55, 61, 63, 64, 66, 74,
   82, 85, 93, 97, 100, 104, 105,
   144, 145, 149, 160; Beveridge
   Report   41–52, 57
Bevin, Aneurin   61
Bevin, Ernest   33, 37, 53, 54
Boothby, Robert   36
Bretton Woods Agreement 1944
   21, 58; *see also* International
   Monetary Fund
Bulpitt, Jim   116
bureaucratic state   22, 24, 47–8,
   60, 64, 82, 89, 90, 95, 97, 151;
   in the United States   125; *see
   also* interventionist state
Business Expansion Scheme   109
Butler, R. A. B.   36, 72n, 104n,
   121n
Butskellism   66, 72n

Callaghan, James   53, 70; *see
   also* Wilson–Callaghan

government
Cambridge Group of Economists
   51, 146; *see also* demand
   management: Keynesian; Keynes
capitalist enterprise   24, 25, 54,
   59, 62, 63, 65, 80, 81, 86; and
   Beveridge   43, 44, 45, 47, 50;
   declining profits of 68, 69, 79,
   80; power of 99; and Thatcher
   governments   108, 114–15, 117;
   in the United States   20, 50,
   51, 125, 129–30, 136; *see also*
   investment; manufacturing
   industry; state aid to industry
Carter, Jimmy   127
Chamberlain, Neville   32, 53
Chicago School of Economists
   90; *see also* Friedman;
   monetarism
Churchill, Winston   37, 38, 53,
   54; war-time Coalition
   government   35–6
City of London   56, 151
Clegg Commission   64
Conservative Party   36, 54, 106,
   116; 'One Nation' Conservatism   103, 116, 120n; 'Libertarian' Conservatism 104
corporatism   80, 85, 86, 87n,
   150, 152; fragility of corporate
   bias   23, 49–50, 65–6, 69, 82,
   151, 152; in United States
   126–7; *see also* Social Contract;
   Tripartism
Crosland, Anthony   150

cyclical unemployment   30, 31–2; in the United States   125, 132, 137; *see also* structural unemployment; unemployment

Dalton, Hugh   37, 55, 56; *see also* Attlee government
declining industrial performance   66–9, 70, 76, 154–5
deindustrialization: in Britain   18, 68, 119, 151, 154–5, 157, 172; in OECD   68, 119, 154; in United States   18, 138; *see also* manufacturing industry: decline of
demand management: in disciplinary state   78–80, 81–2; Keynesian   32–3, 38, 44–5, 53, 54, 55, 56–8, 59, 62–3, 66–7, 78, 104–5, 146, 156–7; in United States   124–5, 126, 127, 135, 137
Democratic Party   125, 126
demographic trends and the labour market   23–4, 37, 49, 57, 62, 119, 157–8, 163; in United States   138, 140
deregulation: in Britain   104, 108, 110–11; in the United States   129, 131, 141n
disciplinary state   25, 26, 74–87, 161
disincentives to work   50, 94, 95; work incentives   106, 108
Disraeli, Benjamin   120–1n
Distribution of Industry Act, 1945 56, 64
Donovan Commission   63
dual society   42–3, 46, 83–5, 100, 119–20, 157, 177; in the United States   135–6, 141

economic planning   55, 146, 147–8, 149, 151–2, 153
Employment Acts   110, 111, 124, 132, 140n
employment patterns: in hunting

and gathering societies   12–13; in nineteenth-century Britain 29; in nineteenth-century employment societies   16, 26–7n; in Soviet-type regimes   12–13
employment societies   11–15, 17, 29, 83, 160, 161; socio-economic class structure in   164–6
enterprise boards   148, 158n
enterprise zones   115
environmentalism   18, 24, 48, 99, 126, 129; and economic growth 82–3; *see also* anti-nuclear groups
ethnic minorities   48, 49, 60, 61–2, 84, 120, 145, 150, 152; in the United States   136, 140
European Economic Community   58, 113, 115, 117, 155, 172

factory states   155
federal budget deficit   134, 135, 136–7, 138
Federal Reserve Board   128, 140–1n
fiscal policy: in Britain   34, 35, 36, 55, 56, 66, 117, 146, 151; in the United States   124, 126, 127; *see also* monetary policy; taxation policy
Friedman, Milton   48, 79, 90–101, 125, 180n; and Reagan administration   123, 127, 130; and Thatcher government   103, 104–5, 106, 108, 109, 110, 113, 114, 116
full employment: abandonment of 69–71; conditions of   58–9; consensus on   28–38; era of 53–71; future of   24–6; nostalgia for   144–58; political pressure for in nineteenth century 16–18 *passim*
full employment welfare state: in Britain   15–18, 41–52; problems

of 18–24, 59–69 *passim*; in the United States 124–5; *see also* bureaucratic state; corporate bias; declining industrial performance; demographic trends; international division of labour; international monetary and trading systems; investment; jobless growth; rising popular expectations; social movements; stagflation

Gaitskell, Hugh 150
Gilder, George 128
Greater London Enterprise Board 148, 158n
Gold Standard 32, 33
Gorz, André: utopian socialism 48, 158, 162–78
government job creation schemes 64, 85, 113–14, 117, 122n; in the United States 126, 132

Hansen, Alvin 44
Hattersley, Roy 150
Hayek, Friedrich 104, 105, 106, 121n
Heath, Edward 103, 104, 116, 121n; Heath government 63, 67, 103, 104, 105
Howe, Geoffrey 107

'imperial visionaries' 32
industrial democracy 140, 149, 152, 157
Industrial Development Act, 1966 64
industrial relations 65, 111
Industrial Relations Acts 63, 69, 111
industrial unrest 60, 61, 78; *see also* strikes
Industry Acts 64
inflation 19, 56, 57, 59, 61, 63, 76, 78, 94, 105, 107–8, 113, 116; and unemployment 66; in the United States 128; and wages 69
Institute of Economic Affairs 104
interest rates 33, 35, 38, 146, 156; and Thatcher governments 105, 107, 146; in the United States 128, 141n
international division of labour 20, 84, 87n, 102n, 118, 155, 156, 158–9n, 169
international monetary and trading systems 21, 31, 58–9, 75, 78, 163, 169; exchange controls 21, 107, 118, 145, 146, 148; exchange rates 21, 59, 66, 146; GATT 58; import controls 21, 36, 146, 148, 155
International Monetary Fund 70; *see also* Bretton Woods Agreement
interventionist state 17–18, 23, 45, 46, 50, 62–5, 69, 75–6, 79; in the United States 126; *see also* bureaucratic state
investment 19, 20, 22–3, 33, 35, 44–5, 50, 51, 57, 58, 68, 98, 108, 109, 118, 148; in the United States 129, 130; *see also* state aid to industry

Japan 21, 114, 115, 138, 158; state industrial planning 147–8
jobless growth 21, 83, 87n, 98, 119, 163–4, 172
Johnson administration 18, 124, 125
Joseph, Sir Keith 104–6, 121n

Kemp, Congressman Jack 141n
Kennedy administration 18, 124, 125, 126, 127
Keynes, J. M. 17, 28, 42, 54, 55–6, 57–8, 59, 62, 66, 93, 97, 104, 105, 124, 146, 160; key concepts of 32–3, 34, 35–8;

Keynes, J. M. (*cont.*)
  see also Cambridge School of
  Economists
Kinnock, Neil 150

Labour Party 25, 36, 54, 55, 61,
  69, 120, 140; contemporary
  policies for full employment
  144–58; Independent Labour
  Party 33
Lafargue, Paul: utopian socialism
  161–2, 168
Laffer, Arthur 128; *see also*
  supply-side economics
Lawson, Nigel 109
Lloyd George, David 33, 34
Local Employment Act 64

McCracken, Paul 75, 81; *see
  also* disciplinary state
MacDonald, Ramsay 35, 36, 39n
Macmillan, Harold 36, 63, 104,
  121n
Manpower Services
  Commission 64, 113, 148
manufacturing industry: decline of
  19, 68, 118, 119, 154, 156,
  164; in the United States 130,
  136, 137, 138, 140; *see also*
  deindustrialization
Marshall Plan 56
Marx, Karl 161, 164
May Committee 35
Middlemas, Keith 65
Mitterrand, François 156, 173
monetarism 93, 94, 105, 106,
  107–8, 115, 116, 117; and state
  coercion 100; in the United
  States 127–8, 133, 134
monetary policy: in Britain 32,
  35, 36, 38, 56, 66, 104, 105,
  106, 107–8, 110, 115, 151; in
  the United States 127, 128,
  133, 134
Morrison, Herbert 37, 54
Mosley, Sir Oswald 33, 35

National Health Service 112
nationalization 57, 64, 65, 117,
  148, 154
nationalized industries 67, 112,
  121n
New Deal coalition *see* Roosevelt
Nixon, Richard 126; Nixon
  administration 126, 127

Organization for Economic
  Co-operation and Develop-
  ment 9, 19, 21, 23–4, 68, 98;
  McCracken Report: Towards
  Full Employment *see* dis-
  ciplinary state
Overseas Sterling Area 58

parliamentary democracy 46–7,
  48, 50, 79, 82
part-time jobs 49, 85, 113, 119,
  163, 164, 174; in the United
  States 140
party system, changes in Britain
  33, 108
Phillips Curve 66, 72n, 94, 126
Polanyi, Karl 99
populism 103, 112, 120, 123,
  127, 140, 103–43 *passim*
Powell, Enoch 104
Prices and Incomes Board 63
private business *see* capitalist
  enterprise
privatization 112, 117
Protestant work ethic 14–15, 16
public expenditure 31, 69, 72n,
  104, 146, 151; and Reagan
  administrations 124, 126, 129;
  and Thatcher governments 107,
  112, 146
public sector borrowing requirement
  106, 107, 115, 116; for the
  United States *see* federal budget
  deficit

Reagan, Ronald 123, 124; Reagan

administrations 90, 120, 123–40

rising popular expectations 22, 48–9, 60–2, 69, 75, 76, 82, 151, 152; in the United States 125–6

Roosevelt, Franklin 124; Roosevelt (New Deal) coalition 124, 125

Say's Law 31, 33, 108

service industries: future job potential of 68, 155–6, 157; in the United States 138

Smith, Adam 14

Snowdon, Philip 34

Social Contract 63, 69, 70, 71, 85, 110, 116

Social Democratic–Liberal Alliance 88n, 108

social democratic model 25, 26, 41–52, 53–71, 74, 82, 89, 93, 160

social movements 18, 22, 24, 48, 49, 86, 99, 126, 129; see also anti-nuclear groups; environmentalism; women's movement

Social Security Act 111

social wage 175–7, 180n

Soviet-type regimes, employment patterns in 12–13, 178

Spencer, Herbert 89–90, 93

stagflation 19–21, 66–7, 68, 78, 79, 81, 108; in the United States 126, 127

state aid to industry 67, 69, 106, 114–15, 117, 148; aid to hi-tech industry 69, 114, 157; aid to hi-tech industry in the United States 130, 140; in the United States 126, 130, 132, 133, 136, 140

Stockman, David 135

strikes 13, 61, 63, 70, 112, 122n; in the United States 131; see also industrial unrest

strong state, free market model 25, 26, 87, 89–101, 104, 106, 160; and Reagan administrations 123, 133; and Thatcher governments 106–20

structural unemployment 67–9; in the United States 132, 135, 136, 141n; see also cyclical unemployment; unemployment

supply-side economics 93, 96; and Reagan administrations 127, 128–32, 133, 134; and Thatcher governments 103, 105, 108–14, 116, 117; see also Gilder; job creation schemes; Kemp; Laffer; taxation; wages and labour market policies; Wanniski

Sweden: unemployment in 18; wage-earner investment funds 149, 153

taxation policy 31, 33, 35, 37, 44, 45, 56, 57, 59, 63, 69, 76, 96, 146; and Thatcher governments 104, 105, 106, 108, 109, 110, 117, 118, 122n, 146; in the United States 124, 128, 129, 130, 133, 134, 135, 141n

Tebbit, Norman 111

technology: effect of on socio-economic class structure 164, 165; and unemployment 20–1, 51, 68, 84, 98, 114, 153, 157, 163; in the United States 138, 139, 140, 142n; see also state aid to hi-tech industries

Thatcher, Margaret 103, 106; Thatcher governments 90, 106–20, 123, 134, 146

Third World, and international division of labour 19, 20, 98, 138, 155

Thorneycroft, Lord 66–7

Trades Union Council 30, 69, 149, 156

trades union movement   17, 19,
20, 22, 23, 24, 25, 30, 54, 55,
60, 61, 62, 63, 65, 72n, 78; and
Beveridge   46, 47, 50; and
disciplinary state model   80,
81, 86; and government   64,
70; and Labour Party policy
147, 149; power of   68, 152;
and Social Contract   69, 70,
71; and strong state, free market
model   94–5, 96, 97, 101; and
Thatcher governments 108, 110,
111–13, 115, 117, 122n; in the
United States   125, 126, 127,
131–2, 140n, 141n; and utopian
socialism   166, 172, 173, 174,
177
transnational corporations   20, 99,
118, 155, 158–9n; *see also*
international division of labour
Treasury: constraint on Labour
governments   151–2; and
Keynesianism   38; Treasury
view   30, 31, 32, 36, 39n:
critiques of   32–5
tripartism   68, 81, 150, 152; *see
also* corporatism

unemployment   18, 21, 22, 24,
28, 29, 30–2, 35, 36, 37, 39n,
41, 56, 57, 66, 67, 160, 164,
178; and Beveridge   42, 44,
45–6; and disciplinary state
model   79; and dual society
100, 120; effects of   10–11,
160; and Labour Party policy
144, 145, 146, 154; patterns
of   9–11, 39n, 56; and strong
state, free market model   93–5,
96, 97–8, 105; and Thatcher
governments   108, 110, 113,
116, 117–18, 119, 120, 121n,
122n; in the United States   9,
18, 125, 128, 131, 134, 136,
141n; *see also* cyclical unemployment; structural unemployment

United States   17–18, 21, 81, 87,
114, 115, 117, 156, 158, 161;
economic conditions in   123,
136–7, 142n; military expenditure in   130, 137; social programmes in   129–30, 135–6,
141n; *see also* Carter; Johnson;
Kennedy; Nixon; Reagan;
Roosevelt administrations
utopian socialism   25–6, 158,
161–2, 166, 168, 172–4, 177

wage and labour market policies
56, 62–4, 66, 67, 69, 80, 106,
110, 112, 153; and Reagan
administrations   131–2; and
Thatcher governments   106,
109–11, 115
Wanniski, Jude   128
Weber, Max   14, 15
Wilson government   63, 104, 151
Wilson–Callaghan governments
63, 67, 69, 104, 151
women's employment: growth of
23–4, 31, 37, 39n, 49, 51, 61–
2, 71n, 145; in the United
States   138, 140, 142n
women's entry into labour market,
restrictions on   16–17, 29, 48–
9,   51, 57, 71n, 152
women's movement   22, 24, 49,
126, 138
work: concept of   11, 13–14;
formal sector   12, 13–15, 16,
26, 29, 49, 83, 145, 158, 160,
162; informal sector   13–14,
16, 29, 49, 62, 83, 145, 158,
160; *see also* employment
societies; full employment;
unemployment; women's employment; women's entry into labour
market